THE COMPLETE ENCYCLOPEDIA OF

SAILING SHIPS

2000 BC – 2006 AD

THE COMPLETE ENCYCLOPEDIA OF
SAILING SHIPS
2000 BC – 2006 AD

JOHN BATCHELOR & CHRIS CHANT

REBO
PUBLISHERS

Published by Rebo International b.v., Lisse,
The Netherlands in association with Publishing Solutions (www) Ltd., England

© 2006 Rebo International b.v., Lisse, The Netherlands and Publishing Solutions (www) Ltd., England

Text: Christopher Chant
Illustrations: John Batchelor
Production, layout and typesetting: The Minster Press, Dorset, England
Pre-press services: Amos Typographical Studio, Prague, The Czech Republic
Cover design: Amos Typographical Studio, Prague, The Czech Republic

Proofreading: Sarah Dunham, Jarmila Pešková Škraňáková

ISBN 13: 978-90-366-1718-5
ISBN 10: 90-366-1718-9

Contents

Introduction   7

Respective Ship Descriptions   26-313

Index   315

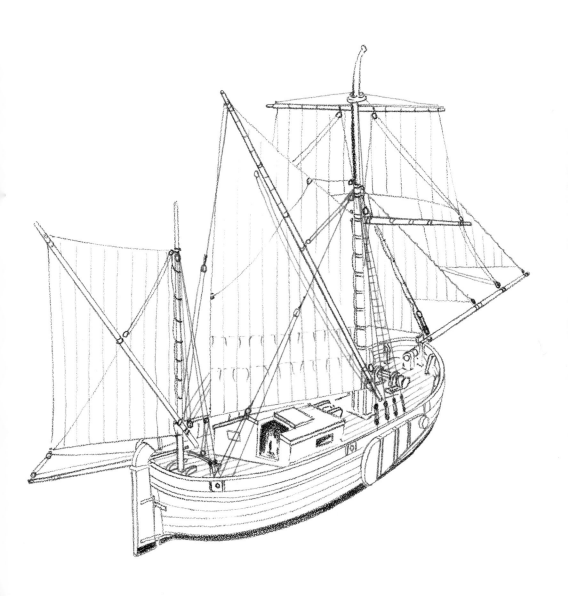

Introduction

The Complete Encyclopedia of Sailing Ships - 2000 BC to 2006 AD.

The word "ship" is used in two senses: first, in general, to mean a sea-going vessel and second, in particular, it is the type of sailing vessel with a bowsprit and three masts, each of the latter having a topmast and top-gallant mast, and square-rigged on all three of these. However, it cannot be denied that the word "ship" was and still is used to denote any and all sea-going vessels.

The origins of the ship are so old that they cannot be determined with complete accuracy, but certainly started with mankind's appreciation of the fact that it could make use of water (lake, river and sea) for transport of persons and goods from one place to another. The vehicle used for such transport was probably at first a floating log, and then a loosely constructed raft (tree trunks and branches, or bundled reeds). The need for greater buoyancy by way of enlarged freight volume was satisfied first by the hollowing out of a tree trunk, and by logical development, the creation of an enlarged and artificial "hollowed-out tree trunk" in the form of a hull created from planks over a frame comprising a central keel, stem and stern pieces, and ribs supporting the sides and, when added, the timbers supporting a deck.

The steady evolution of the ship from the first tentative sea-going examples to the final form of sailing vessels built as standard up to the early part of the 20th century, and since produced in smaller numbers for specialized purposes such as sail training, is related as much to development in the means of propulsion as to changes in the shipwright's art. The reason for this is the fact that the form of the ship is dictated more by its means of propulsion than any other single factor.

The most ancient ship of which present-day knowledge exists is the oared funeral ship of the pharaoh Khufu, dating from about 2525 BC and preserved alongside his tomb. It is improbable that this vessel ever went to sea, or even floated, as it was fabricated specifically as a funeral ship to be buried beside the pharaoh. It is a reasonable assumption that this was not the first such ship to be built, and tomb paintings of the period revealed that similar ships, though probably smaller in size, were used for sea-going purposes in this time during the middle of the third millennium BC. The sole method of propulsion revealed in these paintings is oars worked by men, and it is probable that early Egyptian ships were of just one all-purpose design as there is no discernible difference between the construction of ships used for state purposes, war, trade and simply pleasure. It is worth noting that illustrations of war at sea suggest that they were not exclusive to Egyptian sea-going vessels, but gradually spread out over the eastern end of the Mediterranean sea and the regions surrounding it. The period in which such "one design suits all" purposes extended down to was about 1000 BC.

The first single-role ship ever to be created was probably the Phoenician war galley. Ruling an empire which developed round the Mediterranean littoral between 1000 and 250 BC, the Phoenicians were the people who were the prime movers in the development of the ship during this period. With their sights fixed on trade and colonization, the Phoenicians pushed the evolution of the Egyptian universal ship into a number of specialized forms including the war galley. This was propelled by disciplined banks of oarsmen in various dispositions creating the twin-banked bireme, triple-banked trireme and others. The primary weapon of the war galley was the pointed ram extending forward from the bow either on or slightly below the waterline, but the war galley also carried combat soldiers in the form of archers and stone slingers. As a warship type, the galley was remarkably long lived, remaining in service up to about 1700 AD in the Mediterranean. However, in the waters of northern Europe, where sea and wind conditions are generally more changeable and more extreme, the galley had

given way by about 1000 AD to warships in which sail predominated over oar. The last examples of the "war galley" in northern Europe were the longships of the Scandinavians, or Vikings as they are more commonly called. The longship was not a true galley, but relied on oared propulsion in combat, although it also had a short mast carrying a square sail on a crossed yard which could be braced round to allow the longship to work to windward.

The Phoenicians also reworked the Egyptian universal ship into another role-dedicated type in the form of the merchant ship. This was itself evolved into specific forms such as the small and broad-beamed *gaulus* used for local trade between Phoenicia and her neighbours at the eastern end of the Mediterranean (Egypt and the Greek states of the Greek mainland and Asia Minor) and the larger so-called "Tarshish ship" which traded to the Phoenician colonies in Sicily, Sardinia, north-western Africa and Spain, and also passed through Straits of Gibraltar into the Atlantic before turning south as far south as Mauritania and as far north as the Scilly Islands and Cornwall. In addition to their standard complement of oars, these ships also had a single mast carrying the type of square sail that allowed them to run before the wind. Some of the larger ships were also completed with spritsail on a foremast that was so heavily raked forward that it was just short of a high-angled bowsprit.

By the end of the first millennium AD the oar was giving way to the sail as the primary method of ship propulsion in all of the western world except in the waters of the Mediterranean basin. The initial sail disposition, with a single mast carrying one square sail, as on some Mediterranean galleys to allow the oarsmen to rest when the wind was fair, and also on all Scandinavian longships for the same task as well as a limited capability to sail to windward, was steadily superseded by two and then three masts each carrying one sail and, as progress continued, two, three or even more square sails per mast.

A further fillip to the development of the sailing vessel was the invention, during the 12th century, of the rudder in place of the steering oar extended from the vessel's starboard quarter and later developed into a steering oar on each quarter. Hung from the sternpost, the centerline rudder made sailing vessels considerably more agile. It also combined with developments such as lengthened keels, a reduced beam:length ratio and sails which were cut flatter to pave the way for the consideration and development of sail plans that were considerably more efficient than their predecessors.

As in the earlier age, during the period of the sail's technical improvement in the mediaeval period, the pace of improvement in the dedicated warship lagged behind that of the general-purpose vessel. The common usage in the early days of sail rather than oar power was for those who needed a vessel for naval purposes in times of war to hire merchant ships. This was adequate in the era when the ship was merely the means to deliver soldiers to what was in effect a land battlefield at sea, where an essentially conventional land battle was fought after the ships had come together. But the advent of gunpowder weapons changed all that, for it paved the way for the ship to

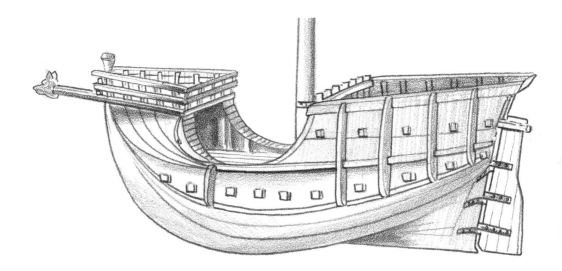

become a weapon of war in its own right. The inevitable result was the development by the seafaring nations of the dedicated warship with no practical alternative role in times of peace. The first true warships were flat-sided vessels with a low freeboard midships, where soldiers were still grouped, and taller fore and after castles (forecastle and poop), where guns were mounted to fire down into the waist, and therefore the soldiers, of any opposing ship.

However, as the art and science of naval gunnery developed, allowing the carriage of larger numbers of heavier guns intended for anti-ship rather than anti-personnel use, stability requirements meant that the guns had to be resited from positions as high as possible in the castles to locations as low as possible in the hull. Thus the wall-sided ship of low freeboard was supplanted by a vessel with higher freeboard and sides of considerable tumblehome. The bow and stern castles were retained and, in some case, actually heightened to provide the area for the siting of light guns intended for anti-personnel use both offensively and defensively. Experience soon revealed though, that such vessels

were poor sailers, especially to windward, as the windage of the tall forecastle caused the bow to be driven down to leeward.

The warships of this early period were generally of about 500 tons, but from a time early in the 15th century English shipwrights sometimes built ships of up to 1,000 tons. In the third quarter of the 16th century and as a direct result of Sir John Hawkins developed the carrack into what became known in Spain as the galleon, warships with a much lower forecastle and therefore considerably enhanced speed and weatherliness. This English lead was soon followed by other European nations, and the result was a generation of warships which were not only similar over the length and breadth of Europe, but generally identical in concept and merely differing in their sizes and the numbers of their guns and gun decks. This tendency continued throughout the 17th and 18th centuries right into the first part of the 19th century. Thus for a period approaching 250 years there was no advance in the concept and basic design of the warship, although experience and greater financial resources combined with

constantly growing naval requirements to increase the size of warships. Thus when the era of the sailing warship ended, in the middle of
the 19th century, the largest warships
were of some 3,000 tons and carried
some 130 guns on three decks.

Since the middle of the 18th century, the navies of most European
nations had categorized their major
warships into six primary groupings,
or rates, by the number of guns they
carried. Ships of the first three rates,
and occasionally the fourth rate, were
seen as having the structural strength
and firepower to lie in the line of battle, and were therefore line-of-battle
ships. Lacking this capability, the
ships of the fifth and sixth rates were
frigates, and the tasks of these lighter
but also faster and more nimble warships ranged from support of the line-
of-battle ships as signal repeating vessels in fleet actions, scouting for the
main fleet, convoy escort and commerce raiding. The vessels of all six
rates were ships with three square-
rigged masts. There were, of course,
large numbers of vessels too small
and lightly armed to be classified in
the rating system, and such brigs,
sloops-of-war, cutters, etc. had auxiliary tasks.

During the period in which the
warship matured as a decisive weapon
in its own right but on the basis of an
essentially unaltered design concept,
the merchant vessel had undergone
a more rapid and also more extensive
development reflecting the altering
nature of an increasingly widespread
trading market. In the early days of
sail, when passage time had been of
little consequence for the delivery of
cargoes such as timber, grain, wine,
etc., the merchant ship had averaged
a length to beam ratio of some 3:1,
which made the hull easy to build and
provided the maximum cargo volume
consonant with adequate sailing capability. Such vessels were generally
rigged in a less complex fashion than
the warship of the time, usually with
two masts each carrying no more than
two sails, for such a rig meant that the
vessel could be sailed adequately by
a small and therefore more economical crew.

Up to the end of the 15th century,
the typical merchant ship was small,
as typified by the caravel of up to 250
tons or so. Then the great voyages of
discovery which had started in the
15th century started to open more distant markets, in both the east and the
west, for the European mercantile
traders of the period. The volume of
the cargoes for which there was now
a market burgeoned, and this
demanded the creation of merchant
shipping that was larger, faster and
more seaworthy to cope with the rig-
ors of passages across the oceans.
The new breed of merchant vessel
was best exemplified by the carrack,
developed in Spain and up to 1,600
tons to exploit that nation's trading
empire. As the volume and value of
trade to the Far East and to the
Americas continued toward what
seemed at the time to be an inex-
orable growth, the carrack gave way

to the galleon. Then as other European nations decided to seek their own slices of the immensely profitable Far Eastern trading pie, and so developed their own interests through East India companies (most importantly in England and Holland but also in Austria, France, Denmark, Portugal, Scotland, Spain and Sweden), further development became not just desirable but inevitable. The East India companies were chartered by the governments of their countries and generally endowed with remarkably wide-ranging powers of expansion and self-government, and demanded the development of

merchant shipping to maximize the profitability of Far Eastern trade. The result was the so-called East India man, which were designed to carry passengers as well as cargo and, most especially when they sailed in convoy, to fight off the warships of other nations as well as privateers and pirates. Thus the East Indiaman grew steadily in size, sturdiness of structure, and elaboration of the decoration that was always a feature of these superb vessels.

Maritime trade continued to grow between the 17th and 19th centuries, steadily placing as much emphasis on speed of delivery as on volume of cargo. Thus there developed the need for merchant

ships that were not only larger but faster, and this was reflected in the introduction of more sails on taller masts and of a finer hull characterized by a length to beam ratio of 5:1 or even 6:1. In the later part of the period the greater length of ships allowed the building of vessels with four or even five masts.

Even after the introduction of steam propulsion, which freed ships from the vagaries of the wind's speed and direction, large numbers of sailing vessels were still profitable. At first the early steam engine's prodigious demand for coal and lack of sufficient bunker volume made the steamship uneconomical except for relatively short voyages. Even after this problem had been overcome, the sailing ship still possessed an advantage for some trades and routes, such as the American gold, Australian wool and China tea trades. Here the sailing ship was so superior to the steamship that it not only survived but in fact flourished, if only for a short time, and spurred the development of the clipper with great speed but only limited cargo capacity. However, the death knell for the clipper, especially for the Far Eastern and Australasian runs round the Cape of Good Hope, was sounded by the 1869 opening of the Suez Canal, which so shortened the routes that steamships could compete

and steadily prevail. The last trade in which the sailing ship still had an advantage was the transport of nitrate fertilizers from the Pacific coast ports of South America, round Cape Horn, until the 1914 opening of the Panama Canal. However, in its short life the South American trade drove the design and operation of the sailing merchant vessel to its peak in great four- and five-masted barques and schooners.

The fore-and-aft rig never became standard in large sailing vessels except in such schooners and also in hybrid types such as barquentines and brigantines. By the 1930s the day of the sailing vessel for commercial purposes was effectively over, although sailing barges continued in service for a number of years after that. Thereafter the only niche left for the larger sailing vessel was that of the training ship. Others are carefully preserved as museums and memorials of the age of sail.

After the first water craft had been created on the basis of tree trunks and bundles of reeds, over the millennia the desire to improve water craft resulted in an interim stage of a light frame over which an animal skin was stretched and lashed, and then probably the first types of what might be termed properly "construction" using flat planks cut from tree trunks. The

first such craft was fastened with leather thongs or vegetable fiber twine, then with wooden pegs (treenails), and finally with iron spikes. The Egyptians knew from an early stage of their civilization how to join timbers by dovetailing and scarfing, and how to make the junction between such timber watertight by rendering it with pitch or resin, camel hair, and teased rope. (Trees sufficiently tall to allow planks to be cut or sawn from them were not abundant in the Nile valley, and the Egyptians had to make do with short lengths of timber until they could import tall cedar from Lebanon.)

By the time of the 18th dynasty in about 1500 BC, Egyptian merchant ships had a length of some 82 ft (25 m) and beam of 16 ft (4.85 m), and carried a single mast (either one or two poles, the latter rising one from each side and lashed together at the top to create an A-frame structure) supporting near its head a yard on which was set a single square sail with a boom at its foot. Relief carvings of the period reveal that this rig was controlled by braces and sheets (yard and boom respectively) so that the sail could be braced round to permit the vessel to sail with the wind almost on the beam. Running before a good breeze, such a vessel might make 9 kt, but in lighter or adverse winds was propelled by between 12 and 16 pairs of oars, worked by standing men facing astern, for a speed of 3 kt.

As in all ancient vessels, steering was entrusted to a long oar usually pivoted at the ship's stern quarter on the starboard side. Using such vessels, the Egyptians navigated the Nile and also journeyed along and off the coast of the Mediterranean Sea and through the Red Sea and Arabian Sea as far south as modern Somalia.

Greater things arrived with the

Phoenicians, who extended the horizons of their trading and colonizing efforts right round the shores of the Mediterranean basin and, as noted above, out of the Straits of Gibraltar in search of the tin that could be alloyed with copper to create bronze, the core of their civilization. Phoenician shipwrights had not yet learned how to built considerably larger wooden hulls with the longitudinal strength to survive in bad weather, so their ships were in general no larger than the Egyptian ships, but were nonetheless more robust and therefore better able to remain at sea under adverse conditions. Like Egyptian ships, Phoenician vessels had a single square sail on a mast which was stepped amidships and could be lowered in unfavorable conditions, when as many as 40 oarsmen assumed the load on their aft-facing benches.

The Phoenician vessel was standard for the rest of the period into the beginning of the Christian era, when the growth of the Roman empire's economy and military requirements demanded a major expansion of shipping capacity. While not innovators in ship design or construction, the Romans were in this, as in many other fields of endeavor, excellent practical engineers with a genius for improving other peoples' concepts and blending a number of differently sourced ideas into a single Roman item. Thus the typical Roman merchant vessel became a type notably different from the preceding Egyptian, Phoenician and Greek vessels. It was based on a very voluminous hull that was broad in the beam, round-ended and based on a significantly more sturdily built hull using a heavy stem, stern post and frames to carry something up to 400 tons of freight. This *corbita* cargo vessel had a single mast amidships carrying one large square sail and two triangular (raffee) topsails above the yard. To improve the vessel's "steerability," an *artemon* (small square sail), was set on a forward-raked mast over the bow. The *corbita* was steered with two deep oars, one on each quarter. Using such vessels, the Romans were able to undertake seasonal voyages between the ports of the Red Sea and the western coast of India by the first century of the common era.

The *corbita* set the pattern for the rest of the Roman empire's existence, and the next major change in the art of designing and building ships was the Norse longship, which was more than adequate for trading and raiding voyages right round the coasts of northern Europe, and also for longer oceanic voyages westward across the North Atlantic and south through the Bay of Biscay before turning east into the Mediterranean. The Vikings shifted away from the Roman pattern of sturdy round-ended vessels back toward the Phoenician concept of long but narrow ships, in this instance of notably light construction and very shallow draught to provide a good combination of easy propulsion by their oars and downwind performance under sail. However, whereas the Mediterranean vessels had been carvel-built with planks butted up against each other, the Viking long-ship was clinker-built with overlapping planks which were fastened with leather thongs. It was to be another four centuries or so before western European shipwrights adopted carvel construction. However, before this took place, a major step forward was the replacement of the curved stern post and one of two lateral steering oars by a straight timber carrying an altogether more effective centerline rudder.

The typical merchant vessel of the mediaeval period reverted to the pattern established by the Romans inasmuch as this "round ship" had a length to beam ratio of as little as 2:1, had square sails on one or, later, two masts, and were dependent on a fair wind and/or a favorable tide as it was too heavy for oar propulsion. The need to fight at sea led to the introduction of raised platforms at the bow and over the stern for the archers and slingers of stones and blazing pitch, and in time these raised additions were built into the hull's structure with their vertical surfaces planked over to become the forecastle (later abbreviated to fo'c's'le) and after castle

(later the poop deck). When gunpowder weapons were introduced, they were initially light weapons that could be carried on the upper deck and even, in the case of the lightest weapons, the castles, but early in the 15th century there appeared the first "great guns" which were larger weapons firing heavier shot. Because of their weight, such guns had to be carried below the upper deck to shoot through ports cut in the ship's sides. This in turn opened the way for the vessel's topsides to receive a pronounced inward slope (tumblehome) to ensure that stability was retained even after smaller guns were added on the upper deck once more.

The firing of heavy guns imposed on the vessel's structure the type of forces that had hitherto not been encountered, especially when broadsides were fired and received in battle. This meant that the warship had to be made immensely strong, with its main timbers locked and bolted together. A similar though not so extreme a demand was imposed on the structures of merchant ships to cope with the longitudinal, lateral and torsional forces imposed on them,

especially in any sort of sea, by the increasingly heavy cargoes they carried.

The matter of ship design and ship construction was a close-held trade secret of the shipwright, based on the rule of thumb and the practiced eye of an art that was passed down from father to son. It was only in the later part of the 16th century that there appeared the first men who could really be described as ship architects, and thus the concept of a ship designed on paper before the keel was laid. Even so, this did not herald a new era in ship design and construction, and the warships with which the Napoleonic Wars (1800-15) were fought were little different in conceptual terms from the ships involved in the fighting of the Spanish Armada (1588), although they were more strongly built. However, within a quarter of a century of Napoleon's final defeat, the sailing ship was reaching the limit of what could be managed in structural terms on the basis of timber as the primary structural medium. Moreover, the situation was fast approaching that timber of shipbuilding grade was becoming an increasingly scarce European commodity.

A new structural material was required, and this had in fact been made available by the industrial revolution of the late 18th century. The material was iron, and the means of producing and working large quantities of this material had already been pioneered by the engineers who created the steam engine, industrial equipment and bridges. The first iron-hulled ships were little more than wooden ships 'translated' into wrought and cast iron, with advantage taken of the new material's capabilities to create longer hulls that lost nothing in their rigidity, but quickly the technology opened the way to a full exploitation of iron's capabilities in both design and construction. The vessel that showed the way forward was the *Great Britain* of 1843, designed as his second steamship by that far-sighted engineer Isambard Kingdom Brunel.

With a gross displacement of 3,270 tons and driven by a propeller, the *Great Britain* properly falls outside the scope of the current title but is worth mentioning as she introduced a number of constructional features that were soon adopted all over the industrialized world. These innovatory features included girder-section iron stringers extending over the full length of the hull, an inner as well as an outer bottom with cellular construction in between, bulkheads dividing the vessel into a number of watertight compartments, and great strength in all directions throughout the hull. The adoption process was not instant, for there was considerably scepticism at first, especially from the builders of traditional wooden ships, but soon the advantages of iron construction were too evident to ignore, and after a short period in which composite iron and wood

structures were used, iron (and later steel) became the dominant ship-building material.

With the introduction of the iron and later the steel hull, the writing was on the wall for the sailing vessel, for hand-in-hand with the development of these materials for hull construction went their use in related technologies such as steam engines and efficient propulsion arrangements, in which the initial paddle wheel was succeeded by the propeller.

As sail gave way to steam though, the rig of sailing vessels had reached an apogee of efficiency and elegance. In overall terms, "rig" is the word used to describe the combination of masts and sails which fix the precise nature of any particular sailing vessel as a ship, barquentine, schooner etc.

The term "square rig" is used to describe the arrangement in which the main driving sails are laced to yards which lie square to the mast, and is the oldest of all rigs. It was designed to exploit a following wind, and the realization that it was possible to sail a square-rigged vessel to windward by bracing the yard round to a pronounced angle to the longitudinal centerline of the vessel is said to have been made by the Scandinavians in the 10th century AD. In

Fore-and-aft staysails were introduced to the square rig during the middle stages of the 17th century, and the jib replaced the spritsail below the bowsprit toward the end of the same century or the very first years of the 18th century. This created what became known as the ship rig (square sails on all masts), and this remained essentially unaltered until the last stages of the 18th century. Then in the course of the 19th century the rapid and very substantial increase in the volume of cargo, especially that delivered over long distances, demanded the development of larger hulls, often made of iron and later of steel, and a rig that was easier to handle and therefore operable by a smaller crew. This led to the introduction of sail plans which included more elements of the fore-and-aft rig. These were developed to create the barque and barquentine among the larger three-

combination with increases in the size of vessels, this paved the way to a greater versatility in rig. As demand for more cargo volume and developments in the shipwright's arts developed, the original one mast gave way to two and later three masts each initially carrying a single square sail. Further escalation in the size of the hull allowed the masts to be made taller by adding to each mast a topmast carrying a topsail, and finally a topgallant mast carrying a topgallant sail.

Local sea and weather conditions were, of course, very important considerations factored into the creation of any particular type of vessel, whether rigged fore-and-aft or with square sails. Thus the Mediterranean peoples opted largely for the caravel and carrack with their very high poops, while northern European peoples opted for the development of the galleon from the high-charged vessel (with its tall fore and after castles) through the cutting down of the high forecastle in order to provide a more weatherly ship for the rougher waters of the north. By the 15th and 16th centuries the typical square-rigged vessel was two- or three-masted with three square sails (course, topsail and topgallant sail) on each mast, a square spritsail under the bowsprit and a lateen or sprit sail on the mizzenmast.

masted vessels, and the brig or brigantine among the smaller two-masted vessels. Experience soon confirmed that these were just as efficient as ship-rigged vessels but with the economically vital advantage of reduced manning requirements.

Another 19th century development was the clipper, though in purist terms this was less a development of the square rig than of hull form. The development of the clipper resulted from the need, in the early part of the century, for those ordering new merchant ships to decide between a beamy hull designed to carry a large cargo load at modest speed or a narrower hull designed to deliver a smaller cargo load at a higher speed. The clipper hull was a development resulting from the desire of American owners to emphasize speed of delivery over volume of cargo, and while the clipper was almost universally adopted by the American merchant marine, its use was considerably less in other parts of the world, where volume of cargo was generally deemed more important than speed of delivery. Even so, there were a number of specialized cargoes, notably tea and wool, in which emphasis was placed on the earliest possible delivery of the new season's stock, and a modest number of clippers were built in

Europe to compete in this limited market.

The square rig's evolution was completed early in the 20th century in response to the demands of the final trade route still economical for sailing vessels, namely that round the southern tip of south America linking Chile and Europe with nitrate fertilizer as the cargo. Offering few coaling stations and with immensely adverse weather placing almost insuperable demands on the propulsion machinery of steamships, this route still provided an advantage to the sailing vessel. The situation changed only in 1914, when the opening of the Panama Canal removed the need to pass round Cape Horn. Much of the nitrate trade was carried by the great three-masted barques of Finland, France, Great Britain, Germany and Spain, but world demand exceeded the capability of these fleets and thus there emerged the final, and wholly classic, ship- and barque-rigged four- and five-masted vessels. Under optimum conditions, the full-rigged five-masted ship set 30 square sails (six on each mast) as well as 13 fore-and-aft sails

(four jibs, eight staysails and one spanker). These great vessels were constructed mostly in Germany.

As noted above, all square-rigged ships carried several fore-and-aft sails, but the designation of the vessel depended on the nature of its primary driving sails. Thus when the main driving sails were set from yards, the rig was considered to be square, but when the main driving sails were set by their luffs, the rig was designated as fore-and-aft. There were also a number of hybrid rigs (the barque, barquentine and brigantine) which were classified as square-rigged even though in some cases these vessels carried as many if not actually more fore-and-aft sails as square sails. In overall terms, fore-and-aft sails were set with their luffs against masts or attached to stays and, with the exception of the jibs and staysails, these sails were normally extended by a boom at their foot and, in the case of four-sided sails, a gaff at their head. It is worth noting, though, that in some rigs, such as the barge and the lug, the boom and gaff combination was replaced by a single diagonal sprit or yard.

The origins of the European fore-and-aft rig can be found in the early part of the 15th century, when it was pioneered by the Dutch from about 1420, though Eastern sailors may had used this type of rig since as early as the 1st century AD in the form of the lateen rig. This was an evolution of the basic square rig into a fore-and-aft rig through the lengthening of a yard now set at a distinct angle to the mast along the hull's centerline. The first European fore-and-aft sail was probably an analogue of the lateen sail in being a four-sided sail set on a sprit but soon replaced by a triangular fore staysail as this was easier to handle and provided a bet-

ter-balanced rig that also eliminated the worst effects of weather helm (the tendency of the bow to come up into the wind, checked only by holding the tiller up to windward).

The gaff and boom were introduced about 100 years later in the first quarter of the 16th century. This development was probably a natural evolution spurred by the growing size of sailing vessel and thus the increasing length, weight and unwieldiness of their sprits. The boom and gaff together were lighter than the single sprit, more easily made from more readily sourced timber, and simpler to handle. Experience soon revealed that the sail with a boom and gaff was more efficient, especially to windward, than the spritsail. Developments at a local level over the next two or three centuries led to the adoption of huge numbers of variations in this basic theme optimized for particular conditions, most especially those typical of the shallow waters of Holland and eastern England, and often with lifting leeboards in place of a fixed keel.

With steady winds and not so much in the way of shoal waters, deep water its norms, the Mediterranean retained the lateen rig, but again in a large numbers of variations optimized for particular conditions, and off the coast of North America there appeared the schooner with four-sided main sails. The standard European fore-and-aft rig of this period, if such could be said to exist, comprised a four-sided main sail set on a gaff and boom, a triangular staysail, a jib set on a bowsprit, and sometimes a small four-sided sail set on a mizzen mast to create a ketch or a yawl depending on the stepping of this mizzen mast relative to the rudder head.

Rigging is the single word used to embrace the total-

ity of the rope, wire and chain used in sailing vessels to support the masts and yards and also to hoist, lower and trim sails to the wind. Within this overall coverage, two terms emerge: standing rigging is the rigging used in the support of the masts, bowsprit and yards, and running rigging is the rigging used to hoist, lower and trim the sails, and also to hoist and strike the yards of a square-rigged ship.

In a square-rigged ship the standing rigging was always a matter of complexity and also of considerable extent. This was inevitable given that the number of masts varied from two to six. Each of these masts could comprise at least three separate parts, and sometimes four when there was a royal mast, and each of these required its own support.

Moreover, each mast was crossed by as many as six yards, each requiring its own support.

The mast was supported athwartships (against sideways movement) by shrouds, which extended between the hounds or a stayband, located just below the top of the mast, to the chain-plates on the outer sides of the hull opposite the mast. The lower ends of the shrouds incorporated provision for the tightening of these primary supports, generally by the use of lanyards threaded through deadeyes, so that any slackness in the shrouds could be taken up. In the square-rigged ship, several shrouds spaced about 2 ft (0.6 m) apart at the chain-plates were needed to bear the forces exerted on the mast by large sails, and these were secured across their span by ratlines which helped to equalize the strains in each shroud and also constituted the ladder up which the crew climbed the mast.

In sailing ships where topmasts and topgallant masts were fitted, their supporting shrouds were led from the hounds or staybands to the top of the mast below them, where the top was a platform (resting on the lower mast's crosstrees and trestle-trees) which provided a width adequate to spread the bottoms of the shrouds sufficiently wide to provide the topmast or topgallant mast with adequate support. Fixed to the crosstrees and trestle-trees, the tops were also braced by futtock shrouds extending downward and inward from the edges of the top to a futtock stave secured to the shrouds or to a stayband round the mast.

It was also necessary, of course, to provide each mast with standing rigging to prevent its fore-and-aft movement, and this was the task of the stays. In the case of a fore mast, par-

ticularly when extended with a topmast and topgallant mast, the angle required to give the stay sufficient leverage was provided by the bowsprit, which could be extended by a jib-boom. These too had to be supported before they could be used to support the foremast, and was achieved laterally by pairs of shrouds led from the end of the bowsprit and the jib-boom to plates at the widest part of the bow, and longitudinally by a bobstay led from the end of the bowsprit to a fitting on the vessel's stem near the waterline, and by martingales led from the end of the jib-boom and similarly secured to the stem. In order to give a wider angle of support, a dolphin striker was fitted to lead the martingales down at a less acute angle than would otherwise be possible.

The foremast was supported by a forestay secured at its bottom to the stem or a point on the deck just inside the stem, and at its top to the stayband. The fore topmast was stayed from the end of the bowsprit to the fore topmast stayband, and the fore topgallant mast from the end of the jib-boom to the fore topgallant mast stayband. These stays supported their masts against movement toward the stern of the vessel, and the other masts were similarly supported by stays led from the mast ahead of them. Support of the masts against movement toward the bows of the vessel was provided by backstays. These were led in pairs aft from the tops of the various masts and secured to the ship's sides, one on each side.

The yards of the square-rigged ship had their own standing rigging. Each yard was supported by a pair of lifts made of rope or chain, one on each side of the mast running from a band round the mast above the yard, and the center of the yard was secured to the mast by a truss or parrel loose enough to allow the yard to turn on the mast when required. Spaced along the yard were short handing stirrups of rope to carry the horizontal horse (footrope) some 3 ft (0.9 m) below it as the foothold for men working the sail.

While the standing rigging ensured the structural integrity of the masts and yards, the running rigging provided the means to control the yards and sails. Running parallel with the masts were the halyards and jeers, which were the purchases which were used to hoist the sails and yards respectively, while in square-rigged ships only the fore-and-aft sails were hoisted with halyards. The square sails were hoisted to their yards in bundled form and then laced to the yards in this form, ready for spreading when required.

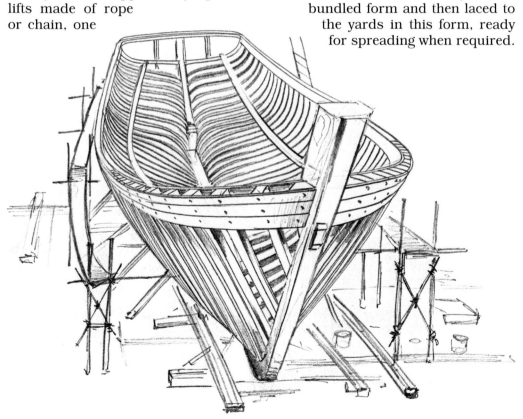

The weight of square sails was such that they were too heavy to be hand-gathered, for reefing or furling, so buntlines (small lines or purchases) were led from the foot of the relevant sail via a block attached to the yard and then down again so that other men could aid in this task, onerous at the best of times and phenomenally difficult in a strong wind. In the same manner as the elements of the standing rigging, individual halyards were designed by the name of the mast they served.

Vessels with a fore-and-aft rig had all their sails hoisted by halyards, originally of hemp. In the case of a gaff-rigged sail there were two halyards, one for the throat and the other for the peak of the sail.

Fore-and-aft sails were trimmed to the wind by sheets. On the other hand, square sails were not trimmed directly to the wind, but rather their yards were trimmed by braces attached to each yardarm and led aft, and the sail's head therefore conformed to this angle. In addition, a forward-led tack and aft-led sheet was attached to the clews of all square sails for finer trimming.

With all plain sails, a square-rigged ship had five sails on each mast, though sometimes a sixth on the main mast is included in this definition. From bottom to top, these were the course, lower topsail, upper topsail, topgallant, royal and, in the case of the sixth sail on the main mast, skysail. With a fair breeze and, most importantly, settled conditions without the threat of a squall, a ship running with a wind abaft the beam, additional kite sail could be set: with short royal masts attached to the tops of the topgallant masts, moonrakers could be set above the royals and skysails, and studding sails set on booms rigged out from the fore and main topsail and topgallant yards as lateral extensions of the topsails and topgallants. In the earlier sails of ships with square sails, the area of the course could be enlarged by lacing a bonnet, which was a long strip of canvas, to its foot, but the bonnet generally disappeared from use in the first years of the 19th century. Reef points were provided on only the courses and topsails, and it is worth noting that while square sails were reefed toward the head, fore-and-aft sails were reefed toward the foot.

The sides of a square sail were the head (top), foot (bottom) and leeches (sides), the latter designated as the weather or lee leech depending on the quarter from which the wind was blowing. The two top corners of the square sail were the earing cringles, and those at the foot the clews (sometimes rendered clues) again designated as the weather or lee units. The square sail's central section was the bunt.

In shape, fore-and-aft sails were either triangular (jib, staysail, etc.) or four-sided (gaff main sail or lug sail), and in common with square sails were designated in accordance with the mast or stay on which they were set. The sides of a triangular sail were its luff (forward edge), leech (rear edge) and foot (bottom), and its corners the tack (foot of the luff), head (top of the luff) and clew (foot of the leech). The sides of a gaff sail were its head (top), foot (bottom), luff (leading edge) and leech (trailing edge), and its corners the throat (top on the leading edge), peak (top on the trailing edge), tack (bottom on the leading edge) and clew (bottom on the trailing edge).

A gaff main sail was frequently extended in working area by the addition of a topsail above it to fill the area between the mast and the gaff. The two types of topsail were the jib-headed topsail stretching from the jaws of the gaff to the masthead, and the jack-yard topsail stretching above the top of the mast to provide a greater area of sail in winds of light or moderate strength. The main sail was set on the relevant mast, either by slides working on a track fixed to the after side of the mast, or by hoops which were arranged to slide up and down the mast as the sail was hoisted or lowered.

All of the standing rigging, running rigging, yards and sails were associated with the vessel's mast or masts. The mast was circular in section and usually inserted through a hole in the deck so that its square-off heel could be fitted into a step in the vessel's keelson. In larger vessels the mast was supported in its deck hole by wedges. In the period into the 17th century, when the increasing size of vessels made another arrangement necessary, the mast was a single spar cut from the trunk of a fir tree, but this type of pole mast was then supplanted by the longer and stronger made mast, which was fabricated from several pieces of timber. From the 17th century onward, lower masts were usually made masts, while the topmasts and topgallant masts were still pole masts.

Papyrus /Reed Boats 6000 BC

We now possess only tantalizing glimpses of the earliest boats. The oldest of which we have any impression are from the pre-dynastic period of Egyptian history. Before the recorded era, which started in about 3400 BC, and certainly before 4000 BC, the peoples of the Nile river valley must have travelled both along and across the great river by raft and later by boat. Contemporary rock and vase paintings sketch primitive water craft.

Among the oldest boats are craft powered by oars or paddles, or alternatively by a sail, and controlled by means of a steering oar. Quite remarkably, these are very similar in basic concept to craft still used on the While Nile, and were probably made of bundled papyrus reed. The most striking feature of the basically similar ancient and modern craft is the combination of a slightly raised bow to help the craft ride over the water and facilitate beaching, and a tall raised stern curved further upward than the bow and ending with a forward-facing section. The reason for this practice remains unknown, but it became a feature of Mediterranean craft and is still evident.

With the river-going boat's concept proved, size was inevitably increased for greater load-carrying, and the oars were supplemented if not replaced by a sail on a primitive mast, stepped well forward, to take advantage of favorable winds. Greater size also opened the way to use of such craft in coastal waters, and then at sea once further size, strength and controllability had been added.

The idea that vessels built of papyrus were capable of making extended sea passages was somewhat derided until the efforts of the Norwegian explorer Thor Heyerdahl (1914-2002). Heyerdahl became world famous for his *Kon-Tiki* expedition of 1947, in which he sailed a balsa raft some 4,300 miles (6920 km) from the western coast of South America to the Tuamoto islands deep in Polynesia. Heyerdahl believed that ancient accounts of Egyptian maritime voyages

The papyrus reed boats used on the White Nile are little changed from those which the ancient Egyptians must have used in 4000 BC and earlier. The paddle was used for propulsion and, when the boat was running before the wind with its sail set, for steering.

The Ra II was the reed-built sailing vessel in which Thor Heyerdahl proved that the ancient Egyptians could have crossed the Atlantic Ocean. The vessel was constructed from tapered cylinders of papyrus reed individually roped and then lashed into a hull with a tall elevated bow. This hull carried a wooden hut providing accommodation and storage space, and also the trellis-like bipod mast that carried the rectangular sail. Steering was entrusted to a long oar extending over the stern.

of discovery might be based on fact, and decided to build a large sea-going papyrus reed boat.

A crucial point of similarity was the design of reed boats shown in Egyptian tombs and those still used on Lake Chad in West Africa and Lake Titicaca in South America. Heyerdahl employed a Chadian reed boat builder to construct a "kaday" vessel using papyrus cut on Lake Tana, the source of the Blue Nile. The finished *Ra* (named after the Egyptian sun god) was built of rope-bound papyrus and then trucked to Safi in Morocco. With a seven-man crew and provisions carried in 160 jars made according to a 5,000-year-old example, the voyage began in May 1969. Though *Ra* made it most of the way across the Atlantic, covering about 60 miles (96 km) per day, the crew was forced to abandon the vessel near the Caribbean island of Barbados because the raft was breaking up.

Convinced that he had chosen the wrong design, Heyerdahl arranged to build the *Ra II* to a Moroccan "madia" design similar to craft used on Lake Titicaca. Four reed boat builders from Bolivia constructed the *Ra II*, which was some 10 ft (3.1 m) shorter than the *Ra*, but had a flatter, broader stern and carried an eight-man crew. In 1970 the *Ra II* sailed from Morocco to Barbados in just 57 days. Heyerdahl thus proved that ancient Egyptians could have sailed across the Atlantic and so kick-started South American civilizations.

Ra II

Type:	ocean-going sailed raft
Construction:	rope-lashed papyrus reed
Dimensions:	length 39 ft 0 in (11.9 m); beam 16 ft 0 in (4.9 m); draught 6 ft 0 in (1.8 m)
Complement:	eight men

Egyptian Ships 2000-500 BC

Given its lack of any effective overland transport facilities, and the availability of navigable waters in the form of the Nile river through most of the region, and of the Mediterranean and Red Seas on its northern and eastern borders, ancient Egypt inevitably made extensive use of oar- and sailed-propelled craft for bulk transport. Over the centuries this waterborne transport clearly grew in capability and importance, and is reflected in a royal ship that is the oldest, the largest, and also the best-preserved ancient vessel. During the course of a clearance excavation at the Great Pyramid at Giza in 1954 a whole but disassembled boat in 651 major groups comprising 1,224 pieces of wood was found. The boat was almost certainly built for Khufu (2551-2528 BC), the second pharaoh of the 4th Dynasty of the Egyptian Old Kingdom.

All but some one-twentieth of the boat was of cedar, the rest comprising other woods for cross-bracing in some deck sections, the tenons, the blades of the oars, and the battens and pegs. This jigsaw of pieces was reassembled over 13 years, a difficult task aided by fact that the boat's pieces had been arranged logically in the pit: bow to the west, stern to the east, starboard timbers on the north side, port timbers on the south, the pieces of the hull at the bottom and sides of the pit, and the pieces of the superstructure at the top of the pile.

Khufu's boat is of the "shell" type of construction: the builders first assembled the external shell of planking and only then added the internal structure to stiffen and stabilize the whole structure. The hull is built not on a keel but around a flat bottom, comprising eight timbers averaging 42 ft 8 in (13.0 m) in

Egyptian thinking in the design of cargo vessels seems to have been strongly influenced by the lines of ancient vessels made of bundles of reeds lashed and tensioned with ropes.

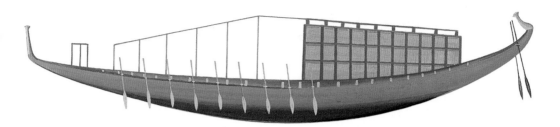

Khufu's boat is the best preserved example of an ancient boat yet found or indeed ever likely to be found.

length and 5.2 in (13 cm) in thickness. From this rise two essentially symmetrical 11-plank sets of side planking. These are lashed together from rail to rail, scarfed together at their ends, and further secured with 467 tenons. In the water, the timbers would expand and the rope lashings shrink, resulting in a strong, watertight fit. Thin wooden battens cover the inboard faces of the seams between the planks. Over the battens are fitted 16 large, curved single-piece cedar floor timbers, lashed to the strakes to strengthen the hull. A long central girder (spine) extends longitudinally amidships, held by forked stanchions attached to the floor timbers. The 66 deck beams are supported by the spine and notched sheer strakes, and in turn, take the deck sections.

The decks carry three independent structures. On the foredeck, 10 slim poles carry a small canopy with a plank roof. Aft of midships is the main deck cabin, consisting of an anteroom and main chamber, its walls comprising 12 cross-braced wooden panels (five on each side and two at each end). Over and forward of the main cabin is a canopy believed to have been covered by reed mats. The graceful forms of the high bow and steeply raked stern were clearly based on the shapes of reed bundle boats, and the stem is carved to resemble a bundle of rope-lashed papyrus.

The boat has five pairs of propulsive oars, varying from 21 ft 8 in (6.6 m) to 27 ft 5 in (8.35 m) in length, and two steering oars are mounted on the after deck.

Khufu's boat

Type:	royal vessel
Tonnage:	94 tons displacement
Dimensions:	length 143 ft 0 in (43.6 m); beam 18 ft 9 in (5.7 m); draught 4 ft 11 in (1.5 m)
Speed:	not available
Armament:	none
Complement:	not available

Greek Merchant Ship 600 BC

During the course of the 8th century BC the Greek peoples began to devote themselves to the development of maritime trade and expansion on a scale altogether larger that they had essayed before this, and were soon capable of offering strong competition to established maritime peoples such as the Phoenicians of the Mediterranean Sea's eastern coast. The success of the Greeks is nowhere more strongly attested than in their establishment of colonies along the coasts of southern Italy, Sicily, North Africa and the Black Sea. Most of these colonies proved eminently viable, and soon grew as major trading partners of the various city states that had

been responsible for their initial foundation. Indeed, so rapidly did the population of the colonies grow that grain and the other staples of life and commerce had to be imported from the regions beyond them, most notably from Italy and the Black Sea. This was in itself a further spur to the development of trade. The only practical means of moving these trade items, especially when they were bulky commodities such as grain, was by sea. It must therefore have been a period of hectic activity for the shipbuilders of the Greek and Phoenician communities, which became increasingly more determined rivals. Although there is no absolute proof,

Like most merchant ships, the Greek trading vessel from about 600 BC was optimized for handling by the smallest, and therefore more economical crew, possible. With no keel and a rectangular sail, the vessel could not sail at all close to the wind, and therefore had to wait for a favorable breeze or rely on slow progress under oar power.

it seems likely that ships of different sizes, and possibly of different types, were soon to be found all over the sea's eastern half and steadily expending Greek and Phoenician influences into the western half.

In general, though, trading ships have always been less obviously interesting than their military counterparts, and therefore less attractive to artists. Much of our knowledge of the early Greek and Phoenician worlds is based on surviving artistic impressions, but of the hundreds of images of contemporary ships available to us, only a very small minority specifically depict trading vessels. A vase in the British Museum shows the ship in which the hero Odysseus tried to return home to Ithaca from the Trojan War. This seems to be a vessel in which warship and merchant ship capabilities were combined: the comparatively great freeboard and high forecastle indicate useful load-carrying capability (supplies for longer voyages or substantial freight for shorter voyages), while the ram bow and the oars on each side suggest the striking power, maneuvrability and speed required for naval operations. It is possible or indeed probable that on longer voyages to areas in which pirate attack might be a threat, a larg-

er crew might be carried to man such oars and provide a force with which to fight off an boarding attack. It is also possible, though, that the extended bow could have represented a cutwater to improve the vessel's sailing capability, or even a combined cutwater and ram.

Trade over shorter routes was generally plied in waters more sheltered than those likely to be encountered on longer voyages. Here, on the routes between the islands of the Aegean Sea, and between western Greece and southern Italy and Sicily, it was possible to sail with a smaller crew. The best image of a Greek trading vessel left to us shows a shorter and presumably beamier vessel with its sail furled against an improbably long spar. There is now evidence of oars, but it is likely that there was provision for rowing when the vessel was becalmed or moving into or out of harbor. Another feature evident in the image is open lateral barriers over the hold, providing for increased carriage of bulky but light cargo items, and perhaps serving as the tholes for the oars, or perhaps as a gangway over the cargo linking the bow and stern.

Monoreme, Bireme, Trireme

For many centuries following the dawn of the ship's use for fighting purposes, the oar was preferred to the sail as the primary means of propulsion in action. The sail had its place for cruising to and from the battle, so conserving the energies of the oarsmen. But in combat the oar was far superior to the sail for outright speed and greater maneuvrability independent of the wind. Early warships carried men armed with missile weapons (arrow-firing bows, spears and slings) to pepper the crew of an opposing vessel and so render it ripe for boarding, but by the 6th century BC the Phoenicians had introduced the bow-mounted ram as the dominant weapon, although marines were still embarked to "keep down the heads" of the opposing ship's crew and so enhance the chances of their own ship in making a decisive hit.

It is believed that the Egyptians had oared warships, perhaps better known by the term galley, as early as 1600 BC, and by the time of the Trojan War of about 1100 BC the Achaeans (Greeks) had warships with 20 or more oarsmen. The advent of the ram increased the need for oarsmen, for the availability of a large

and well-trained crew made it feasible for the ship to reach a speed in the order of 8-9 kt, although this could be maintained for only a short time. The ram extending from the bow on the waterline was designed to strike the side of the opposing vessel at right angles, so piercing the side on the waterline and then, as the oarsmen of the attacking vessel backed water, pulling clear of the victim and opening the way for water to flood into the vessel and start the process of sinking it. Backing away from the stricken vessel also removed the threat of being boarded by the crew of the sinking vessel.

The need for additional oarsmen could be achieved in the first-generation monoreme (single bank of oars) during the 6th century BC only by lengthening the hull, although the hull was also made effectively narrower to produce less drag and therefore aid the oarsmen in their tasking of generating the highest possible speed. One disadvantage of this process, which produced vessels with as many as 50 oarsmen, was that agility was reduced. The monoreme was controlled with the aid of two steering oars, and a logical development whose

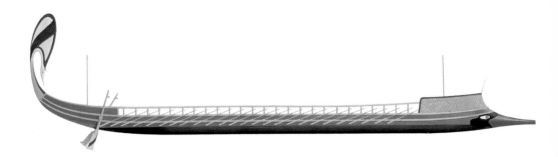

The monoreme was the first-generation ramming warship with semi-open oarsmen's benches on a single level, two steering oars and a wicker or woven hide bulwark over the bow.

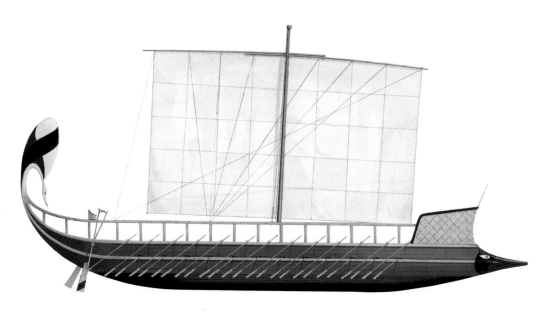

The bireme had a mast and sail for cruising, oarsmen's benches on two levels, and provision for a smaller number of missile-armed marines.

introduction could not have been long delayed, was the partial decking of the hull over the level of the oarsmen to provide a measure of protection against the enemy's missile weapons. Another development was a bulwark of woven construction, in hide or light wood, to provide additional protection against head-on fire without adding significantly to weight.

Development of the monoreme to increase its power, without adding to its length and thereby reducing its maneuvrability, led to the second-generation bireme. First appearing as early as 700 BC, this was probably a Greek or Phoenician development with the oarsmen in two superimposed banks, so doubling the number of oarsmen for each unit of hull length. The men on the lower bank worked their oars through ports in the side of the hull comparatively close to the waterline, while the men on the upper bank had oars held by thole pins on the gunwales. The vessel normally carried a single mast and a single rectangular sail, and

these were struck down to deck level before the ship entered action. As before a small number of marines was also embarked to harass the crew of the enemy vessel as the attacker closed for its ram attack. A favorite preliminary tactic was a glancing blow along the side of the enemy vessel to shatter on that side, thereby leaving the enemy without the power to maneuver effectively.

Later in the 6th century, apparently in Corinth, there emerged the third-generation trireme with three banks of oars. The key to the trireme was the addition of an outrigged hull section above and outside the upper oarsmen of the bireme. Manned by up to 170 and later 230 oarsmen as well as a small number of marines, the trireme was about 120 ft (36.6 m) long with a waterline beam of 12 ft (3.65 m) increasing to 16 ft (4.9 m) on the upper rowing deck. Fitted with a multi-pronged ram, the trireme became the workhorse of the naval forces operated by the Greek maritime city states, and proved decisive

Monoreme, Bireme, Trireme *continued*

in history-making naval engagement such as the Battle of Salamis (480 BC), when the Greek forces finally halted Persia's attempts to conquer mainland Greece. The oarsmen of the three banks were staggered longitudinally to facilitate their work, and while the thranites of the upper bank had oars some 14 ft (4.25 m) long, the zygotes of the middle bank had oars 10 ft 6 in (3.2 m) long and the thalamites of the lower bank had oars 7 ft 6 in (2.3 m) long and were seated only 1 ft 6 in (0.45 m) above the water.

After the land Battle of Thermopylae, in which a Greek army spearheaded by the Spartans had checked the Persian advance and bought time for the other Greeks to prepare their final line of defence on the Isthmus of Corinth, the Persians advanced and took Athens. The Athenians had refused to fall back, though, and under the leadership of Themistocles most of the population had been ferried to the island of Salamis, just off Athens. Themistocles sought a naval engagement in the strait between Athens and Salamis, and the naval contingents of the other Greek states remained with him. The Greek fleet, with Cimon as its able second-in-command, took up position in the narrow western end of the strait with the Athenians on the left, allies in the centre, and the Spartans on the right. The Persians advanced into the eastern strait in three lines after landing troops on the island of Psyttaleia in mid-strait. The geography of the strait, narrowing from east to west, soon compacted the Persian fleet, and soon the Persian formation had been rendered completely unwieldy as it approached the western end where the Greek fleets was waiting with the whole of the 6,000-man Athenian army on board. As the fleets closed, a well-timed counterattack by Cimon threw the Persians into disarray, and the final closing of the fleets turned the battle into what was in effect a land action in which the hoplite heavy infantry of the Greeks were altogether superior to the Persians.

The fighting lasted seven hours, and for the loss of 40 of their own ves-

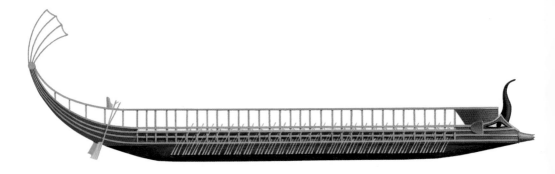

The trireme was the logical development of the bireme with three, rather than two, levels of oarsmen who were protected from plunging fire from the enemy vessel by the light but complete fighting deck above them. This deck also provided the area from which the vessel's own marines could bombard the enemy vessel.

A cross section of the trireme's hull reveals the arrangement of the three banks of oarsmen. As in the monoreme and bireme, control was exercised by two steering oars as well as the application of differing power to the oars on each side of the ship.

sels the Greeks sank, burned or captured more than 200 and possibly as many as 350 of possibly 700 Persian ships. The Persians eventually managed to break off the battle and fall back, leaving the men they had landed on Psyttaleia to be mopped up. With his huge army reliant on supply from the sea but his fleet crushed, Xerxes had abandon Athens and fall back northward to the Hellespont, which separates Europe from Asia, and the immediate threat to Greece was lifted. Well handled and carrying high-grade infantry, the trireme had more than proved its worth in battle.

A number of ancient texts mention vessels with more than three banks of oars, up to a maximum of 17, but for obvious physical reasons this cannot indicate banks of oars stepped vertically. There must be a different explanation, one suggestion being that the banks were divided in the horizontal rather than vertical plane, and possibly stepped with the lowest bank aft, the middle bank amidships, and the highest bank forward.

The trireme remained the supreme warship of the classical and post-classical era, and although galleys were to be found in major service with Mediterranean navies until the early years of the 18th century, the pure galley of the trireme type was superseded in more far-sighted navies by lateen-sailed two-masted vessels from about 1200 AD.

The last trireme "in commission" anywhere in the world is the Greek navy's *Olympias*, built of Oregon pine and completed in 1987 as a historical research and "feel good" ship for the Greek nation. The vessel had two steering oars and two masts carrying a larger mainsail and a smaller foresail.

Type:	trireme
Dimensions:	length 121 ft 5 in (37.0 m); beam 17 ft 1 in (5.2 m); draught 4 ft 11 in (1.5 m)
Speed:	8 kt
Complement:	180 including 170 oarsmen in the form of 65 on each beam in three banks

Roman Ship 200 AD

The earliest merchant ships relied for propulsion under favorable wind conditions on a single rectangular sail hanging from a yard on the single mast that was at first stepped well forward toward the bow but then gradually moved to a position almost amidships. This change made the ship more maneuvrable, but without altering the fact that the ship was still limited in practical terms to running before the wind. Later the ship was revised with a forward-raked fore-post that can be regarded as the precursor of what later became known as the bowsprit. This helped to make the ship more agile relative to the wind, but it still carried only a single rectangular sail that, like the mainsail, was controlled by two sheets and could be brailed up against a yard controlled by two guys. With the concept of the merchant ship by now comparatively fixed, the differences that emerged were in the development of a sturdier structure and a greater size, and to a lesser extent refinements such as topsails carried in the triangles bounded by the upper part of the mast, the yard and the lifts that supported the mainsail yard. Other

changes included fore- and back-stays to support the mast against fore and aft loads, allowing the carriage of a larger mainsail, and a system of deadeyes and lanyards to allow the tightening of the stays and also the shrouds that braced the mast against lateral loads.

Whereas the Greek merchant ships of the 4th to 2nd centuries BC regularly carried freight loads in the order of 20 to 165 tons, the type of merchant ships that became standard for maritime trade in the 1st and 2nd centuries AD, during the heyday of the imperial Roman empire, had evolved steadily into somewhat larger and therefore more capacious type of vessel with a full deck supported by through-beams. Within the same basic concept, there thus emerged substantial numbers of smaller ships carrying between 20 and 100 tons of cargo, many medium-sized ships for the movement of freight totalling between 100 and 300 tons, and a few ships of considerably larger size for the carriage of cargoes turning the scales at 600 or more tons. It is probable that the smallest of these three basic sizes of merchant ship were used primarily for short-distance "run of the mill" coastal routes carrying local trade, the middle-ranking size for longer voyages

This line drawing is of a Roman merchant ship of the large grain-carrying type in the period around the end of the 2nd century AD.

The lineal descent of Roman merchant ships from the earliest types of Egyptian vessel is evident in the rounded bow and stern, the latter centered on a sternpost extended upward and forward, and often ornately carved. However, the Romans developed Phoenician and Greek merchant ship concepts into larger and more refined sizes.

such as those that linked southern Italy and mainland Greece for the delivery of cargoes such as wine, and the largest size for long voyages either across or along the Mediterranean Sea with bulk freight such as grain or stone.

The features of the largest size of Roman merchant ship, typically of the type common in about 200 AD as a fully decked type, included a balcony extending abaft the stern and covered with an awning for the comfort of the captain and his most important passengers; two large steering oars that could be lifted from the water by tackles; a deckhouse providing cabin accommodation for the ship's officers and important passengers; two or three hatches providing access through the deck to the holds; a single large pole mast; a boat generally carried on deck and employed for easy movement of passengers and other light loads between the shore and the ship when the latter was at anchor rather than alongside a quay; a cathead on each side of the bow to carry the single- or doubled-hooked anchors; a gallery round the bow as the ship's "heads"; a brailed mainsail; triangular topsails; and the fore-post projecting above the bow to carry the foresail.

Roman merchant ship from about 200 AD

Displacement:	not available
Dimensions:	length 175 ft 0 in (53.3 m) or more; beam between 45 ft 0 in and 50 ft 0 in (13.7 and 15.2 m)
Cargo capacity:	600 to 700 tons of grain or a similar bulk freight commodity
Speed:	about 6-7 kt
Complement:	about 12 to 15

Kvalsund Ship

Built around 700 AD, the so-called Kvalsund ship is a vessel of genuinely Norse origin, and was found in a bog about 150 miles (240 km) north of Bergen on Norway's western coast. With an overall length of some 59 ft (18 m), the Kvalsund ship is smaller than the similar ship found at Sutton Hoo in eastern England, but can be dated to within 50 years of the later vessel. Of clinker-built wooden construction, with eight or, according to one authority, seven strakes on each side strengthened internally by 13 frames, the Kvalsund ship probably carried 20 oarsmen (10 per side). The overlapping strakes were edge-joined with iron rivets and the rib frames were attached to the upper strakes by treenails (oak pins), but lashed to cleats cut into the lower strakes. It is possible that this last may have been facilitated by the partial assembly of the lower portion of the hull as a shell with the rib frames lashed to the cleats, before the upper strakes were treenailed to the ribs. The keel and the garboard strakes (the planks immediately outboard of the keel) were not attached to the ribs at all. The keel was itself a substantial plank of considerable thickness with a carved external fillet creating a broad, flat T–section. There was a sturdy gunwhale plank, carrying the kabes (rowlocks), at the top of the planks constituting each side, and the tholes were attached to the gunwhales with treenails rather than iron spikes.

The hull was broad and the rudder oar was deep, which suggests that the Kvalsund ship was designed for sailing as much as rowing. There was no evidence in the archaeological dig which recovered the vessel of a mast or any mast fittings, but it is believed that when boats of the Viking period were abandoned or used deliberately for burials, rather than just being wrecked, valuable components such as masts, mast steps and associated fittings were often taken for re-use. We must conclude, therefore, that the lack of any evidence

Although there is no direct evidence that the Kvalsund ship had a sailing capability, it is possible that it had the type of mast, rigging and single sail depicted here.

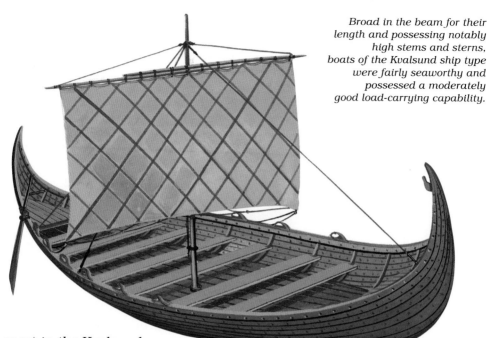

Broad in the beam for their length and possessing notably high stems and sterns, boats of the Kvalsund ship type were fairly seaworthy and possessed a moderately good load-carrying capability.

of a mast in the Kvalsund ship does not wholly remove the possibility of an original sailing capability.

The keel fillet strengthened the hull against the tendency to hogging (the sagging of the bow and stern), and also made it feasible to make the hull sufficiently beamy for adequate sailing performance. Two other interesting features of the Kvalsund ship were associated with the steering arrangement. Firstly, the rudder oar was attached to the relevant frame in the standard fashion (as also in the Sutton Hoo ship), but the rudder loom was seized (bound) to an oak boss on the outside of the hull by a withy passing through holes in the hull and the center of the boss, and then round the loom; the boss held the steering oar's loom clear of the hull's side. This improved the surface's steering capability and its facility to serve as a leeboard with the vessel under sail. Secondly, the frame supporting the steering oar assembly was actually a triangular piece of timber constituting a bulkhead and

notched to fit over the clinker planks. A similar piece was installed forward, and these two units provided a strengthened base for the treenailing of the side planking at the stem and stern, so reinforcing the hull at those highly stressed points at which the side planks were forcibly curved into the stem and stern posts and, in the stern, providing the basis for the short platform on which the steersman stood to see properly over the vessel's stem. This shaped bulkhead replacing the first and last rib frames became a standard element of Viking boatbuilding.

The Kvalsund ship was similar to the smaller but almost contemporaneous Barsett boat (in which the upper strake was sewn to the next strake down but the remaining strakes were lashed to each other in the standard fashion) and also to the Fortoft boat. Most of the features evident in this vessels became typical of the later Viking ship, although of course this last had a mast as standard.

The Vikings

Among the earliest of the great sea-faring races were the Vikings (otherwise known as the Norsemen or Northmen) of what is now Scandinavia. The Vikings were seafaring warriors best known for their raids along the coasts of Europe between the 9th and 11th centuries AD, but should also be noted for their colonization and subsequent trading across wide areas of Europe and still farther afield, and their influence on the development of European civilization and history over a period of some 250 to 300 years.

The Vikings were a pagan people from what are now Denmark, Norway and Sweden, and were originally farming folk who were probably tempted if not actually driven into their marauding and colonizing efforts by factors as diverse as the steadily increasing overpopulation of their home areas, the comparative wealth of those whom they raided, and the generally indifferent resistance that the raided communities could offer against the surprise attacks that the Vikings could deliver from the sea. The Vikings were land-owning chiefs and clan heads, the retainers of these senior figures, freemen, and any young men of the clan wanting adventure and the chance of booty. Thus a people who on land were independent farmers at

A Norse longship under way with the captain or another senior man "conning" the vessel from the bow. Before the vessel entered action, the mast was stricken to the three supports over the crew's heads.

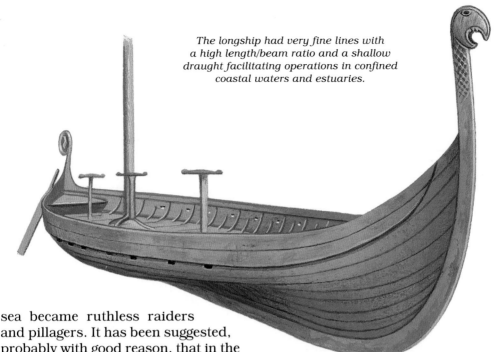

The longship had very fine lines with a high length/beam ratio and a shallow draught facilitating operations in confined coastal waters and estuaries.

sea became ruthless raiders and pillagers. It has been suggested, probably with good reason, that in the Viking period Scandinavia was characterized by what was in effect a limitless supply of men not required for day-to-day farming purposes, and also a useful number of intelligent and resourceful leaders able to organize the available manpower. This combination opened the way for the melding of men who saw themselves primarily as individual warriors first into effective raiding bands and later, as the power of the Vikings grew, into larger armies.

The Viking bands negotiated the seas right round Europe in their longships to undertake hit-and-run attacks on religious institutions, towns and cities between western Russia and the eastern end of the Mediterranean Sea. The depredations of these bands, as they plundered, burned and killed before departing once more, led to the use of the word *vikingr* ("pirate" or "sea warrior" in the early Scandinavian language). The precise make-up of the Viking armies is not known in many cases, but in general it can be said that

the expansion of the Vikings into the Baltic Sea, the lands round it, Russia and down the great Russian rivers to the Black Sea and Byzantium was probably undertaken by Swedish Vikings. The attacks on settlements in southern England and round the coast of western Europe to southern Italy were attributable mainly to Danish Vikings, who also sailed up the coast of Norway and into the White Sea. The exploratory and colonizing journeys to the Orkneys, Shetland, Faeroes, Iceland, Greenland and probably the northeastern corner of North America were the exploits of the Norwegian Vikings, who also raided the north and west coasts of Scotland, along either side of the Irish Sea and as far south into France as the mouth of the Loire river.

At the heart of the Vikings' physical capacity to undertake these exploits was their deep understanding of the sea and their development of the longship, which was the

The Vikings *continued*

Vikings' particular take on the galley and admirably suited to their particular requirements. The heyday of the longship for raiding and war purposes was between 600 and 1000 AD, and the type was developed on the basis of the same concept and design parameters from the small *snekkja* vessel with some 30 oars, via a medium-sized vessel with between 40 and 50 oars, to a large vessel with some 65 or, in some cases, as many as 80 oars. By the time of their definitive raiding and exploration, in about 800 AD, the Vikings had developed the early type of comparatively primitive vessel into the classic Viking longship.

This last was a notably sturdy vessel of the galley type, double-ended with a sharp stern as well as a sharp bow, clinker- rather than carvel-built (i.e. with a planked hull in which each lengthways plank overlapped that below it rather than being butted up against it) overlapping planks on a relatively light frame, and assembled with the aid of iron nails and caulked with tarred moss or rope. The longship had a mast which was stepped on

the keel, and this carried a single rectangular sail on one yard. The mast and yard were always struck to the rear before the oarsmen took over the propulsive effort and before the vessel entered battle. With sheets controlling the foot of the sail, and bowlines and bearing-out spars working on the tips of the yard, the sail could be braced round sufficiently for the vessel to work its way to windward rather than merely run before the wind. Other elements of the design were a high bow and stern with removable dragon, snake or monster heads, and a single side rudder on the starboard (steerboard) quarter.

The longship was, in essence, a large open boat, and lacking either a keel or a deck, offered its crew no protection from the conditions. The hull's open nature, combined with a comparatively flat bottom and low freeboard made the longship a poor seaboat, and in general the Vikings did not venture to sea in the winter for fear of being swamped and drowned. Instead, the longships were

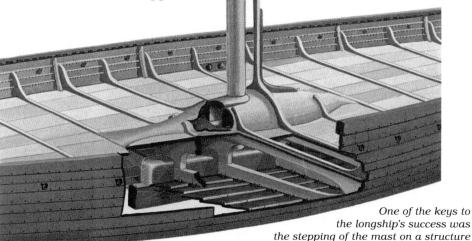

One of the keys to the longship's success was the stepping of the mast on a structure that carried the loads right through to the keel.

42

The cross section of a longship highlights the vessel's notably shallow draught and the seating arrangement for the oarsmen.

hauled up on shore in the autumn and restored to the water only in the following spring. The longship was not well suited to long ocean voyages, although such voyages were often made, as a result of its shallow draft and comparatively narrow beam. The other side of the coin however was considerable speed under sail or oar, as well as the ability to penetrate deeply into estuaries and inlets to beach safely on most shore lines so that the men could vault ashore, and the agility to extract themselves from danger even in the most confined of waters.

In the early period of their maritime history, the Vikings at first regarded the longship in its initial *skuta* (round ship) form as a dual-purpose merchant and war ship with oars intended for use only when the wind was too light or from the wrong quarter. In their golden age, around 1000 AD, the Vikings saw the need for longships fully dedicated to the warlike role with the oars more important than the sail. These definitive longships were built in three basic sizes: fewer than 20 thwarts for 40 oarsmen, up to 30 thwarts for 60 oarsmen, and more than 30 thwarts for more than 60 oarsmen in the "great ship," which can be regarded as the decisive warship of the period in northern Europe. Costly to build and lacking a high level of agility on the water, the "great ships" were not produced in large numbers however, so it was the vessels of the middle group, both fast and agile, which were the most important ships in the Vikings' "armoury."

In war, the sides of the longship and its crew were protected by the men's round, painted shields, which were hung from the gunwales. The men themselves frequently wore mail shirts and a helmet, and were generally well armed with weapons including a sword, axe, spear, javelin, and bow and arrow according to individual preference.

Havhingsten fra Glendalough (sea stallion from Glendalough) reconstruction of the *Skuldelev 2* ship in the Roskilde Viking Ship Museum, completed in September 2004

Type:	longship
Dimensions:	length 98 ft 5 in (30.0 m); mast height 47 ft 7 in (14.5 m); yard length 39 ft 4 in (12.0 m); sail area 1,205.6 sq ft (112 m²)
Speed:	10 kt under sail and 5 kt under oar
Complement:	80 including 60 oarsmen on 30 thwarts

Cinque Ports Ships

The Cinque Ports were an association of towns on the southeast coast of England, and dates from a time earlier than 1278 AD. The original five ports were Dover, Hastings, Hythe, Romney and Sandwich, soon joined by the ancient towns of Rye and Winchelsea, and then an increasing number of smaller towns in a grouping that extended finally from Essex to Seaford in Sussex. The Cinque Ports had unique responsibilities and rights. The former were based up the 16th century on the requirement to provide most of the ships and crews required for service under the English crown in time of war. Secured by a number of important charters, of which the earliest known is dated 1278, the latter giving the ports certain rights in the matters of tolls and fishing, and in the maritime jurisdiction over the waters of the English

Channel's eastern end. Though the Cinque Ports still exist, their importance as an organization declined from the reigns of Henry VII and Henry VIII (1485-1558) as a permanent navy was established, and as the growth of oceanic trade began to make western ports, such as Bristol and Plymouth, more significant in terms of the English economy.

The ships which carried the flag of the Cinque Ports in the later part of the 13th century were typical of the vessels used throughout the waters of northern Europe. The hull was a logical development of the classic "round ship" type with a length to beam ratio as low as 3:1 to maximize the volume available for the embarkation of the freight that was these ships' economic lifeblood. There was normally a single mast carrying one large rectangular sail, and the mast was braced lateral-

The English single-masted ship of the late 13th century was sturdily built and capacious, and intended for mercantile and military service.

ly by shrouds and longitudinally by stays running to the stern and to the bow and also to the tip of the high-steeved bowsprit. The most evident changes were large fore and after castles over the bow and stern, and often a combined crow's nest and fighting platform above the lifts for the yard. These were essential features in any ship that had to carry armed men either to fight off pirates or to undertake any commitment the king might impose in time of war.

Such a ship is depicted on the seal of Dover, the greatest of the Cinque Ports. The ship has large fore and after castles extended farther over the ship's ends than had earlier been the case. Even so, it is evident that the ship lies in a direct line of descent from the Viking longship in its high fore and after ends, its clinker construction, and large steering oar. This is depicted on the port rather than starboard side, presumably for artistic reasons, as the port side was always left clear of such protrusions so that all ships could come alongside the quay in an identical fashion.

Somewhat more massive than the Viking longship, though without significant enlargement of the overall dimensions, the typical ship of the Cinque Ports was still clinker-built, and was fully decked for the maximum of seaworthiness and the minimum of water damage to any cargo. The ship was worked from the deck, and evidence of the smaller size of the crew and the larger area of the sail is provided by the use of two windlasses just forward of the steering oar position. Their improved seaworthiness meant that while such vessels generally opted for coastal routes, they were also able to make sea passages such as those across the North Sea and across the width of the English Channel towards its western end.

Cinque Ports ship of the late 13th century

Type:	dual-role mercantile vessel and warship
Weight:	80 tons
Dimensions:	length 78 ft 0 in (23.8 m); beam 22 ft 0 in (6.7 m); draught 3 ft 6 in (1.1 m)
Complement:	15 sailors and, in time of war, up to 70 soldiers

Poole Seal Ship

The generic term for European ships of the mediaeval period, up to the 15th century and most especially in northern Europe but to a lesser degree in the Mediterranean, is the "round ship." The exceptions were the largely Mediterranean galley and universally northern longship, which were designed for propulsion by oars rather than by a sail, although a sailing capability was provided for cruising purposes. As suggested by the designation, the "round ship" was characterized by a low length to beam ratio, typically in the order of 2.5:1, for maximum carrying capacity. However, within the "round ship" term there were several subvariants including the cog and the dromon. These retained the round ship's basic features. including a single rectangular sail hoisted by a yard on the single mast.

The cog was the standard trading vessel of the 13th, 14th and 15th centuries, and was a clinker-built vessel with a rounded bow and stern, prominent fore and after castles, and notably broad in the beam. Such vessels carried the vast majority of the cargoes delivered to ports round the Baltic and the North Sea, and along the Atlantic seaboards of France and Spain. Though normally used for mercantile purposes, the cog was sometimes used as a warship in times of conflict: at the Battle of Sluys (1340) against the French off the

The large cog typical of the first part of the 14th century. The large bowsprit and substantial stern structure allowed the use of strong fore and back stays, opening the way for a taller mast carrying a larger sail whose area could be changed by the use of the reef points, of which two rows are shown toward the foot of the sail.

coast of Flanders, for instance, the cog *Thomas* served as the flagship of King Edward III of England. Otherwise called the dromond, the dromon was a Mediterranean vessel of the period between the 9th and the 15th centuries, and was of Byzantine origin. The dromon was at first an imperial ship, but the term was gradually adopted for any very large vessel with a single rectangular sail on a yard carried by the single mast, and a large number of oars. The dromon was used mainly for trading purposes in peace and as a transport in times of war, and knowledge of the dromon reached northern Europe largely as a result of the fact that many crusaders and their horses reached the Levant after embarking in dromon vessels at southern European ports.

The cog type of round ship developed, so far as the hull was concerned, from the concept of the Viking longship. The first stage of its further evolution was the introduction of a fixed rather than strikable mast to carry the single rectangular sail. Next came the adoption of fore and after castles as lightly framed structures that stood free of the hull proper merely as platforms for any fighting men embarked on the vessel. It was soon seen that the supports for these castles could be covered in to create additional volume for accommodation and light stowage. Another change, and certainly one of the most important in turning the hull based on the Viking longship into a more effective seagoing form, was the replacement of the starboard-side steering oar by a rudder hinged to the sternpost and generally operated by means of a tiller or ropes. The rudder made its first appearance in the middle of the 13th century, as suggested by the seals of some of the Hanseatic ports on the North and Baltic Sea coasts of northern Germany, which started to show cogs with rudders from about this time. The need to improve the installation and operation of the rudder itself paved the way for the further evolution of the hull shape, the round stern gradually giving way to a less rounded stern and then to a flat transom stern, both of which were better suited to the carriage of the ringed gudgeons into which the spikes of the rudder's pintles fitted.

47

Ships of the Crusades

The 2nd Crusade (1147-49) was undertaken mainly under German and French leadership, and while the forces of both Emperor Conrad III and King Louis III departed from Constantinople with the intention of advancing to the Holy Land by land, they were forced by circumstances to change their plans and divide their efforts, part of the forces then being forwarded by sea.

Many of these men, horses and supplies shipped to the Holy Land travelled in local vessels. By this time the hull of such vessels had remained essentially unaltered over many centuries, but more recently the square sail of the classical period had been almost wholly superseded by the triangular lateen sail, certainly by the 9th century AD but possibly as much as 200 years before that. The rig of the mediaeval lateen-rigged vessel comprised two masts each carrying a single sail, the larger of them forward, and this rig was carried on a built hull with flush planking attached to a framework stem, sternpost and ribs. The deck beams still often extended through the side planking, and steering was still entrusted to a semi-permanent oar-shaped rudder on each quarter.

Other elements of the crusader army were carried in ships which had sailed round from northern Europe, and derived largely from the *knarr*, which was the definitive form of the Viking longship for the trading role. In these vessels, which were double-ended with a stern that was in essence a mirror image of the bow, one of the primary problems of the early shipbuilders, namely the ends, had been solved by the use of a stem and a stern post. The planks were nailed together in clinker-built fashion, the cut ribs were still lashed to cleats on their inside, and steering was entrusted to a single

The larger type of northern European vessel derived from the knarr had a single square sail, side-mounted steering device, and fore and after castles.

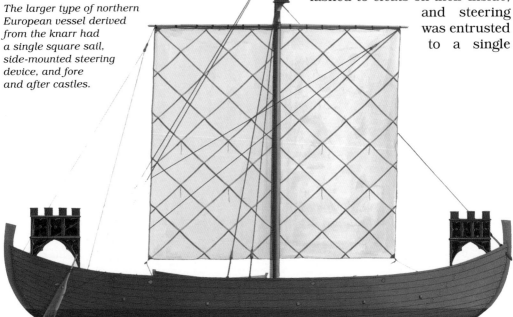

Slow and unwieldy, the trading vessels typical of northern European waters were nonetheless capacious by the standards of the day, safe, and could be used for warlike as well as peaceful purposes.

side rudder on the starboard quarter. Propulsion was provided by the simplest of sailing rigs, namely a single square sail.

This type of double-ended vessel remained in use for several centuries, but the practice of lashing the ribs to cleats was replaced by nailing, and the keel plank was replaced by a true keel. This stage of development had been reached by about 1000, and it is arguable that the replacement of cleated lashing by nails was the result of saws rather than adzes for shaping the planks. The vessels used by William I in 1066 were probably of this type, and some had their pole masts supported by shrouds, indicating that they were able to sail with the wind at least abeam.

There was little change in the 11th and 12th centuries except the addition on larger vessels of light "castles" at each end to provide elevated fighting platforms and a measure of protected accommodation below them. In this period, though, came one of the most important developments in history of sail, namely the introduction of the rudder hinged to the stern post. Where and when this took place is unknown, but it was probably in the Low Countries and possibly about 1200. However, the vessels at the time of the 2nd Crusade still had a side-mounted steering device.

Eastern Mediterranean trading vessel (typical)

Type:	two-masted lateen-rigged trading vessel
Tonnage:	30-40 tons burthen
Dimensions:	length 49 ft 3 in (15.0 m); beam 16 ft 8 in (5.1 m); draught not available
Speed:	not available
Armament:	none
Complement:	not available

Hansa Cog 1450

A reconstruction of a type of vessel that once plied the waters of northern Europe in large numbers, the *Hansekogge* (Hansa cog) is one of three modern replicas of a cog of the Hanseatic League. The original vessel was built in about 1379-80, and is supposed to have been swept away in unballasted form from the port of Bremen during a spring flood, and to have hit a sandbar and been submerged in the River Weser some 2,200 yards (2000 m) below the city. When recovered in the early 1960s, the remnants revealed that the cog's hull had been completed, but the after castle had still been under construction. Examination of the salvaged vessel revealed that it was a lineal descendant of the Viking longship in terms of its hull construction: the hull was clinker-built of long planks before the supporting frame was built into it. Less than 100 years later this concept was later abandoned for vessels in which the process began with the hull's frame or skeleton, onto which carvel planking was then added.

The vessel had a typically low length to beam ratio, and as such was boxy vessel of heavier and more rigid construction than any longship. The keel was 51 ft 2 in (15.6 m), with the angled stem and stern posts adding overhangs of 15 ft 9 in (4.8 m) forward and 7 ft 10 in (2.4 m) aft. The height from keelson to deck was 10 ft 4 in (3.15 m), and this provided a carrying capacity of 50 or slightly more tons, making the vessel in the middle of three basic sizes of which the largest could carry up to 150 tons. Somewhat strangely, the vessel's construction combined two basic types of joinery. There were 12 strakes on each side of the keel, each made up of three or four planks, and the innermost four strakes combined clinker and carvel planking. The fore part of the ship was completely clinker planked and amidships the planking changed to the carvel type: so on each side of the ship the first four strakes comprised one clinkered, eight mixed and five carvel planks. The vessel's sides were continued with four

The workhorse of northern European maritime trade, the cog in its definitive form in about 1450, as seen here, had a crew of about 10 to manage a vessel about 77 ft 0 in (23.5 m) in length and 24 ft 0 in (7.3 m) in beam, and with a burthen of some 130 tons.

The cogs of the ports and other cities which made up the Hanseatic League were suited to all types of transport tasks, the smallest vessels carrying up to about 20 tons and the largest up to 150 tons or perhaps slightly more. The vessels could operate on rivers as well as along the coast and across seas.

clinker strakes on either side. The hull was strengthened by five transverse crossbeams extending though each side immediately under the deck, which was laid cross- rather than length-wise and included a number of loose planks with finger holes so that they could be lifted easily to provide access to the hold.

The vessel had been fitted with no mast or rigging, but the propulsion arrangement would have been a single rectangular sail (traditionally of red and white vertical stripes) on a mast stepped amidships. Steering was provided by a centerline rudder controlled, by means of a tiller, by a helmsman on the main deck under the sterncastle. This was 15 ft 1 in (4.6 m) long with a width declining from 22 ft 4 in (6.8 m) forward to 21 f

(6.4 m) aft overhanging the stern, and had port and starboard extensions 11 ft 6 in (3.5 m) long and 5 ft 11 in (1.8 m) wide.

Two full-scale replicas of the Bremen cog have been built. One was built in Kiel using 14th century techniques as much as was possible, and the other in Bremerhaven to conform as much as possible with current safety requirements and an engine so that the replica can retrace Hansa shipping routes without the assistance of tugs. Both replicas have performed well in a number of sea and weather conditions, and made a significant contribution to the modern understanding of how such ships were handled.

Reconstruction of a Hanseatic cog lost off Bremen in 1380

Type:	merchant vessel
Burthen:	about 50 tons
Dimensions:	length 76 ft 5 in (23.3 m); beam 24 ft 11 in (7.6 m); loaded draught 7 ft 6 in (2.25 m); height of mast 82 ft (25 m); sail area about 2,153 sq ft (200.0 m²)
Speed:	about 5-6 kt
Complement:	about 15 men

Niña and Pinta

The caravel was a small trading vessel that was used in the Mediterranean between the 14th and the 17th centuries, and was used from a time later in the 15th century by the Portuguese and Spanish not only for trading purposes but also for their great voyages of discovery. The caravel was in essence a scaled-up boat, and therefore lacked a beakhead and any after castle. These were replaced by a simple curved stem and a plain, flat transom stern with a centerline rudder.

The original variant of the caravel was the *caravela latina* of the Mediterranean Sea with lateen (triangular fore-and-aft) sails on two or sometimes three masts, but this was soon discov-

ered to be a cumbersome arrangement as tacking required the long yards to be lowered to the deck before they could be shifted to the other side of the mast. This became even more evident on longer oceanic voyages, in which it could be both wearisome and tiring. The result was the evolution of the *caravela latina* into the *caravela rotunda*, which had three masts which were square-rigged on the fore and main mast, but retained the lateen sail on the mizzen mast. By comparison with the *caravela latina*, the *caravela rotunda* provided a considerably better-balanced sail plan which greatly eased the tasks of its crew on longer deep-ocean voyages.

In common with other ship types of the era of sail, the *caravela* was built in several sizes. The definitive *caravela rotunda* is known in three basic sizes: the smallest of these had a length of 55 to 60 ft (16.75 to 27.2 m), the middle size a length in the order of 75 to 80 ft (22.9 and 36.3 m), and the largest size

The Niña set off toward the Americas as a caravela latina with lateen sails on all three of her masts.

India and the East Indies. It was also in vessels of this type that Ferdinand Magellan departed on the voyage that led to the first circumnavigation of the Earth in 1519-22.

The *Niña* was a *caravela Latina* lateen-rigged on three masts with the largest sail and foremost sail being set almost amidships. Owned by Juan Niño de Moguer and officially named *Santa Clara*, the vessel is known to history as the *Niña* because it was Spanish custom to give ships the feminine form of the owner's surname. Taken by Columbus in satisfaction of a fine owed by the citizens of Los Palos to King Ferdinand and Queen Isabella, the *Niña* was commanded by Vicente Yáñez Pinzón, whose brother Martín Alonso was master of *Pinta*. The *Niña* sailed from Palos in company with the *Santa María* and *Pinta* on August 3, 1492. At Las Palmas Pinzón changed the *Niña* from a *caravela latina* to a *caravela redonda* with a lateen mizzen, a square sail on the mainmast (the old foremast) and a square sail on a new foremast stepped near the bow. This made the vessel better suited to running before the trade winds across the Atlantic. The vessels reached the Bahamas on October 12th and continued the exploration, but after the *Santa María* grounded on a coral reef on December 25th, it was obvious that the 40 men of her crew could be accommodated in the *Niña*, the *Pinta* having separated. A fort was erected from the *Santa María's* timbers and 39 men volunteered to stay. Columbus transferred to the *Niña*, and after the *Pinta* had rejoined, the two vessels set off toward Spain on January 16, 1493 but were separated in a storm on

with a length of up to 100 ft (30.5 m). The largest size was comparatively uncommon, and of the other two sizes the middle was perhaps more numerous, and certainly more important in trading terms, than the small size.

All three of the ships with which Christopher Columbus departed Spain in 1492 to find a westward route to Cathay but instead discovered the Americas were caravels, and the importance of the caravel in the Iberian voyages of discovery before and just after the end of the 15th century is attested by the fact that it was in a vessel of this type that Bartholomew Diaz rounded the Cape of Good Hope at the southern tip of Africa in 1488 and thus paved the maritime way to

Niña and Pinta *continued*

February 12th. It was March 15th before the *Niña* reached Los Palos, just hours before the *Pinta*'s arrival and eight months after the squadron's departure.

Columbus was promoted to "Admiral of the Ocean Sea," and almost immediately set about planning a second voyage. The *Niña* was too small to be the flagship of a new fleet, for which a new *Santa María* was selected. The new fleet consisted of no fewer than 17 ships, which sailed from Cadiz on September 25, 1493 and reached Dominica on November 3rd after an uneventful passage. In April 1494 Columbus selected three caravels, the *Niña* which he now half-owned, the *San Juan* and the *Cardera* for an exploring expedition which lasted four

months. On March 10, 1496 the *Niña* and one other vessel sailed for Spain, embarking between them about 255 people, reaching the Bay of Cadiz on June 11th.

As Columbus was preparing his third voyage to the Americas, *Niña's* captain, Alonso Medel, decided to undertake a trading voyage to Rome, but was captured by Sardinian pirates. But the vessel was recaptured by its crew, and returned to Cadiz in time to sail from Sanlúcar on January 23, 1498, under the command of Pedro Francés, shortly before Columbus's main fleet sailed on his third voyage. The *Niña's* later career in the Caribbean is not known, and the last written record of the vessel is datable to 1501.

The smallest and least known of the three vessels on Columbus's first voyage to the Americas in 1492-93, the *Pinta* was a *car-*

From the beginning of the 1492 voyage to Cathay, the Pinta was rigged as a caravela redonda with square sails on her fore and main masts and a lateen sail on her mizzen mast.

avela rotunda (or in Spanish *car-avela redonda*), which had been built as a trading vessel with a single rectangular sail on the fore and main masts, and a single lateen sail on the mizzen mast. As was the case with the *Niña*, Columbus requisitioned the ship for the voyage in satisfaction of a fine levied by Spain's King Ferdinand and Queen Isabella. Acquired from Cristóbal Quintero, who sailed as a seaman on the voyage, the *Pinta* was commanded by Martín Alonso Pinzón and sailed from Los Palos in company with the *Santa María* and the *Niña* on August 3, 1492. Three days later, the *Pinta* had trouble with her rudder, and this was properly repaired only after Pinzón put into Las Palmas, on Grand Canary Island. Columbus pressed on to Gomera, in hopes of finding a replacement vessel, and when they returned to Las Palmas on August 25, two weeks later, the *Pinta* had been ready only slightly more than one day. With repairs to

Pinta complete, the squadron departed once more on September 1st, and after two days at Gomera resumed its westward voyage on September 6th. Early in the morning of October 12th, the *Pinta's* lookout Rodrigo de Triana made the first verifiable sighting of land. The *Pinta* later separated from the other two ships, but rejoined Columbus, whose *Santa María* had been wrecked, on January 6, 1493. Two days later, the *Niña* and *Pinta* sailed for Spain. The two vessels were separated by a storm on February 13. The *Pinta* made her way to Bayona, north of the Portuguese border, probably by the end of February. While there, Pinzón sent letters to Ferdinand and Isabella asking for permission to tell them of the voyage's success. Denied permission, Pinzon returned to Los Palos, which he reached just after Columbus had arrived. Ill, Pinzón returned home and soon died, and the *Pinta's* fate is not recorded.

Niña

Type:	three-masted caravela redonda
Displacement:	55 tons empty and 94 tons laden
Dimensions:	length 49 ft 3 in (15.0 m) on the waterline and 68 ft 11 in (21.0 m) overall; beam 16 ft 5 in (5.0 m) on the waterline and 19 ft 8 in (6.0 m) overall; draught 6 ft 7 in (2.0 m)
Armament:	one 3.5 in (90 mm) lombard and several 1 8 in (45-mm) falconets
Complement:	24 men

Pinta

Type:	three-masted caravela redonda
Displacement:	75 tons empty and 116 tons laden
Dimensions:	length 55 ft 9 in (17.0 m) on the waterline and 75 ft 6 in (23.0 m) overall; beam 16 ft 5 in (5.0 m) on the waterline and 23 ft 0 in (7.0 m) overall; draught 6 ft 7 in (2.0 m)
Armament:	one 3.5 in (90 mm) lombard and several 1.8 in (45-mm) falconets
Complement:	26 men

Santa María

One of the single most important voyages in history was the first of Christopher Columbus' four crossings of the North Atlantic between Spain and the Americas in the period between 1492 and 1502. Columbus's intention was the discovery of a direct westward route to the Orient or, as it was put at the time, "the land of India and the great island of Cipango (Japan) and the realms of the Great Khan (Cathay or China)." One of the many people now sure that the Earth was round, Columbus was nonetheless well wide of the mark about the Earth's diameter when he estimated the distance from the Canary Islands, Spain's most westerly possession, to Japan and China as 2,400 and 3,550 miles (3860 and 5715 km) respectively, whereas the real straight-line distances are 10,600 and 11,765 miles (17060 and 18935 km) respectively. Though he reached South and Central America on his last voyage, Columbus went to his death bed believing that the Far East lay only 10 days' sailing west of Honduras.

1   The "Great Cabin" occupied by Christopher Colombus
2   Ports for light cannons
3   After Hatch – used by crew when the main hatch was covered by the ship's boat
4   Tiller
5   Main Hatch - leading to hold
6   Ship's boat - whose tarpaulin would be used for collecting drinking water from rain squalls

The Santa María was a comparatively small caravel by contemporary standards, but was nonetheless the flagship of Columbus's first transatlantic voyage.

Columbus made his first approach for funding to King João II of Portugal, who refused to provide any support for the endeavor even though Portugal had been bearing the cost of launching exploratory expeditions down the west coast of the African continent over the last half century. In 1485, Columbus therefore shifted the base of his operations to Los Palos de la Frontera in Spain as he had now decided to approach two new sponsors, namely King Ferdinand and Queen Isabella. The joint monarchs took their time in considering the proposal that Columbus put to them, but finally approved it. When Columbus received his commission, the citizens of Palos furnished him with two small caravels, *Niña* and *Pinta*, as a means of satisfying a fine which had been imposed on the town by Ferdinand and Isabella, and Columbus also hired a larger *nao* (ship) of the caravel type. This was the *Santa María*, a merchant vessel from Galicia, and *Santa María's* owner, Juan de la Cosa, sailed as pilot.

Although the *nao* was larger than the caravel, with the size that persuaded Columbus to make the *Santa María* the *capitana* (flagship) of his little squadron of three vessels, she was not an especially large vessel for her day. Sometimes called *La Gallega* in reflection of the vessel's Galician origins, the *Santa María* was a three-masted vessel: the foremast carried a single square sail, the main mast two square sails and a topsail, and the mizzen mast a single fore-and-aft lateen sail; the bowsprit also carried a square spritsail. In favorable conditions the mainsail could be increased in overall area and this in driving power by the addition of two bonnets, which were lengths of canvas laced to the foot of the course (mainsail) to increase its

depth. The *Santa María* had a centerline rudder on her transom stern, and this was controlled by the helmsman with a tiller. With only one deck and loaded with provisions for a year away from any source of resupply, the *Santa María* was able to offer her crew only the barest of personal comforts, and even by the standards of the day the sleeping quarters were sparse. In this last capacity, though, it is worth noting that the provision for the crew's rest were considerably improved by the adoption of the hammock, a device which the crew first discovered on arrival in the Caribbean. The hammock was soon the standard "bed" of sailors the length and breadth of Europe. When required, the *Santa María* could be towed by a heavy yawl or herself rowed by the working of large wooden sweeps. Columbus discovered the *Santa María* to be an indifferent vessel, and he was also unhappy with the fact that she was too deep in the draught for real utility in exploratory purposes when it was necessary to be close to unknown shore that might have shallowly submerged reefs or rocks just off it.

The squadron departed from Los Palos on August 3, 1492. The *Santa María* and *Niña* arrived at the island of Gomera in the Canary Islands on August 12th, but rudder problems had forced the *Pinta* into Las Palmas, to which the *Santa María* and *Niña* returned on August 25. Reunited, the squadron sailed to Gomera and finally set off on the main leg its westward voyage on September 6th. The lightness of the wind prevented the three ships from making more than the most vestigial progress until three days later, but then the wind came round to a most favorable quarter and gained strength. The ships reached the Sargasso Sea in about 32° W longitude

Santa María *continued*

on September 16, but three days later came out of the area favored by the trade winds and had to endure about seven days of light and fluky breezes. On September 25, Vicente Yáñez Pinzón of the *Niña* made the first false landfall, presumably in an effort to secure for himself the prize of 10,000 *maravedis* (10 months of a seaman's typical pay) that had been offered by Ferdinand and Isabella. Conditions then improved once more, and the squadron covered something over 700 miles (1125 km) in the five-day period up to October 6th. On October 7th there was another report of a landfall, but the squadron was still 400 miles (645 km) east of the nearest land, in the Bahamas. However, Columbus appreci-

ated the significance of birds flying southwest, and followed this lead. By this time, though, there was considerable disaffection, and indeed talk of a mutiny by October 10th, and it is believed that Columbus was so disturbed that the agreed to turn back across he Atlantic if land was not sighted within the next few days. Just one day later, the ships encountered man-made objects and tree branches floating in the sea, and this was sufficient to persuade all that land was in the immediate offing.

At about 10 o'clock in the evening Columbus believed that he saw a distant light, and about fours hours later, early in the morning of October 12, the *Pinta's* lookout, Rodrigo de Triana, saw the island of Guanahaní, inhabited by Taino "Indians," in what is now the Bahamas, where the Spaniards landed later on the same morning. Columbus gave this island the

The Santa María was the flagship of the small squadron of Spanish vessels led across the Atlantic by Christopher Columbus in 1492. She was three-masted and had a crew of some 40 men.

name San Salvador: the English later renamed this as Watlings Island, but the name was finally changed back to San Salvador in honor of its historical importance. What immediately caught the eyes of the Spaniards was the fact that the Taino islanders wore jewellery made of gold.

The squadron cruised through the Bahamas for two weeks and then on October 27 headed south to Cuba, whose north coast, as far to the west as Puerto Padre, it explored for the next six weeks. Early in November, Columbus sent an embassy inland to the village of Holguín in the hope that this might be revealed as a large town in Asia. Columbus was sadly disappointed when he learned that his interpreter, Luis de Torres with languages including Arabic, Aramaic and Hebrew, achieved nothing. On November 20 the squadron sailed east once more in the direction of the Bahamas, but the *Pinta* separated to investigate Great Inagua Island, and rejoined the other two vessels only in the first days of 1493.

After completing a preliminary exploration of the northeastern coast of Cuba, on December 5th the *Santa María* and the *Niña* sailed eastward to Cape St. Nicholas, the northwestern tip of the island of Hispaniola, in what is now Haiti, and a week later claimed possession of the land in the name of Ferdinand and Isabella. The presence of more gold artifacts and the friendliness of the local cacique (headman) gave considerable encouragement to the Spaniards. Then a disaster overtook the voyage, for as the two ships were sailing to the east on December 24, the *Santa María* grounded on a coral reef just after midnight; the only person awake aboard the ship seems to have been a ship's boy, who was steering, for the master of the watch and the helmsman had fallen asleep. No one lost his life, but the *Santa María* was beyond any redemption and the Spaniards spent December 25 salvaging what could be saved from the vessel. With the *Pinta* still absent, Columbus faced the prospect of a crossing of the Atlantic in the little *Niña*, loaded with more than 60 men and their supplies, so 39 men from the *Santa María* and the *Niña* volunteered to remain at La Navidad, in a fort which was extemporized from the salvaged timbers of the *Santa María*. The *Niña* sailed on January 4, 1493, and two days later met the *Pinta* at Isla Cabra before sealing eastward for Spain. None of the men who stayed on Hispaniola lived to be recovered by Columbus on his return during November 1493, all having been killed as they attempted a foray inland in search of booty.

Santa María

Type:	three-masted nao of the *caravela rotunda* type
Tonnage:	108 toneladas empty and 239 toneladas laden (the tonelada was about 2,030 lb/920 kg)
Dimensions:	length 59 ft 1 in (18.0 m) on the waterline and 88 ft 7 in (27.0 m) overall; beam 19 ft 8 in (6.0 m) on the waterline and 26 ft 3 in (8.0 m) overall; draught 9 ft 10 in (3.0 m)
Armament:	one 3.5 in (90 mm) lombard and several 1.75 in (45 mm) falconets
Complement:	40 men

The Lateen

Derived from the word "latin" as pertaining to the Mediterranean region, the lateen sail is defined as a triangular sail set on a very long yard bowsed well down at its forward end so that it sets obliquely on the mast and has a high peak. The yard is generally of two of more pieces bound together to yield a center more rigid than the ends, and because with this type of sail no forestay was possible, the mast was normally raked well forward, and the yard was generally connected to the mast by an easily released slip knot, or an equivalent mechanical device. The forward end of the yard was usually hauled down by two bow tackles, and the after end was braced down, thus producing curvature on the yard.

Although it was long believed that the lateen sail was an Arab creation, it is now thought that it may have had its origins in the sails of the Greek and Roman civilizations. Though square, these sails were carried by yards whose tips could be moved vertically as well as horizontally. The sails also had brails and could thus be furled in sections, and this meant that it was feasible for the square sail to be turned virtually into a lateen sail by bracing the yard right round, hauling down its forward end, and brailing up the portion of the sail forward of the mast. Such a rig allowed the ship to sail far closer to the wind than would otherwise have been the case, a fact that would not have been lost on sailors, who could well have demanded that their sails be cut to facilitate this practice.

Even so, the square sail predominated right into the 4th century AD, and was then probably challenged by the more lateen-type sail. The lateen sail became wholly dominant in the Mediterranean in the 9th century, and preserved this position into the 13th century and the re-emergence of the square sail.

While the square sail offered dis-

The lateen rig, with a large triangular sail set on a two- or three-piece yard bowsed well down at its forward end, was very efficient and could be handled by a small crew.

60

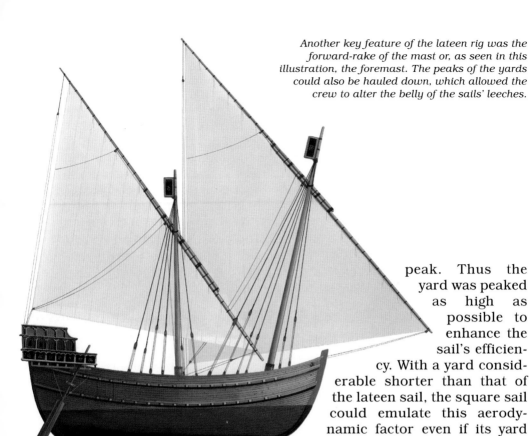

peak. Thus the yard was peaked as high as possible to enhance the sail's efficiency. With a yard considerable shorter than that of the lateen sail, the square sail could emulate this aerodynamic factor even if its yard could have been elevated to the almost vertical position.

The almost universal adoption of the lateen sail in the Mediterranean during the mediaeval period reflects the fact that shipping was probably more scattered over the sea than it had been in ancient times, during which ships generally cruised between major ports as and when the wind suited. In the mediaeval period there was greater demand for shipping able to sail to and from larger numbers of more scattered ports in diverse conditions. The lateen sail improved the ability of ships to beat to windward, so opening the way for trade as demanded by economic conditions rather than at the dictate of weather conditions. The lateen-sailed vessel was also more agile than its square-rigged counterpart, with obvious advantages for warlike purposes.

tinct advantages to the vessel running before the wind, the lateen sail offered unrivalled capabilities for vessels sailing in more changeable conditions. Even if a square sail can be braced round virtually fore-and-aft, it is not as efficient for upwind sailing as a lateen sail created specifically to be rigged fore-and-aft. In a vessel beating into the wind, the closer its sails are set to the vessel's longitudinal axis the more capably the rig will perform, and the lateen sail can be set much closer to this axis than a square sail. It is also worth noting that, either by accident or by design, the lateen sail of the mediaeval period was notably efficient because of its large windward bagginess: air trapped at the foot of the sail's luff (leading edge) spiralled upward within the bag of the sail, increasing in pressure toward the

Junks

The junk was developed in the Far East as a type of sailing vessel and is particularly associated with the Chinese and Javanese. This type of vessel was produced with varying numbers of masts and in sizes ranging from small up to monsters with a displacement of between 3,000 and 4,000 deadweight tons. The most characteristic features of the junk, which was always of wooden construction, were a flat bottom without any keel, a notably high stern, a comparatively low, square bow, and typically two or three masts each carrying a single lugsail and, in the larger vessels, provision for one or two more masts that could be raised or lowered as required by the weather conditions. This type of sail was four-sided and set on a lug or yard about two-thirds of the length of the foot, and in the case of the junk was normally set with about one-quarter of the sail area extending forward of the mast. The lug or yard carried a strop by which it was hoisted up the yard on a traveller until the luff of the lugsail was taut. In the junk the lugsail was generally made of matting stiffened with horizontal battens, generally of bamboo, which greatly improved the aerodynamic efficiency of the sail. But from the early part of the 19th century matting was often replaced by matting-reinforced canvas. Reefing was simple with the type of sail used on junks: with the luff controlled by a number of sheets extending into a large number of crowfeet, the lug or yard was merely lowered to create a sail of the desired area.

The name *junk* is derived from the Portuguese *junco*, itself based on the Javanese djong (ship). The junk has survived for a very long time without significant change, and among its other features are the point of maximum beam about two-thirds of the length from the bow, and a chamfered bow without a stem. The junk had a very full stern, and was steered by a single large rudder that was lowered beneath the level of the bottom once the vessel was at sea. Less obvious to any external view, moreover, were features such as the pontoon deck and the very considerable com-

The junk was a capable and adaptable type of vessel which served the maritime needs of the Chinese empire for many centuries without significant conceptual change.

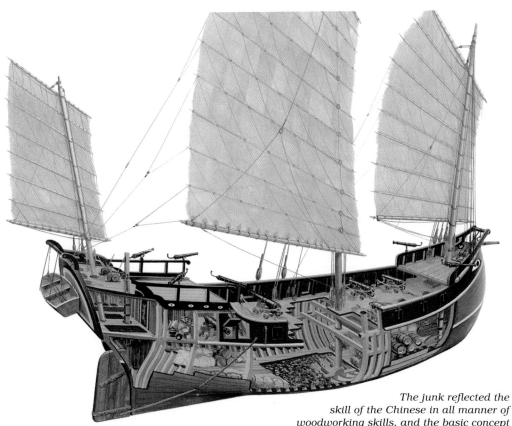

The junk reflected the skill of the Chinese in all manner of woodworking skills, and the basic concept proved highly adaptable for the ocean-going as well as coastal tasks imposed on it.

partmentalization within the hull. The pontoon deck was curved downward from the longitudinal centerline to the point of widest beam, facilitating flow of water from the deck, and above this was a flat fore-and-aft deck of narrower beam. The use of large numbers of bulkheads (up to 20 in total for major vessels) provided additional structural strength, helped to ensure that in the event the vessel sprang a leak the water would be confined to the smallest possible part of the vessel, and with the various decks allowed the establishment of large numbers of cabins for the merchants and their wares on long trading voyages.

In its larger ocean-going form, the junk was the standard merchant vessel of the Chinese empire right into the western reaches of the Pacific Ocean, as far south as the Philippine Islands on a regular basis and on a more irregular basis the Indian Ocean as far west as East Africa, and perhaps as far east as the western coast of North America. The junk was also the standard general-purpose fighting ship of the Chinese empire, the vessel being armed with guns on its deck.

Junks built in south China began to a reveal a distinct western influence from the 18th century, a wide housing often being added round the rudder, a large platform being added over the railings at the bow, and a bowsprit making its appearance to carry a jib.

Caravel 1520

The caravel was the vessel typical of 15th and 16th century seafaring, and was a comparatively short but broad-beamed vessel with a larger after castle and smaller fore castle. The caravel was one of the most important types of sailing vessel ever developed, and instrumental on the epoch-making journeys of discovery undertaken by Portuguese and Spanish captains in the century starting from about 1425 AD. From the 1440s, the caravel appeared throughout Atlantic Europe and the Mediterranean as a versatile vessel readily adaptable to local practices. The caravel's heyday lasted almost one century until the popularity of lighter vessels waned from the 1530s.

The earliest known Iberian caravels date to the 13th century, when it was an offshore fishing and coastal trading vessel probably related to the *caravo* or *qarib*, a lateen-sailed vessel used by the Muslims of the Iberian peninsula and northwest Africa into the 15th century. The caravel came to be used for voyages of discovery some time between 1420 and 1440, which coincides with the first known use of the caravel outside the Iberian peninsula. Between 1440 and the death of Prince Henry "the Navigator" of Portugal in 1460, more than 80 caravels sailed south into the Atlantic. Information about the first exploratory caravels is scanty, but these were probably vessels of about 18 to 60 tons burthen. There remains no evidence about the dimensions of these ships, but illustrations of the late 15th and early 16th

In its later forms the caravel was a mix of influences, the most obvious being the combination of "northern European" square sails forward and "Mediterranean" lateen sails aft. The combination was designed to yield a satisfactory combination of sailing characteristics on and off the wind.

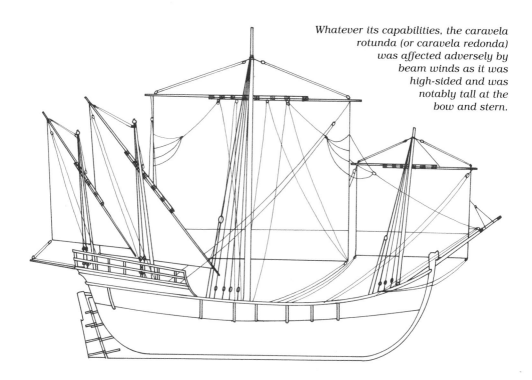

Whatever its capabilities, the caravela rotunda (or caravela redonda) was affected adversely by beam winds as it was high-sided and was notably tall at the bow and stern.

century suggest that the smallest caravels were open boats and had only a single mast. Fully decked Portuguese caravels stepped two or three masts with lateen sails, and their length to beam ratio may have been 5:1. They had no forecastle, and the low after castle sometimes extended almost to the foot of the main mast or a little forward of it. The main advantages of the caravel over the preceding *barque* and *barinel* were its higher speed, greater agility and shallower draught. The caravel could also point higher into the wind, and its low sides reduced windage and thus leeway, and mounted a sternpost rudder at a time when Mediterranean *barques* still had steering oars. However, the lateen rig was not best suited to long downwind passages, though a solution was soon discovered in the rerigging of the fore and sometimes the main masts with square sails, though some captains then reverted to the lateen rig for upwind passages.

The limitations of the lateen caravel had become clear by about 1480, and were reflected in the Portuguese evolution in the 16th century of the *caravela da annada* with two square sails on a forward-raked foremast and lateen sails on the other three masts, so opening the way to a more capacious vessel, but retaining the basic caravel's speed and ability to sail close to the wind. Square-rigged caravels appeared much earlier outside Portugal, however, possibly as early as the later 1430s for the ruler of Burgundy, and in Andalusia the square-rigged *caravela redonda* certainly no later than 1475. By 1520, however, the caravel was being superseded by small full-rigged ships (square sails on three masts), especially as on longer voyages as the full-rigged ship was wider in the beam and so offered an attractive combination of the greater payload and lesser handling risks without significant degradation of windward sailing capability.

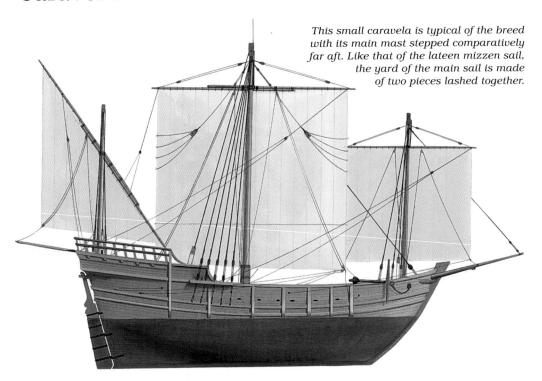

This small caravela is typical of the breed with its main mast stepped comparatively far aft. Like that of the lateen mizzen sail, the yard of the main sail is made of two pieces lashed together.

The caravel was used primarily for fishing and trading, or alternatively for escort and patrol in times of crisis. The fisheries off Morocco and West Africa had been worked by caravels for many years right into the early years of the 16th century, and from 1500 Portuguese caravels moved northwest to the new cod fisheries off Newfoundland. Closer to home *caravelões* (small caravels first appearing in 1484) were the core of the Algarve's tuna fleet in the 1570s. It should be noted that caravels also distributed preserved fish to European markets, and such was the importance of this trade that by the middle of the 1450s larger caravels were being built. Caravels were also at the heart of the gold and silver bullion, slave, spice and sugar trades. Up to about 1550 and then again in the late 16th and early 17th centuries, therefore, the caravel was vital to the trade of Portugal and Spain.

The growth of this commercial empire also demanded expansion of naval capability, and the caravel served well in tasks as diverse as shorter-distance supply and troop transport to longer-endurance warship. By the later part of the 15th century the caravel was perceived as a decisive weapon of war. By 1494, Portugal had heavy guns on caravels built to guard the Portuguese coasts and the Straits of Gibraltar. The small 40/50-ton caravels or *caravelões* of the 16th century carried only light guns, but there were also smaller numbers of very heavily armed large caravels mounting up to 40 guns by comparison with the typical figure of 14 to 18 pieces.

Between 1430 and 1470 the caravel had also become a vessel typical of western Europe between England and Sicily. This reflected not only the caravel's capabilities, but also the period's shift toward smaller, faster and more versatile vessels which could be loaded and unloaded rapidly and could operate between a more diverse range of ports. The shipping slumps of the 1430s and 1440s began the process whereby the dominance of the great carracks of the early 15th century was terminated, and the process was almost complete by the 1480s.

By the middle of the 16th century the first inklings that the caravel was becoming outmoded had started to appear. By this time the caravel's technical development had peaked with the advent of the four-masted *caravela de armada*, which carried a square spritsail, fore sail and fore topsail, and three lateen sails. A heavy warship of 140 to 170 tons with a length to beam ratio of only 2.9:1, the *caravela de armada* was in effect a hybrid combining elements of the round ship and the caravel, and as such offered advantages as a gun platform but also lacked some of the caravel's better sailing and handling characteristics. There were, of course, still a number of older caravel warships of the finer-hulled type, these including the a small type of 95 to 115 tons with a length to beam ratio of 3.3:1 but rigged like the *caravela de armada*,

other small two-deck caravels with a length to beam ratio of between 3.6:1 and 3.8:1, and smallest of all the *mexeriqueira* dispatch carrier. The naval thinkers of the later 16th century disapproved of the caravel for naval purposes in both its square- and lateen-rigged forms, the latter more than the former on the grounds that it had a tendency toward heavy heeling and the lack of the protection that would have been afforded by a fore castle to the men on the poop deck, and especially the helmsman together with the tiller.

For whatever reason, the caravel was drawing to a close soon after the end of the first quarter of the 16th century as emphasis switched to larger vessels such as the newly developed galleon. When smaller vessels began to reacquire a commercial validity in European waters from 1570, the caravel reappeared but was soon overtaken by the barque in a modernized form, the *saetta*, the *patache* of less than 100 tons and essentially similar to the same period's full rigged three-masted pinnace of northern Europe, and the *bergantin*. Despite its different name and a number of significant differences, the *saetta* of 50 to 100 tons can be seen as a revitalized caravel with a long, light hull and three lateen-rigged masts, while the full-rigged *saetta-polacra* can by the same token be seen as the final flowering of the *caravela redonda*.

Barcelona caravel (1465)

Type:	two-masted caravel with a sternpost rudder and two steering oars
Tonnage:	53 tons burden
Displacement:	length 60 ft 8 in (18.5 m); beam 14 ft 9 in (4.5 m); hold depth 5 ft 7 in (1.7 m)
Speed:	probably 4-5 kt
Complement:	not available, but probably in the order of 7 or 8 men

Great Harry

The step up from the caravel in terms of size and, reflecting the need for the carriage of greater cargo loads as European trade boomed, if payload was the carrack. This became the standard larger vessel of northern and southern Europe between the 14th and 16th centuries. The type was in essence an enlarged, beamier and structurally strengthened version of the *caravela rotunda* combining the square-sailed rig of the northern Europeans with the lateen-sailed rig of the Mediterranean peoples, as well as notably tall fore and stern castles. As such, the carrack can be regarded as an intermediate stage between the caravel and the galleon which paved the way for the fully fledged three-masted ship. The carrack was square-rigged on its fore and main masts, and lateen-rigged on its mizzen mast, and was built in tonnages up to about 1,200. Such was its success that the carrack became the standard trading ship used by the Portuguese and Spanish between the Iberian peninsula and their imperial and trading interests in the Americas, India, China and South-East Asia.

Like the caravel, the carrack was used as a trading vessel and also as a warship, and the most celebrated

of the latter was the *Henry Grâce à Dieu*, otherwise known as the *Great Harry* and, in her time, the largest warship in the world. One of the most important features of the reign of Henry VIII (1509-47) was the furtherance of his father's work in beginning a permanent navy, and to this end Henry VIII was responsible for three notably important warships in the form of the *Mary Rose* (1505), and *Great Galley* (1513) and *Henry Grâce à Dieu* (1514). Among the many features that characterized these vessels was their construction as dedicated warships rather than as merchant vessels which could be adapted as warships in times of crisis. The ship was built at Woolwich Dockyard (at Erith in Kent) by

A huge warship by the standards of the time, the Henry Grace à Dieu was a four-masted carrack armed, at one period, with 231 small and 21 large guns.

The "great guns" of the Henry Grâce à Dieu were of a primitive breech-loading type with the hoop-strengthened iron or bronze barrel lashed to the "carriage." Handling rings are attached to the breech section, and the gun fired stone shot.

William Bond, master shipbuilder, under the supervision of Robert Brygandine, clerk of the ships, and launched in June, 1514. The tonnage of the *Great Harry* is given variously as 1,000 or 1,500 tons, and she was a vessel with four pole masts; all but the bonaventure mizzen mast had two circular tops, and the vessel set three square sails each on the fore and main masts, and lateen sails on the mizzen and bonaventure mizzen masts. On state occasions, the sails were of damasked cloth of gold. The vessel's armament varied considerably with the period, but at one time comprised 231 small-calibre brass and iron guns mainly of the trainable murderer type, as well as 21 large guns mounted below the vessel's waist on three decks. The low siting of the heavy guns improved the *Great Harry's* stability, and at the same time enhanced the guns' capabilities in ship-against-ship fighting, in which

the enemy vessels could be more easily hulled on or below the waterline. The smaller-calibre guns were designed mainly for use against masts, rigging, and people, and were most effective mounted in the fore and stern castles, which rose four and two decks respectively and allowed the guns to fire down on the decks of any opposing vessel.

Though conceived in a time of almost continuous war between England and France, the *Henry Grâce à Dieu* saw no action until 1545 when, in the course of the French attack on Portsmouth, during which the *Mary Rose* sank, the vessel was engaged by Admiral Claude d'Annebault's more agile galleys. Upon the accession of Edward VI (1547-53), the vessel was renamed for that monarch and remained in service to August 23, 1553, when she was destroyed in an accidental fire at Woolwich.

Henry Grâce à Dieu

Type:	four-masted carrack warship
Tonnage:	1,500 tons
Dimensions:	length about 200 ft 0 in (61.0 m) on the main deck; beam about 50 ft 0 in (15.2 m); draught not available
Armament:	varied with period, but typically 43 heavy and 141 light guns
Speed:	not available
Complement:	700 men in 1536

Mary Rose

In wars up to the first part of the 16th century, ships had been used largely for the transport of troops, and naval battles generally took the form of side-by-side boarding engagements. Even after the development of cannon, during the 14th century, naval guns were merely an adjunct to this practice in an effort to cripple the enemy's crew before a boarding was attempted. Fighting ships therefore had tall fore and stern castles from which gunners and archers could fire down onto their opponents, massed on deck for a boarding. The development of anti-ship rather than anti-personnel gunnery became feasible only with the advent of guns possessing increased range with heavier shot. For reasons of stability, such guns had to be mounted low in the vessel, and this became practicable only after the development of a water-tight gun port in the early part of the 16th century.

The earliest surviving vessel of this new type is the *Mary Rose*, which was carvel-built in Portsmouth as the flagship of the navy built up by Henry VIII (1509-47), named after the king's younger sister, and one of the first purpose-built English warships. The growing importance of anti-ship gunnery is attested by the fact that the *Mary Rose* carried 200 sailors, 185 soldiers and 30 gunners, whereas ships of the previous generation carried a greater proportion of soldiers: the somewhat larger *Sovereign* had 300 sailors and 400 soldiers.

In 1511 the *Mary Rose* was the flagship of Sir Edward Howard's English fleet of 20 ships patrolling, with a Spanish force, between Brest and Calais. The Lord Admiral was killed during the blockade of Brest in April of the following year, and was replaced by his older brother, Sir Thomas Howard, and in the summer of the same year the *Mary Rose* helped to deliver an English army to Calais. The *Mary Rose* remained in commission until 1536, when Henry ordered her rebuilt with 91 guns.

It is believed that the Mary Rose broached, the sudden heel to starboard causing water to flood through the open gun ports and sink the vessel.

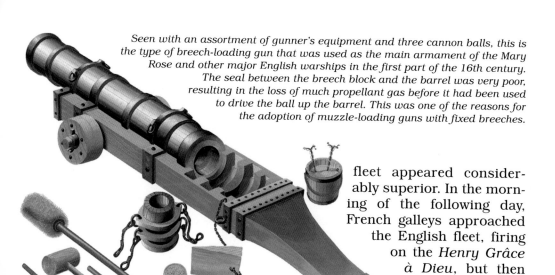

Seen with an assortment of gunner's equipment and three cannon balls, this is the type of breech-loading gun that was used as the main armament of the Mary Rose and other major English warships in the first part of the 16th century. The seal between the breech block and the barrel was very poor, resulting in the loss of much propellant gas before it had been used to drive the ball up the barrel. This was one of the reasons for the adoption of muzzle-loading guns with fixed breeches.

During 1544, the *Mary Rose* took part in Henry VIII's operations against France. Then in 1545, Francis I countered with an invasion of Portsmouth with 30,000 troops in 235 ships. The defence comprised only 60 vessels at Portsmouth with another 40 on their way. On July 18, the French fleet arrived between the Isle of Wight and Portsmouth, and the English fleet weighed anchor. The *Mary Rose* was the flagship of Sir George Carew, and despite the loss of *La Maîtresse*, which sprang a leak and sank off St. Helen's, the French fleet appeared considerably superior. In the morning of the following day, French galleys approached the English fleet, firing on the *Henry Grâce à Dieu*, but then a northerly wind allowed the English fleet to advance. The *Mary Rose* had a poor crew, however, and the guns had not been secured or their ports closed. The vessel suddenly heeled, water poured through the ports, and the *Mary Rose* sank with the loss of all but 35 men. The French landed troops on the Isle of Wight and the coast of Sussex four days later, but their effort was lacklustre and by August 17 the French fleet was back at Le Havre.

An immediate attempt to raise the *Mary Rose* resulted only in the salvage of some guns. In 1982 a major effort led to the recovery of part of the vessel's starboard side and a mass of specialized and everyday equipment.

Mary Rose

Type:	four-masted carrack warship
Tonnage:	600 tons burthen increasing to 700 tons after the ship's 1536 reconstruction
Dimensions:	length 105 ft 0 in (32.0 m) for the keel; beam 38 ft 3 in (11.65 m); draught 15 ft 1 in (4.6 m)
Speed:	not available
Armament:	78 guns increased during the ship's 1536 reconstruction to 91 guns
Complement:	about 415 men

Venetian Galley 1571

The 16th century was characterized by a major revolution in naval warfare as the age of the galley, which had extended over a period of 2,100 or more years, ended shortly after reaching its definitive form in the hands of three of the most capable galley admirals of history, namely the Ottoman Khair ed-Din, the Genoese Andrea Doria, and the Spanish Don Juan of Austria. The war galley continued to serve in the Mediterranean for more than another 100 years, but was increasingly the support for the sailing ship with broadside batteries of cannon.

Naval tactics had changed little between the Battles of Salamis in 480 BC and Lepanto in 1571, the object of combat being to close the enemy in preparation for ramming or boarding. The galleys of this period little different in basic concept from those with the Romans had used in the Punic Wars (264-146 BC). Thus they were long, narrow-beamed and single-decked vessels, about 150 ft (45.7 m) in length and 20 ft (6.1 m) in beam, propelled by about 54 oars. In addition they had two or three lateen-rigged masts, the sails being useful to provide the oarsmen (four to six on each oar, and normally slaves) with periods of rest and to give added speed in a favorable breeze. In Christian vessels the galley slaves were usually protected by mantelets, but Ottoman vessels generally lacked this feature. The crew was therefore in the order of 400 men in the form of the oarsmen, sailors and soldiers.

Mounted exactly on the centerline of the galley's foredeck was an 5,000-lb (2268-kg) bow gun some 15 ft (4.6 m) long and usually loaded with scrap metal that was fired only at the last moment. Flanking this were batteries

The name Bucintoro (derived from buzino d'oro, or golden beak in the form of the lion of St. Mark) was reserved for the state galley of the Venetian Republic, whose head of state was the doge.

of smaller ordnance: half-culverins, which were small-caliber weapons fired an iron ball weighing about 12 lb (5.4 kg), and swivel-mounted light guns. Extending ahead of the bow, just above the waterline, was a metal beak, some 10 to 20 ft (3 to 6 m) long, to provide the punch for a ramming attack. Two post-mounted moschette weapons, which were breech-loading swivel guns, were carried on each side of the stern to repel boarding attempts. Also at the stern of the ship was a high poop surmounted by a large lantern and enclosed in a wooden framework over which a canopy could be stretched. The galley was steered from this deck with a tiller, and here too the captain controlled the rate at which the oars struck the water. The oars were pivoted on outriggers that ran the length of both sides of the vessel, extending about 3 ft (0.9 m) outboard of the gunwales.

The galley's oared cruising speed was about 3 kt and, rowing in shifts and by a method essentially peculiar to Venetian galleys, her crew could maintain this speed all day. When necessary, it could drum up a maximum short-range speed of 7 kt at a rating of some 26 strokes per minute, but even the best crews could not maintain this for anything over 20 minutes. Under canvas, the galley could achieve 12 kt.

As a result of its narrow beam and shallow draught, however, the galley performed very poorly into the wind and was also very vulnerable to high seas.

The two important variations on the galley theme at the time of Lepanto were the Ottoman galiot, which was a smaller and faster vessel based on an earlier Byzantine warship, with 18 to 24 oars and a crew of about 100, and the Venetian-developed galleass, which was a larger double-sized galley, slower but stronger than the galley with improved seaworthiness and carrying more soldiers. The galleass represented a not notably successful effort to create a hybrid between the fast Mediterranean war galley and the new heavily armed sailing vessels of northern Europe. The galleass mounted between 50 and 70 cannon, but these were generally of small caliber and intended for killing men rather than piercing the hulls of vessels.

The apogee of the galley's career was the Battle of Lepanto on October 7, 1571. In his fleet Don Juan had 108 Venetian, 81 Spanish and 32 other galleys (the last provided by the Papal and other small states) as well as six great Venetian galleasses. The Ottoman fleet under Pasha Ali Monizindade had 270 galleys, generally smaller than those of the Christian fleet with crews somewhat less experienced than those of the Christian ships.

The two fleets formed up in a traditional battle formation which had varied little since the Battle of Actium in 31 BC. Each fleet was disposed over a length of some 5 miles (8 km) in

Venetians *continued*

a long line of three divisions, backed by a reserve. The Ottoman left wing was larger than the right wing, suggested that Ali planned a battle of envelopment, but neither side had any real tactical plan other than to close the enemy and secure victory by ramming and boarding. The vessels of the Christian fleet included 20,000 soldiers in a total of 84,000 men, and those of the Ottomans carried 16,000 soldiers in a total of 88,000 men. The only real difference between these fleets and those of the Punic Wars, almost two millennia earlier, was the mounting of a few small cannon in the bows of the galleys and in the broadsides of the galleasses. The Christian soldiers, including a number of arquebusiers in their number, wore light armor, but few of the Ottomans had such protection, and most were armed with bows or crossbows.

The fleets collided in a series of great clashes. By noon, about 90 minutes after the start of the fighting, the main bodies of both sides were wholly engaged. The galleasses broke the Ottoman line,

but this failed to open the way for a swift victory, and a melee raged for about three hours, during which the superior skill and armament of the Christian forces steadily made their effect felt.

The Ottoman right flank, which had not been able to get very far from land, was driven back against the shore and exterminated. The fighting in the center continued somewhat longer, but here too the Christian superiority prevailed. The Ottoman left flank, which was far

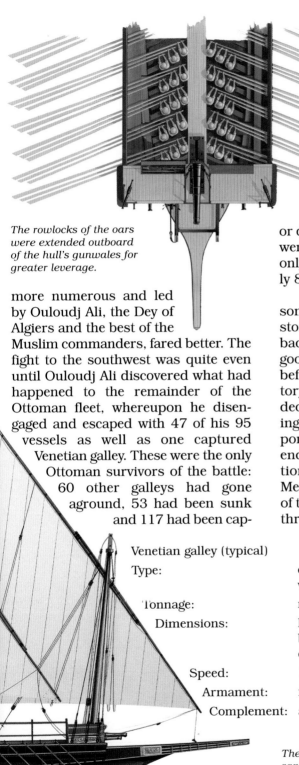

The rowlocks of the oars were extended outboard of the hull's gunwales for greater leverage.

tured, and some 15,000 Christian oarsman slaves were freed from captured or sunken Ottoman vessels, though at least 10,000 more must have drowned as they were chained to their benches. At least 15,000-20,000 Ottoman sailors and soldiers were killed or drowned, and a mere 300 prisoners were taken. The Christian fleet lost only 13 galleys, 7,566 dead and nearly 8,000 wounded.

more numerous and led by Ouloudj Ali, the Dey of Algiers and the best of the Muslim commanders, fared better. The fight to the southwest was quite even until Ouloudj Ali discovered what had happened to the remainder of the Ottoman fleet, whereupon he disengaged and escaped with 47 of his 95 vessels as well as one captured Venetian galley. These were the only Ottoman survivors of the battle: 60 other galleys had gone aground, 53 had been sunk and 117 had been cap-

Because of the lateness of the season and the likelihood of autumnal storms, the Christian fleet then pulled back to Italy to await the rearrival of good weather in the spring of 1572 before trying to exploit the great victory. Lepanto was one of the world's decisive battles. This success, resulting from the creation, if only temporarily, of a united Christendom, ended the growing Ottoman domination of the central and western Mediterranean, and marked the end of the full flood of Islam's second great threat against Christian Europe.

Venetian galley (typical)

Type:	one- or two-mastedlateen-rigged warship
Tonnage:	not available
Dimensions:	length 137 ft 0 in (41.75 m); beam 17 ft 0 in (5.2 m); draught not available
Speed:	12 kt under sail and 7 kt under oar
Armament:	five guns
Complement:	about 400 men

The galley combined lateen sails for long-range cruising and the resting of the oarsmen, and oars for high speed and maneuvrability in combat.

Golden Hinde 1580

Francis Drake made two privateering voyages to the Spanish territories round the Caribbean Sea between 1566 and 1568 in company with Sir John Hawkins, his cousin and in 1570 the creator of the galleon. Though his primary goal was profit, Drake was a fervent Protestant who hated Roman Catholicism. In 1576, Queen Elizabeth (1558-1603) gave Drake permission to sail round the southern tip of the Americas through the Strait of Magellan, scout the Americas' Pacific coast and, if possible, return to England by means of the sup-

The Golden Hinde was a wooden galleon built in 1576 as the Pelican, and completed the first English circumnavigation of the world as well as capturing much Spanish treasure.

Golden Hinde *continued*

posed Northwest Passage, to establish relations with peoples not yet subject to European states, and to plunder Spanish shipping.

Drake had a force of five vessels and about 180 men. His own ship, the *Pelican*, was a galleon built in Plymouth in 1576. The other ships were the 80-ton *Elizabeth* of 16 guns, the 30-ton *Marigold* of 16 guns, the 50-ton *Swan* of five guns, and the 15-ton *Christopher* of one gun. These departed Plymouth on December 13, 1577. After a pause at Mogador in Morocco, the vessels sailed for the Cape Verde Islands, capturing half a dozen Spanish ships and, more importantly, a Portuguese pilot named Nuño da Silva, whose *Santa Maria* was renamed *Mary*. The force reached the South American coast in southern Brazil on April 5, before sailing to the River Plate and then Puerto San Julian, where the English ships remained at anchor for a month. Drake decided to abandon his three smallest vessels (the *Swan, Christopher* and *Mary*), and set sail once more on August 17 with the *Pelican, Marigold* and *Elizabeth*. Three days later, the little squadron entered the Strait of Magellan and Drake renamed his ship the *Golden Hinde* as Sir Christopher Hatton,

a principal backer, had a golden hind on his coat of arms. Drake emerged into the Pacific on September 6 after only 14 days, but his luck changed as a great storm drove the ships south and caused the loss of two vessels: the *Marigold* sank with her 29 men, and the *Elizabeth* turned back to England.

Drake was finally able to head north along South America's west coast, where his presence was not even suspected. Looting Valparaiso on December 5, Drake swooped on Arica, whence silver from the mines of Potosí was shipped. But when the *Golden Hinde* reached Callao on February 15, Drake discovered that his presence was now known, although there was still little that the Spanish could do about it. Learning that a treasure ship had departed only days before, Drake followed with all speed and on March 1, 1579 captured the *Nuestra Señora de la Concepción* off the Colombian coast, taking bullion valued at about half of the English crown's yearly revenues.

Searching for the Northwest Passage, Drake now sailed as far as 48° N, just south of the Strait of Juan de Fuca, before returning south. On June 17 the *Golden Hinde* anchored in what is thought to be Drake's Bay

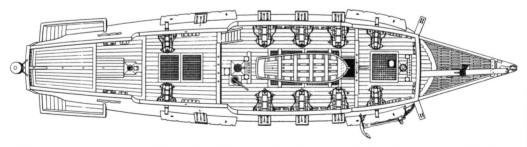

A deck plan reveals many of the Golden Hinde's salient features including the stepping of the three masts, the ship's boat, the upper-deck cannon, and the catheads for the anchors.

A sketch of the Golden Hinde in the waters of North America's western coast highlights the vessel's tall stern castle and comparatively low forecastle.

in California, which Drake claimed as "New Albion." On July 25 the *Golden Hinde* headed west across the Pacific, neared the Filipino island of Mindanao on October 16, and changed course south toward the Moluccas, where a local king permitted the English to load spices and refit their vessel. Drake sailed on the last leg of his voyage round the world on December 12, but spent a month finding his way through the Indonesian archipelago. On January 9, 1580 the *Golden Hinde* struck a reef but slid off into deeper water a day later. At taking on fresh water on the south coast of Java, Drake set sail on March 26 on a non-stop leg of some 9,700 miles (15610 km) to Sierra Leone. The *Golden Hinde* completed her voyage on September 26, 1580 as she reached Plymouth after a voyage of 2 years 10 months and 18 days with 59 of her crew still alive.

Golden Hinde (formerly *Pelican*)

Type:	three-masted galleon
Tonnage:	about 150 tons burthen
Dimensions:	length about 70 ft 0 in (21.3 m) between perpendiculars; beam about 19 ft 0 in (5.8 m); draught about 9 ft 0 in (2.75 m)
Speed:	not available
Armament:	18 guns
Complement:	80-85 men

Spanish Armada 1588

At the suggestion of the Marquis de Santa Cruz, King Philip II in 1586 ordered the preparation of a great fleet (armada) to force its way up the English Channel to the Spanish Netherlands, where it would embark the Duke of Parma's army for an invasion of England. Spanish preparations were hampered by Drake's "singeing of the king of Spain's beard" when, in April 1587, he led 23 English vessels into Cádiz and destroyed 33 Spanish vessels. Santa Cruz died in January 1588, the armada then being entrusted to the inexperienced Duke of Medina Sidonia.

The 20 galleons, 44 armed merchant vessels, 23 transports, 35 smaller vessels, four galleasses and four galleys (2,431 cannon including 1,100 heavy guns, 8,500 sailors and galley slaves, and 19,000 soldiers) sailed from Lisbon on May 28, 1588 but was hit by adverse weather and put into Corunna for repairs before sailing again on July 12.

The English fleet was split between Plymouth (94 vessels under Lord Howard of Effingham) and Dover (35 vessels under Lord Henry Seymour). The English ships carried about 1,800 heavy cannon, most of

Smaller, more nimble and generally armed with longer-range cannon than the Spanish vessels, the outnumbered English ships used darting attacks to harass the armada and pick off any stragglers before making their escape.

them long-range culverins of which the Spanish vessels had only 600. The western squadron sailed from Plymouth the day after the armada was sighted off the Lizard, and the first shots were fired off the Eddystone on July 21. The armada was too strong for the English ships to attack in formation. Smaller and handier than their Spanish opponents, though, the English vessels attacked individually, exploiting their greater agility and the longer range of their cannon, and for four days the English harassed the Spanish, who lost only two vessels. By the evening of July 25 the two forces were abreast the Isle of Wight. The English ships were running short of ammunition, and Howard reported that he intended to attack only after receiving more powder and shot.

The Spanish anchored off Calais on July 27 to await Parma's army. Howard's force also dropped anchor, and was strengthened by the advent of Seymour's vessels. The English force lay just to windward of the armada, and was thus well placed for a fireship attack. Eight fireships were committed on the following night, and there followed great confusion among the Spanish. The Spanish captains cut their cables and ran before the wind, followed by the whole English fleet. A major battle was then fought off Gravelines, the armada losing three of

The English galleon Ark Royal is seen on a St. Vincent stamp.

its finest vessels and being driven toward Dutch shoal waters. At the very last moment the wind backed and allowed the Spanish vessels to claw their way to deeper water.

Medina Sidonia's only option was a return to Spain. He could not fight his way down the English Channel, so the armada had to pass north round Scotland. Leaving Seymour's force, Howard pressed the armada as far north as the Firth of Forth but then broke off. A few English pinnaces followed the Spanish until they passed the Orkney Islands and turned west, thus committing themselves to a passage west of Ireland. The weather worsened steadily, and many Spanish ships were wrecked. Of the 130 Spanish ships, only 67 returned; the English had sunk or captured 15, 19 were wrecked on the coasts of Scotland and Ireland, and the other 29 disappeared in storms.

Ark Royal (formerly *Ark Raleigh*, built at Deptford Dockyard in 1587)

Type:	four-masted galleon
Tonnage:	694 burthen
Dimensions:	not available
Speed:	not available
Armament:	four 60-pdr, four 30-pdr, 12 18-pdr, 12 9-pdr, six 6-pdr, and 17 smaller guns
Complement:	not available

Ships of the Spanish Armada 1588

Apparently formidable, the armada included too many types of vessel, including a few completely unsuitable oared warships. The primary strength lay with 20 galleons, generally larger than their English counterparts, well built and heavily armed, but with a higher proportion of shorter-range cannon than the English vessels. The Spanish galleons were also hampered by their lack of agility and poorly trained crews. The galleons ranged in size between 250 and 1,000 tons, the largest carrying up to 50 heavy guns and a crew of 500 men. The galleons were supported by eight oared warships in the form of four galleasses and four galleys. The galleass had much of the galleon's form in its hull shape, fore and stern castles, and two or three masts. To provide a means of maneuvring independently of the wind, the galleass was also driven by oars, the three-masted type having up to 20 oars on each side. A typical galleass was 150 ft (45.7 m) long to the tip of its iron-shod ram, and also carried up to 50 guns. The compromise between galleon and galley features had the inevitable result of indifferent capabil-

Although it was not as effective as the galleon in pure warship terms, the three-masted carrack taken up from trade was turned into a moderately useful warship by the enhancement of its armament and the installation of tall bow and stern castles.

The main advantages of the patache were its speed and agility, allowing the type to operate effectively in the scouting, dispatch carrying and screening roles.

ities. With their lateen sails on two masts and shallow-draught hulls carrying up to 30 oars on each side, the galleys were useless for northern European water. The fighting strength of the armada was completed by 33 carracks pressed into naval service, fitted with more guns, and revised with raised fore and stern castles to improve their capabilities in close-quarter combat by providing platforms for smaller-caliber guns. Support for the larger vessels was provided by smaller three-masted vessels including more than 20 patache 70-ton vessels used mainly as dispatch carriers, scouts and screening vessels. Finally there were 23 urca broad-beamed transports, which were indifferent sailers but carried the fleet's stores.

Nuestra Señora del Rosario
(built in Galicia in 1587)

Type:	galleon
Tonnage:	1,150 toneladas
Dimensions:	not available
Speed:	not available
Armament:	51 guns
Complement:	443 men

San Martín
(built in Portugal shortly before 1588)

Type:	three-masted galleon
Tonnage:	1,000 tons
Dimensions:	not available
Speed:	not available
Armament:	48 guns
Complement:	650 men

Spanish Galleon

The galleon was created, in fact if not in name as the term was never used for English vessels, by Sir John Hawkins in 1570. Discovering that the carrack was a poor sailer in adverse conditions as its high fore castle was driven down to leeward by beam winds, Hawkins cut down the bulk of the forecastle. Thus the typical massive triangular superstructure, almost as high as the poop (after castle), was reduced to a shallow, rectangular unit set farther from the stem, where it would have caught the wind and acted as a lever driving the ship's bow down to leeward. As a result, the galleon sailed better upwind, in general as little as six points (70°) to the wind.

This revised type of carrack was adopted in Spain in the 1580s, initially as a warship and then steadily as a merchant vessel replacing the car-

rack, and became instrumental in the development of Spain's imperial and trading empires in the Americas and in the Far East. Spanish galleons were the most important transporters of silver from the Philippines across the Pacific to central America where, with silver and gold from the Spain's American possessions, it was transferred to other galleons for delivery across the Atlantic to Seville. The great treasure galleons that traversed the Pacific and Atlantic Oceans in the 16th and 17th centuries were among the most advanced deep-ocean vessels of their time. Success on these long crossings demanded that the galleon had to carry a sizeable cargo and large quantities of stores, but also to embark a heavy armament and a numerous crew to fight off any attempts to capture the ship, and the definitive form of the galleon reflected both these requirements.

The galleon's most striking physical feature was the considerable tumblehome, whereby the hull sloped sharply inward from a point just above the waterline and tapered to a top deck that was therefore much narrower than the ship's waterline beam. This allowed the very considerable weight of the galleon's ordnance, which could comprise as many as 60 guns, to be concentrated close to the ship's centerline with consequent advantages in sta-

With its small number of large sails and massive fighting tops, the Spanish galleon was a notably impressive type of vessel.

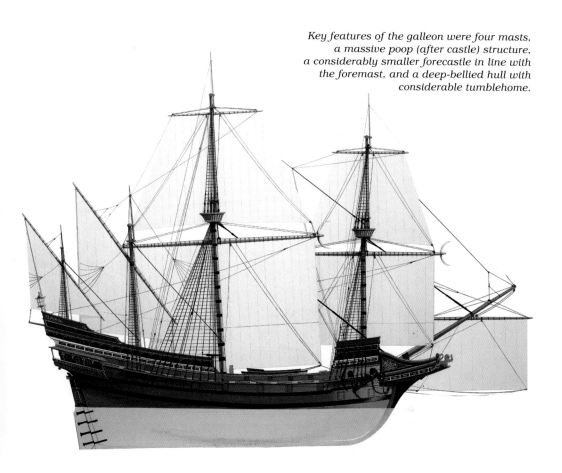

bility. This tumblehome factor also made it more difficult for an attacker to board the vessel.

This notwithstanding, her high sides and tall stern castle rendered the Spanish galleon somewhat tender and therefore easy to roll. At the same time, the short length of the keel in relation to the overall length of the hull also made the galleon pitch badly in heavy conditions. In short, therefore, the galleon could often be uncomfortable. What cannot be denied, however, is that the galleon was also notably seaworthy. With a length to beam ratio of about 3.5:1, the galleon was less bluff than other types of vessel in this period, and therefore faster than the broader-beamed vessels that were typical of the period before the galleon's introduction.

The single most important aspect of the Spanish treasure galleon's life was the delivery of her cargo, so captains were ordered to avoid contact with other ships. If challenged, the galleon's captain therefore sought to escape if his vessel could possibly manage this, and a particular feature of the treasure galleon was the provision of large scimitar-shaped blades on her yards to cut the rigging and sails of any vessel seeking to come alongside and board. The blades were designed and disposed so that they would disengage easily when required, and so facilitate the galleon's escape.

In the event that hand-to-hand combat was unavoidable, archers filled the pair of fighting tops above the main yards of the fore and main masts. From these vantage points the

Spanish Galleon *continued*

archers could pepper the deck of the enemy vessels with arrows from their bows and harder-hitting bolts from their crossbows. Gunpowder weapons would have provided harder-hitting and longer-range firepower (although at a slower rate), but firearms were expressly banned from the fighting tops for fear that a spark would set fire to the galleon's sails.

The fore and main masts each carried square sails, as did the bowsprit, whereas the mizzen mast and the bonaventure mast, the last the abaft the mizzen mast, were rigged with lateen sails, which enhanced the agility of the vessel, particularly into the wind. With a good wind well abaft the beam, this was sufficient to drive the galleon at a maximum of 8 kt, though an average of 4 kt was typical of long trans-oceanic voyages, especially when heavily laden. To cope with the great strain imposed on her masts and yards by the wind in the sails and also working on other elements of the top hamper, the masts were each stepped onto one of the main structural members of the vessel's hull. The bonaventure and mizzen masts were stepped on deck beams, and the main and fore masts extended though deck openings to mast steps in the keelson or keel. Lashed to the beakhead and morticed at its after end into the riding bitts, the bowsprit was angled slightly off the centerline so that its after end passed to one side of the foremast.

While the galleon might have the outward bulk and general aspect of a heavily armed warship, internally the galleon was primarily a cargo carrier. The most important stowage, for the bullion, was a specially strength-

ened and strongly sealed compartment deep in the hull, on her orlop deck. On this deck and in the hold below it were stored the barrels carrying fresh water and the ship's provisions as well as the rest of the cargo, which was selected on the grounds of high value and, if possible, low volume. Typical of these types of cargo were colored hardwood, sugar, tobacco, and llama wool. Soldiers guarded the cargo, protected the officers, and provided a powerful deterrent against boarding attacks, and the vessel's crew of some 200 men lived on the gun deck, increasingly in hammocks rather than cots after the concept of the hammock had been discovered from the indigenous peoples of the Americas. In the stern castle were cabins for the more senior persons

Cutaway and plan views of the galleon reveal the salient internal and external features of this type of vessel, so important to the growth of Spain as an imperial and economic power.

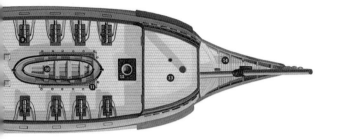

1	Lantern
2	Poop Deck
3	Quarter Gallery
4	Hood over Helm
5	Knight (for securing rigging)
6	2 Pound Culvern
7	Stern Hatch
8	1 Pound Swivel Gun
9	4 Pound Gun
10	Ship's Boats
11	Main Hatch
12	Firebox and Kettle
13	Forecastle Deck
14	Beakhead
15	Sailing Master's Cabin
16	Great Cabin - for Captain
17	Bonaventure Mast
18	Gun deck
19	Tiller
20	Whipstaff
21	Mizzenmast
22	Bronze 9 Pound Gun
23	Capstan
24	Treasure Room
25	Small Arms
26	Water Casks
27	Keel
28	Mainmast Step
29	Hold
30	Mainmast
31	Hanging Knee
32	Bilge Pump
33	Orlop Deck
34	Lower Main Hatch
35	Anchor Cables
36	Frame
37	Deck Beam
38	Lumber
39	Riding Bitts
40	Foremast
41	Hawsepipe
42	Stem
43	Gammon Lashing
44	Bowsprit

on board, namely the captain, officers, sailing master and up to 40 passengers.

The helmsman stood well aft on the gun deck and peered out through a wooden hood in the deck above him, and operated a whipstaff, which was an upright pole pivoted in the deck below the helmsman and attached at its lower end to the forward end of the tiller. Below the waterline the galleon's hull planking was liberally coated with a thick and sticky amalgam of tallow, sulphur, white lead and crushed glass: this was designed to prevent teredo worms (wood-boring marine organisms) from piercing and weakening the hull.

Nuestra Señora de la Concepción (built at Cavite, Manila, in 1636)

Type:	three-masted galleon
Tonnage:	not available
Dimensions:	length 147 ft 7 in (45.0 m); beam 49 ft 3 in (15.0 m); depth in hold 19 ft 9 in (6.0 m)
Speed:	8 kt
Armament:	40 guns
Complement:	350-400 men

Dutch Crompster 1600

Whereas most early ships had been built on the basis of creating the outer skin of planks and then adding inside these the structural framework that supported the outer planking and gave the vessel its physical integrity, there gradually developed in the south of Europe the reverse of this practice. Here the rigid skeleton of the vessel was built first, and only then was the outer skin of planks added. This planking was initially of the clinker type, with the lower edge of each plank overlapping the upper edge of that below it, but then there was a shift to carvel planking, in which the lower edge of one plank was butted up against the upper edge of the plank below it, the whole arrangement being made watertight by the swelling of the planks after the vessel had been launched, and by the caulking of the planks with fibrous matter driven into the inevitable gaps and then covered with hot pitch or some similar substance to prevent the water from entering and rotting the caulking material. The concepts of skeleton construction and carvel planking then spread to northern Europe.

A good example of the way in which these concepts were used in their definitive forms is provided by the crompster (otherwise known as the cromster or crumster), which was developed in the Netherlands during the 16th century as a type optimized for use on coastal and estuarine waters, and therefore characterized by the combination of a considerable beam and a shallow draught. Measuring up to 200 tons, the crompster was sturdy and steady, and therefore well suited for the carriage of a useful payload, which could comprise a substantial cargo in the commercial role,

or a notably heavy armament in the naval role.

The crompster generally had a rounded, bluff bow with a bowsprit but no raised forecastle, and a high stern with a long main deck and a short poop deck. The crompster was two-masted (occasionally three-masted) and carried a fore-and-aft rig comprising a lateen sail on the comparatively short mizzenmast and a spritsail and staysail on the mainmast. The feature most typical of the crompster was the spritsail, basically similar to that later used on Thames barges. This sail was four-sided with a loose foot, a luff hooped to the mast, and a peak supported by the sprit. This last was a long spar extending diagonally across the sail with its heel held in a snotter near the base on the mast forward of the spritsail's tack and a lift bearing the main weight of the spar from a point about two-thirds along its length to its upper end to the mast just above the sail's throat. The staysail was hanked to the stay bracing the mainmast, at a point about two-thirds of the way up its height, to the bow, while the bowsprit was probably used only as a support for the lighter stay that braced the head of the mainmast.

The Dutch made good use of crompsters in the Battle of Scheldt Estuary against the Spanish during 1572, and also in another naval engagement at Rummerswael near Antwerp, and it was the capability of these vessels in confined waters which attracted the attentions of a great British mariner, Sir Walter Raleigh. He was all too aware of the lack of any real coast-defence capability in southern England, especially against the Spanish galleys based in the Netherlands and which might be used for hit-and-run raids against ports in the southeastern corner of England. It was quickly appreciated that some 200 hoys, based at Newcastle for the coasting trade as single-masted vessels of about 60 tons, could be adapted for the carriage of a powerful armament and also for the carriage of men and equipment, thereby turning them into extemporized but capable river monitors and landing craft. But the English also wanted to evaluate a coastal warship of full crompster type, and in 1590 but the *Advantage*, *Answer*, *Crane* and *Quittance* to a three-masted standard which included a tonnage of about 200 burthen, keel length of 60 to 65 ft (18.3 to 19.8 m), beam of 24 to 26 ft (7.3 to 7.9 m), and crew of about 100 men. The vessels each carried 24 guns including culverins, demi-culverins, verins and sakers, and in the course of long lives saw active service at Cádiz in 1596, the Azores in 1600, Ireland in 1601 and Lisbon in 1602. The Spanish galley leader Federico Spinoza was killed in 1603, and with him died any realistic threat of a galley attack across the narrower end of the English Channel, so the British built no more crompster warships.

The crompster was developed by the Dutch for mercantile and naval work in confined waters, and combined a good load-carrying capability with a shallow draught and considerable agility.

Crompster (typical of about 1600)

Type:	two-masted shallow-draught warship
Tonnage:	80 tons burthen
Dimensions:	length of keel 46 ft 0 in (14. 0m); beam 20 ft 0 in (6.1 m); depth of hold 8 ft 0 in (2.4 m)
Speed:	not available
Armament:	12 heavy cannon and probably numbers of smaller cannon
Complement:	not available

Eendracht/Hoorn 1610

During 1602 the Vereenigde Oostindische Companie (VOC or United East Indies Company) was established by a Dutch merchants to amalgamate and regulate the trading ventures to the East Indies already in existence. Among the VOC's rights were a monopoly of the East Indian trade, exemption from import taxes, and the right to maintain armed forces, make war and peace, build forts, and mint its own coinage. The charter also prohibited all but the company's ships from using the 'only' two routes to the East Indies by means of the Cape of Good Hope round the southern tip of Africa and the Strait of Magellan through the southern tip of South America.

An Amsterdam merchant, Isaac le Maire wished to break the monopoly. In 1610 he received a charter to create a company with permission to trade in Tartary (China), Japan, 'Terra Australis' and the islands of the South Seas. Le Maire knew from the start that his success would depend on finding a new route into the Pacific, and was in fact convinced that such a route existed to the south of the VOC's Strait of Magellan passage. This belief found support from Willem Cornelisz Schouten, a capable navigator who had already logged three voyages to the East Indies. Le Maire and Schouten therefore decided to launch an expedition of two vessels to look for this more southerly route into the Pacific. The expedition was prepared in great secrecy.

The two vessels selected for the voyage were the *Eendracht* (19 cannon and 12 swivel guns) with a 65-man crew under Schouten's command, and the 110-ton *Hoorn* (eight cannon and four swivel guns) with a 22-man crew under Jan Schouten, Willem's younger brother. Jakob le

The Hoorn was a comparatively small vessel for the lengthy voyage to the East Indies via the passage round south America, and was a three-masted galleon square-rigged on the fore and mainmasts, and lateen-rigged on the mizzenmast. The vessel was lost to fire while beached on the coast of Patagonia.

Maire, the eldest of Isaac le Maire's 22 children, was in overall command. The leaders of the undertaking fully appreciated that there would probably be the need for large numbers of smaller craft for scouting and landing purposes, so the *Eendracht* carried a large sailing pinnace, a smaller oared pinnace, a launch and a small workboat, and the *Hoorn* carried two small boats.

The expedition sailed from Texel on June 14, 1615, called in southern England and then at Cape Verde, the vessels made an uneventful voyage to Port Desire, where their bottoms were found to be foul. The vessels were beached, but as their bottoms were being burned and scraped clean, the *Hoorn* caught fire and was effectively destroyed, though much of the vessel's equipment and stores were brought aboard the *Eendracht*. After a month the vessel set sail, and on January 20, 1616 was south of the Strait of Magellan's eastern entrance. Five days later the vessel passed into what is now known as the Strait of le Maire, emerging into the Pacific and sighting the western end of the Strait of Magellan. The *Eendracht* called at Juan Fernandez, then headed across the Pacific. At the beginning of April Jan Schouten died.

After trading its way through the East Indies, the *Eendracht* arrived at the VOC's port of Bantam, and the crew was ordered to surrender its vessel and all its cargo as the VOC's agent refused to believe that the *Eendracht* had found a new passage round South America. Schouten, le Maire and several crew members were given passage home in the VOC's vessel *Amsterdam*, but le Maire died during the voyage. After two years of litigation, Isaac le Maire was compensated for the VOC's seizure of his vessel and cargo, and the existence of Schouten and le Maire's different Cape Horn passage was recognized.

Mayflower 1620

The small vessel which took the "Pilgrim Fathers" to Plymouth Rock in 1620 is one of the most celebrated in US history, but its origin and end are problematical. However, there is mention in 1609 of a London-registered *Mayflower* under Christopher Jones, a part-owner. Built in Leigh in about 1606, this vessel traded mainly between England and the French ports of the Bay of Biscay, and was also involved in the Norwegian and north German trades. At this time the Church of England, separate from Rome since 1534, included many who believed that Anglicanism was more Catholic than Protestant. Among these were Puritans who wanted Anglicanism's internal reform, and Separatists who did not adhere to the concepts of the Church of England's authority or the monarch as the church's head. In 1607 several groups of Separatists emigrated to the Netherlands, but over the following decade developed a wish to settle in the New World under English rule. Appeals to the Company for Virginia, which had established the Jamestown colony in 1609, yielded no result, but the would-be emigrants' charter of the *Mayflower* was eventually arranged through the Merchant Adventurers, including representatives of the Virginia, London and Plymouth Companies, all with the right to make land grants in North America. The Separatists were involved most directly with two men with a Virginia Company patent to settle in "the neighborhood

The Mayflower has a secure place in history as the vessel in which the "Pilgrim Fathers" journeyed to the Americas to establish the first permanent colony in New England.

of" Hudson's River in the northern part of Virginia.

The Separatists departed from Leyden in the *Speedwell* to meet the *Mayflower* at Southampton in July 1620, and the two vessels departed Southampton on August 5th with 90 "pilgrims" on the larger *Mayflower* and 30 on the smaller *Speedwell*. It soon became clear that the smaller vessel was not suitable and, after leaks had forced both vessels into Dartmouth and then Plymouth, it was decided to continue with only the larger vessel. The task of accommodating the passengers was eased by the decision of about 18 or 20 of the would-be emigrants not to continue, and when she departed Plymouth on September 6th the *Mayflower* was carrying 104 passengers (50 men, 20 women and 34 children), divided about equally between Separatists and members of the Church of England.

The voyage's first part was beset by adverse weather, but then conditions improved and on November 9th the *Mayflower* sighted land at Truro, Cape Cod, some 200 miles (320 km) north of the Virginia Company's lands. Jones tried to sail south, but the *Mayflower* was checked by contrary winds, which drove the vessel round the tip of Cape Cod. Thus on November 11 the *Mayflower* anchored at Provincetown Harbor. The voyage had lasted 67 days, and in that time one of the pilgrims had died and one child had been born. Before landing, some 41 of the passengers signed the Mayflower Compact, which was the document by which all the members would be governed. On November 15 a small group of pilgrims started a first scouting expedition along the neck of Cape Cod. At the end of the month, some Pilgrims undertook a second, in this instance by shallop (a small boat which had to be assembled after the *Mayflower's* arrival) to the Pamet River near Truro, and a third took them across Massachusetts Bay. This last seemed to be a good wintering spot, and on December 16 the *Mayflower* arrived at what appeared to be the place called "Plimouth" on a chart of just a few years earlier.

By April the weather had moderated, but the harsh winter is reflected in the fact that about half of the *Mayflower's* crew had died. The vessel sailed on April 5, 1621 and reached the Thames estuary in only 31 days. The *Mayflower* is last mentioned in connection with Jones in December 1621, when she unloaded in London. In 1624 a vessel of the same name and in which Josian Jones, the captain's widow, was a part owner, was surveyed at Rotherhithe, but its later history is not known.

Mayflower

Type:	mercantile galleon
Tonnage:	244 tons displacement and 183 tons burthen
Dimensions:	length 111 ft 0 in (33.8 m) overall and 90 ft 0 in (27.4 m) on the waterline; beam 26 ft 0 in (7.9 m); draught 9 ft 0 in (2.7 m)
Speed:	not available
Armament:	none
Complement:	crew of 20-30 and 101 passengers

Vasa 1628

Departing on her maiden voyage, the *Vasa* (otherwise *Wasa*) was the most impressive line-of-battle vessel in the Swedish navy. But she sank only a few minutes later, and it was 333 years before her salvage opened a new era in archaeology. Named for the Swedish royal house, the *Vasa* was built for the navy of King Gustavus Adolphus (1611-32), then the dominant military force in the Baltic at the height of the Thirty Years' War (1618-48). The campaign in the southern Baltic began early in 1628, and by May some 34 ships were blockading Danzig to prevent the maritime reinforcement of the city. Designed by Henrik Hybertson de Groot and Henrik Jacobson, and built by the Royal Dockyard in Stockholm, the *Vasa* was scheduled to join the Swedish force, and on 10 April 1628 sailed from Stockholm.

The breeze was very light, and the crew had to warp the vessel out of the harbor to Slussen, where the fore and main courses and topsails started to draw. Soon after this, a gust laid the *Vasa* on her beam ends, water poured into the open gun ports, and the vessel immediately sank.

Attempts to salvage the *Vasa* were soon put in hand. The Englishman Ian Bulmer succeeded in putting the vessel on an even keel, but the equipment of the time was too limited to raise the *Vasa* from 115 ft (35 m). However, in 1663-64, Hans Albrecht von Treileben and Andreas Peckell raised 53 of the bronze guns. With the most valuable element recovered, interest in the *Vasa* faded, and it was 1956 before the wreck was rediscovered. After an amateur archaeologist had extracted a sample of the hull and Swedish naval

Caught by a sudden squall, the Vasa was blown onto her beam ends, filled with water. It sank almost immediately.

divers confirmed the find, a program to raise the wreck was planned.

Naval divers excavated six passages between the hull and the mud into which it had settled, and slings were then passed beneath the hull and attached to a pair of pontoon vessels. On August 20, 1959, the *Vasa* was pulled from the mud, and four weeks later was moved, still submerged, to a point where the water was only 50 ft (15 m) deep. Over the next year and a half, patches were applied to hull openings such as the gun ports and the 5,000 holes where iron bolts had rusted away. On April 24, 1960 the *Vasa* was brought to the surface, and two weeks later she was floated into a dry dock on her own hull. Ballast and a host of artefacts were removed, and by the autumn of that year she was safely housed in a museum building, where she remained under continuous water spray to prevent the disintegration of her timbers.

As the recovery of the *Vasa* was the first of its kind, virtually all of the preservation set a precedent. The wood and all artefacts were soaked with glycol, leather items were preserved in the same fashion, and six sails were slowly and very carefully unfurled in a shallow pool. Divers also rescued an additional 3,000 sundry artefacts from the wreck site. The *Vasa's* carvings and fragments constitute one of the largest collections of

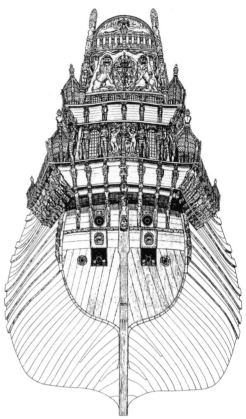

Designed by a Dutchman, the Vasa revealed many influences of the Low Countries including the ornate and superbly executed carving round the stern.
Picture courtesy of
Sjöhistoriska Museum, Stockholm.

17th century wooden sculpture in the world. One of the most popular visitor attractions in Sweden, the recovered *Vasa* is the heart of the Statens Sjöhistoriska Museum in Stockholm.

Vasa

Type:	three-masted line-of-battle vessel
Tonnage:	1,300 tons displacement
Dimensions:	length 180 ft 0 in (54.9 m); beam 38 ft 4 in (11.7 m); draught 15 ft 5 in (4.9 m)
Speed:	not available
Armament:	48 24-pdr, eight 3-pdr, two 1-pdr, one 16-pdr, two 62-pdr and three 35-pdr guns
Complement:	145 crew plus 300 soldiers

Heemskerck & Zeehean 1642

During August 1642 Antoonij van Diemen, the governor general of the Dutch East Indies, instructed Abel Janszoon Tasman and Franchoys Jacobsen Visscher "to discover the partly known and still unreached South and Easternland," now known as Australia. This voyage of discovery was intended not for any altruistic purpose such as the furthering of mankind's knowledge of world geography or the garnering of scientific information, but for "the improvement and increase of the general welfare of the Vereenidge Oostindische Companie [United East Indies Company, generally translated at the Dutch East India Company]." The two most important tasks imposed on Tasman and Visscher were the establishment of whether or not there existed a passage from the Indian Ocean to the Pacific Ocean

(permitting an increase in Dutch trade with Peru and Chile) and the search for the elusive passage south of New Guinea into the Pacific Ocean.

For the expedition he was to lead, Tasman was allocated two vessels, namely the war *jacht* (large dispatch vessel) *Heemskerck*, which had sailed to the East Indies in 1638, and the *fluyt* (transport) *Zeehaen*. The two vessels sailed from Batavia on August 14, 1642, and their first landing was on the island of Mauritius, where they spent a month effecting essential repairs to the *Zeehaen*. The ships departed from Mauritius on October 8 and headed south to about latitude 50° S before altering course to the east. On November 17 the ships arrived off hitherto uncharted land, which Tasman named Antoonij van Diemensland in honour of the expedition originator. This new land is now known as Tasmania, a large island off the south of Australia's eastern coast, and here the explorers landed several times. Though they saw smoke on some occasions, the Dutch sailors saw no people. Tasman claimed the island for the Dutch East India Company.

Unable to make westward headway though the Bass Strait separating Tasmania from Australia, Tasman's expedition steered east once more and after an eight-day crossing of what is now known as the Tasman Sea, reached the

The Heemskerck was smaller than the Zeehaen, and was a jacht of the type commonly used as a dispatch vessel.

The Zeehaen was a substantial four-masted fluyt, designed mostly for the transport role and generally used as a supply vessel.

South Island of New Zealand. Tasman believed that this was a continuation of Staten Island off Cape Horn, which is in fact some 5,000 miles (8050 km) or more to the east, and therefore named Statenland. Tasman now opted to turn north, and on December 18 four of the Dutch sailors were killed by Maoris in Murderer's Bay. From there the expedition sailed east and almost passed through the Cook Strait separating the North and South Islands of New Zealand, but bad weather then inter-

vened to prevent Tasman from making this discovered of another passage into the southern part of the Pacific Ocean. The Dutch expedition sought unsuccessfully to land near Cape Maria van Diemen, so named for the governor general's wife, and then directed its course to the northeast in the correct estimation (later disbelieved by van Diemen) that the vessels had entered the Pacific.

On January 21, 1643 the ships took on provisions in the Tonga islands, and on February 1 headed north and then west. In the next seven weeks the Dutch vessels covered only some 300 miles (480 km), but on March 22 caught sight of Onthong Java and from there adhered to the 1616 route of Schouten and le Maire in the *Eendracht*, reaching Batavia on June 15, 1643.

Heemskerck

Type:	three-masted *jacht*
Tonnage:	120 tons
Dimensions:	not available
Speed:	not available
Armament:	light guns
Complement:	60 men

Nonsuch 1688

The *Nonsuch* was built at Wivenhoe in Essex as a trading vessel but was bought during 1654 as an eight-gun vessel for naval service, and remained in this latter employment until 1667. The vessel was a ketch, that is with two masts including a mizzen mast stepped before rather than abaft the rudder head: the *Nonsuch* was square-rigged on her main mast with a course and a top sail, and the combination of a lateen driver and square top sail on her mizzen mast; there was also, of course, provision for other sails such as staysails and jibs. In February 1659 the *Nonsuch* was captured by a pair of Dutch privateers while escorting a merchant ketch through the English Channel, but was recaptured by the English two months later. In 1667 the *Nonsuch*

was sold out of the service into the hands of Sir William Warren, and then became the primary instrument in the establishment of the Hudson's Bay Company.

As these events had been taking place in European waters, on the other side of the North Atlantic the Huron allies of the French fur traders Médard Chouart, Sieur des Groseliers, and his brother-in-law Pierre Esprit Radisson had been defeated by the Iroquois, who were allied with the English, and thus their trade via the St. Lawrence River and the Great Lakes was made very problematical. Seeking an alternative route for their furs to reach the sea for shipment to Europe, Chouart and Radisson proposed to inaugurate a simpler but geographically more complex route to

The ketch-rigged Nonsuch was a small vessel, but suitable for navigation in the inhospitable waters of northern Canada.

and from the area in which the fur trappers operated via the waters of Hudson's Bay. Angered by the high rates at which their furs were taxed, and denied any redress by the French government, the two French fur entrepreneurs turned their attention to England, where the great pioneering chemist Robert Boyle introduced the two Frenchmen to the court of King Charles II (1660-85).

By 1667 the core of the Hudson's Bay Company had coalesced around these two men, and on June 5, 1668 the *Nonsuch* and the *Eaglet*, the latter lent to the undertaking by Charles II, set sail from London. The vessels main cargo was *wampumpeag*, the Algonquian Indian word for the small marine shell beads which were extensively used as a medium of exchange among the Indian nations of the northeastern part of North America. The *Eaglet* was damaged in the middle of the Atlantic Ocean and turned back to England with Radisson, but the *Nonsuch* sailed into Hudson's Bay and thence south to the shores of James Bay. On September 29, 1668 the men of this pioneering trading enterprise came ashore and started to construct Charles Fort, which was later named as Rupert's House, on the Rupert River. After almost a year of trade with the Indians, Groselliers returned to England in the *Nonsuch* during October 1669 with a cargo of furs. In the next year the Hudson's

To give them a broader base in their task of preventing the masts from moving sideways, the shrouds extended upward from dead-eyes in the chains, which were platforms extending outside the vessel's hull and themselves braced by the chain plates.

Bay Company was formally established and allocated, by royal grant, an area equivalent to nearly two-fifths of modern Canada.

The later fate of the *Nonsuch* is not recorded, but a near-replica of the vessel is exhibited at the Manitoba Museum of Man and Nature in Winnipeg.

Nonsuch

Type:	ketch-rigged vessel
Tonnage:	43 tons burthen
Dimensions:	length 50 ft 0 in (15.2 m) on the keel; beam 15 ft 0 in (4.3 m); draught not available
Speed:	not available
Armament:	8 guns
Complement:	between 12 and 24 men

Dutch Tjalk & Boeier 17ᵗʰ Century

Given their location toward the middle of the primary coastal trading routes along the north coast of continental Europe, the Dutch were ideally suited to rise to prominence as a trading people. Moreover, the shallow nature of the Dutch coast and the fact that major rivers, which were among Europe's most important trading arteries, debouched into the sea along this coast, meant that the Dutch inevitably developed coastal and riverine trading vessels ideally suited to the precise requirement of Dutch traders.

The *tjalk* was a barge-type Dutch vessel for the carriage of freight, and dated from the 17th century virtually to the present. The *tjalk* had the stan-

dard barge rig of a main mast carrying a course and a top sail, a mizzen mast carrying a sprit sail, and a staysail and jib forward of the main mast. To combine the type of capacious hull suitable for operations in shallow, coastal waters with at least an adequate capability to hold a course to windward, the *tjalk* had a rounded hull and two leeboards. Pivoted at its upper end and raised when nor required, the relevant leeboard was lowered when the vessel was on the wind to increase the hull's effective draught.

The *boeier* (or *boier*) was developed in the early part of the 16th century as a comparatively flat-bottomed seagoing trading vessel with a length of some 65 ft (19.8 m)

The tjalk was a maid-of-all-work for Dutch mariners specializing in the coastal trade along the north coast of the European mainland. The hull was capacious, the provision of leeboards allowed a shallow draught in combination with an adequate windward sailing capability, and the rig could be operated by a small crew.

With its combined fore-and-aft and square rig, the tjalk could hold a course well up into the wind with one of its leeboards lowered.

and a beam in the order of 23 to 26 ft (7.0 to 7.9 m). As with the *tjalk*, an adequate capability for sailing to windward with a shallow yet capacious hull was provided by the provision of two leeboards, and the rig was originally based on a sprit sail or boomless main sail of the brailed type (for easy modification of area) possessing a standing gaff, often with a square top sail above it. Some of the oldest and largest of the boeier vessels had a small mizzenmast carrying a lateen sail. The *boeier* was later developed into a smaller vessel, with a single mast stepped in a tabernacle so that it could be lowered and raised easily, for mercantile use on inland waters. In this form the boeier was normally rigged with a boomed main sail, a foresail set on the forestay, and a jib set on a running bowsprit. In the most recent parts of their commercial lives, both the *tjalk* and *boeier* were further developed with steel rather than the original type of wooden hulls, and both types were finally evolved as the *pavilijoen tjalk* and *pavilionenjacht* pleasure yachts.

Tjalk (typical)

Type:	single-masted coastal merchant vessel
Tonnage:	not available
Dimensions:	length 75 ft 0 in (22.85 m); beam 16 ft 1 in (4.90 m); draught 3 ft 3 in (1.0 m)
Speed:	not available
Armament:	none
Complement:	4 or 5 persons

Jacht 1660

The Dutch word *jacht* was initially applied to any sailing vessel notable for its speed, but during the 17th century became applied more specifically, as the *staten jacht*, to small single-masted vessels used mainly for courier (such as dispatch carrying and the delivery of important persons) and scouting purposes. However, the basic term was still used for any comparatively fast transport or fishing vessels, especially when possessing more elegant lines than most, or even for pleasure sailing.

Possessing a hull of elegant line and fitted with two leeboards, the *jacht* was originally fore-and-aft rigged with a spritsail, but then developed

with a gaff mainsail, which could more readily be furled with clewlines, and a square topsail together with a fore staysail and a jib. The concept proved successful and was then expanded to encompass two- and three-masted vessels.

A good example of the last was the *Duyfken*, with was built in the later years of the 16th century. When the Dutch declared their independence from Spain in 1581, King Philip II retaliated by closing the port of Lisbon, with its rich spice trade, to Dutch shipping. The Dutch therefore decided to open their own trade with the Far East, and in 1595 the *Hollandia* (400 tons), *Mauritius* (400 tons), *Amsterdam* (200 tons) and *Duyfken* sailed for Java. The voyage enjoyed mixed success, for although the *Amsterdam* was lost and a mere 80 of the 249 crewmen lived, the voyage was considered fruitful in financial terms.

An early result was the despatch, in December 1603, of another expedition, this time of 12 vessels including a further *Duyfken* under Willem Jansz. Reaching the East Indies, Jansz was detached to seek other trading opportunities, espe-

A gaff-sailed staten jacht vessel under all plain sail in a lively breeze.

cially in "the great land of Nova Guinea and other East- and South-lands." Thus on November 18 1605 the *Duyfken* departed Bantam to Banda, through the Kai Islands and thus to Tanjung Deyong in New Guinea. The *Duyfken* rounded False Cape and then crossed the Arafura Sea into the Gulf of Carpentaria (thereby missing the Torres Strait) and charted some 250 mils (400 km) of the Australian north coast, which Jansz though to be part of New Guinea, but this was in fact first recorded European visit to Australia. Finding the land poor and its peoples hostile, Jansz turned back to regain Bantam in June 1606.

More typical of the smaller species of the *jacht* in its *staten jacht* form was the *Avondster* (evening star), built in England during 1640 as the *Blessing*, a vessel of 250 tons burthen with a crew of 65. The *Blessing* was operated by the East India Company for some 12 years before being captured by the Dutch East India Company during 1653 and renamed *Avondster*. This sank on the night of June 23, 1659 while in the process of loading cargo for India: anchored at Black Fort at Galle, toward the southern tip of Ceylon, the vessel lost her anchor and drifted onto the rocks.

The staten jacht had an elegant hull with a cutwater bow, two leeboards, and comfortable accommodation in the large poop.

Duyfken (built about 1600)

Type:	three-masted jacht
Tonnage:	60 tons
Dimensions:	length 63 ft 0 in (19.0 m); beam 17 ft 0 in (5.0 m); draught 7 ft 0 in (2.0 m)
Speed:	not available
Armament:	10 guns
Complement:	20 men

HMS Sussex

The system of categorizing warships into six rates, differentiated by the number of guns they carried, was formalized in Great Britain only during the initial period (1751-56) in which Admiral Lord Anson was First Lord of the Admiralty. However, the concept has occasionally been extended backward in time by up to 150 years as a convenient way of describing older warships. In its initial form, the rate system described vessels with 100 or more guns as first-rate ships, those

with between 84 and 100 guns as second-rate ships, those with between 70 and 84 guns as third-rate ships, etc. By retrospective application of this system, therefore, the Sussex was a third-rate ship as she carried 80 guns.

The ship was also described as a "two-decker" as the main weight of her armament was carried on a main gun deck (26 x 24-pdr guns) and an

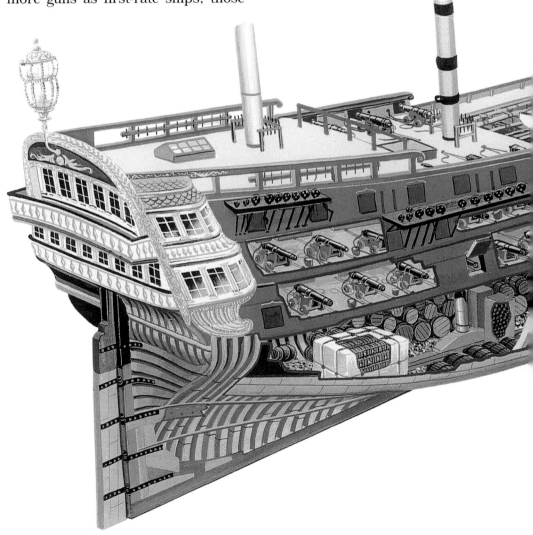

upper gun deck (28 x 12-pdr guns). This arrangement of the guns on several decks allowed the carriage of heavy armament in a vessel of comparatively short overall length, and also ensured that the main weight of the armament was installed low in the hull and therefore destabilized the vessel as little as possible. The evolution of the warship with several decks of heavy guns had been made possible only by the development of gun ports. Known as lids, these were watertight hatches in the sides of the vessel, and were hinged on their upper edges so that they could be opened with blocks and tackles to permit the guns to be run out through the ports before they were fired, the recoil then taking the guns inboard before they were checked by their breechings, when they were swabbed put and then reloaded before being hauled back into battery for firing once more. The need to create powerful warships with their guns on several decks was also the spur for the evolution of the "classic" cross-section of a warship's hull with a broad beam close above the waterline and a distinct tumble-home (inward angling) above this point so that the decks decreased steadily in width to keep the upper guns as far inboard as possible.

The *Sussex* was built at Chatham Dock Yard under the supervision of a master shipwright named Lee, and was launched on April 11, 1693 for commissioning into the English navy later in the same year, and was lost less than one year later when the vessel foundered in a gale near the Strait of Gibraltar. The *Sussex* was one of 27 vessels (four three-decker third-rates of 80 guns, 13 two-decker third-rates of 80 guns, and 10 fourth-rates of 60 guns) ordered as part of the programme ordained in 1691. The fourth-rate vessels were comparatively effective, but the same could not be said of the third-rate vessels as they were initially completed, for they were built down to a price rather than up to a standard. In an effort to keep down their costs, therefore, the ships were designed to a somewhat reactionary concept that harked back to the "great ships" of the 1650s rather forward into the 18th century. Thus the additional length that was properly required for the planned armament

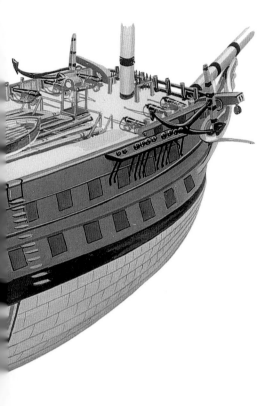

The Sussex was of typical overall design for her period in the later part of the 17th century, but carried too great a weight of guns on the forecastle and quarterdeck, resulting in a tendency to sag at the ends.

HMS Sussex *continued*

was not provided, and instead the additional guns were mounted on the upper works and as fore- and aft-firing weapons. This placed a disproportionately great weight in the bow and stern, which were narrow and therefore possessed less buoyancy, and the effect was a tendency for the vessels to sag at their ends, resulting in a distortion of their frames and thus in leakiness.

The loss of the *Sussex* took place as the vessel was the flagship of Admiral Sir Francis Wheeler's squadron despatched to the Mediterranean to harass the French forces in and around the Mediterranean during the War of the Grand Alliance (1688-97). The *Sussex* also had another mission, namely the delivery of a very large quantity of bullion (several tons of gold and perhaps £3 million in sil-

An impression of the Sussex as she approaches the point at which she founders depicts the vessel with her fore topmast gone.

ver coinage) to Eugene, Duke of Savoy. The object of this payment is disputed, and in the absence of any clear evidence the two most likely reasons were an attempt to persuade the Austrian leader to join the war on the side of the English against the French, or on the side of the French against the English. The former notion is favored by the modern British, who see the event as an effort to persuade Eugene to raise privateering and land force to attack the French by sea and land. The latter notion is preferred by those who look for more complex causation, and see an effort launched by the political establishment in England after the 1694 death of the very popular Queen Mary II (1689-94) left the unpopular King William III (1689-1702) as sole ruler. The conspiracy theorists therefore see the attempted payment to Eugene as an establishment effort to intensify pressure on William III and so pave the way for the restoration of King James II (1685-88), who had been forced into French exile by the "Glorious Revolution" of 1688. The case of the conspiracy theorists is perhaps strengthened by the fact that Admiral Wheeler is known to have been a strong supporter of James II.

Whatever the reason for the carriage of a very large cargo of bullion in the hold of the *Sussex*, it was more than effectively negated by the loss of the ship in a storm on February 19, 1694. Wheeler's squadron was caught by the sudden on set of a levanter (strong Mediterranean wind and accompanying storm blowing from the east or northeast) with the rocky coast of Spain immediately under its lee. The ships of the squadron attempted under very difficult circumstances to tack up into the wind and so gain additional sea room for a maneuvre that would allow them to run back toward Gibraltar and perhaps through the strait into the Atlantic Ocean if required by the conditions. The *Sussex*'s gun ports were open, however, and as the ship was tacked and heeled, water started to pour through the lower ports. In only a very short time the vessel filled and foundered so swiftly that the admiral died in his bed, clad only in a nightshirt, and just one of 500 men who went down with the vessel. The loss was ascribed at the time to the poor design of the class of vessels to which the *Sussex* belonged, but this is unfair as the severity of the storm was such that the British lost another five warships and six merchant vessels in the same catastrophe.

Sussex

Type:	third-rate line of battle ship
Tonnage:	1,263 tons
Dimensions:	length 157 ft 2 in (47.90 m) on the gundeck; beam 41 ft 4 in (12.60 m); depth in the hold 17 ft 1.5 in (5.22 m)
Speed:	not available
Armament:	26 x 24-pdr guns on the gun deck, 28 x 12-pdr guns on the upper deck, 16 x 6-pdr guns on the quarterdeck, 6 x 6-pdr guns on the forecastle, and 4 x 3-pdr guns in the coach
Complement:	500 men

Dutch Fluyt 1700

There is little doubt that at the beginning of the 17th century the Dutch had an enormous merchant marine, and although the establishment of precise numbers is not possible, it seems likely that more than half of all European merchant shipping was in the hands of Dutch owners. The predominant type vessel used by the Dutch was the *fluyt*, generally rendered as the flute in modern English or as the fly-boat or flite in the English of the period. The *fluyt* was essentially a development of the pink with a more rounded stern, a hull with a flat bottom and sides of pronounced tumblehome that was reduced after 1670 as a result of a change in the way customs dues were calculated, an upper line that was strongly curved up to the bow and stern from the position of the main mast, and three masts. The last carried two square sails on the fore and main masts, and a lateen sail on the mizzen mast, and a square spritsail was set below the sharply elevated bowsprit. The rig was effective and, worked with the aid of large numbers of blocks and tackles, required only a few relatively men for effective

Capacious and sturdy, the fluyt had only a limited number of sails on its three masts.

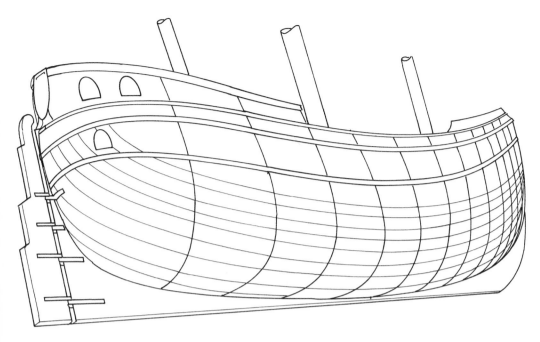

Notable features of the fluyt were its deep belly and rounded stern.

operation. This was an important economic factor in the profitable operation of the *fluyt*.

Flat-bottomed with full ends, its considerable tumblehome gave the *fluyt* an almost pear-shaped cross section, even at the stern. This latter was rounded to a level as high as the main deck, but above this was square but notably narrow. The rudder head was located outside the vessel, and the lower part of the counter was concave where the tiller passed through an oblong port. A carved quarter piece surrounded the lower part of the counter, and the wales were taken over the full quarters to terminate against the stern post. Depending on the desire of the owner and the type of trade for which it was intended, the *fluyt* could have an elaborate head or just a plain stem without gammon knees.

The *fluyt* was particularly useful for the carriage of bulk cargoes including timber, and for this type of cargo the *fluyt's* considerable length was a decided asset, especially when ports were cut in the bow or stern for this purpose. The *fluyt* was also extensively used for whaling and for long trading voyages such as those to India and the East Indies. During the course of the 18th century, the *fluyt's* tumblehome was considerably reduced, a fact which resulted in wider decks and also, of course, a beamier stern. The *fluyt* had become extinct by the end of the 17th century's third quarter, but its success is further attested by the fact that direct descendents of the type included successful types such as the *bootschip*, *hekboot* and *kat*, the last two generally being known in English as the hagboat and cat. The latter was extensively operated as a collier with a load of some 600 tons.

Whydah 1717

Named for the important slaving port in the West African region of Dahomey (now Ouidah in the state of Benin), the merchant ship *Whydah* was a slaver built in 1716 in London for a trade which involved triangular transatlantic voyages between Britain. West Africa and the islands of the Caribbean Sea. In the last week of February 1717, the vessel was returning to London from the West Indies with a cargo comprising sugar, indigo, dried cinchona bark (from which quinine is extracted) and between £20,000 and £30,000 of bullion (both gold and silver), representing the profit in trade goods and specie of a voyage from Dahomey with slaves. While still on the western side of the Atlantic Ocean, however, the vessel was captured by the celebrated

pirate Samuel "Black Sam" Bellamy off Long Island in the Bahamas group after a three-day chase from the initial point of interception in the Windward Passage between the islands of Cuba and Hispaniola (now Haiti and the Dominican Republic).

So impressed was he with his latest acquisition that Bellamy made the *Whydah* his own vessel, and as such the flagship of his pirate fleet. This now comprised the *Whydah*, the sloop *Mary Anne*, the snow-rigged galley *Anne*, and the ship-rigged pink *Mary Anne* (different from the sloop). This fleet was manned by some 200 pirates, and in board the various vessels were also a substantial number of prisoners and, on the *Whydah*, an additional 12 or so cannon in her hold as well as her 28 guns, increased in number from the original complement of 18 guns probably by the addition of

The Whydah was designed in a fashion that optimized her capacity for carrying slaves and for delivering them between West Africa and the Caribbean as quickly as possible.

weapons on the quarterdeck and on the erstwhile slave deck. Another change was probably the internal revision of the ship by the elimination of the pilot house and the bulkheads that created officers' cabins abaft the slave deck prop. This latter change would have facilitated fore and aft movement inside the vessel.

The *Whydah* reflected not only her intended role, as reflected in the considerable slave and cargo volume in her hull, but also the transitional nature of sailing vessel design in this period. The vessel was thus a hybrid of three types of vessel, namely the galley, the galleon, and the ship. The galley feature was the provision for the vessel to be rowed with 25 pairs of oars extended through small ports in the sides of what had been the slave deck, the galleon feature was the retention of a lateen sail on the mizzenmast, and the ship features included the setting of square sails on all three masts as a topsail was set on the mizzenmast above the lateen sail.

After taking a French vessel in the Bahamas, Bellamy sailed with his fleet toward the Virginia capes, but during this passage the *Whydah* was dismasted in a storm. Once the *Whydah* had been repaired, Bellamy captured a number of vessels off the Virginia and Delaware capes, and also farther north off Cape Cod. This last was an area not well known by Bellamy, so he chose from one of these vessels a pilot who agreed to guide the four pirate vessels, currently four in number as the sloop *Mary Anne* had become separated a few days earlier but Bellamy had meanwhile captured the sloop *Fisher*, to Provincetown in the British colony of Massachusetts. However, during the night of April 26/27, 1717, Bellamy's vessels were caught in a violent New England storm off Wellfleet and ran aground, although it is claimed by some sources that the pilot used the excuse of the storm deliberately to run the ships ashore as a means of saving his fellow merchants and the citizens of Provincetown from the attentions of the pirates.

The *Whydah* and the pink *Mary Anne* ran aground off Eastham, while the snow *Anne* and the sloop *Fisher*, carrying a cargo of tobacco and hides, sailed away, then anchored offshore

Whydah *continued*

and was able to ride out the storm. After this had blown itself out, the *Anne* and the *Fisher* sailed to Maine, and were there abandoned by their crews, now led by Richard Noland, who had been the fleet's quartermaster and treasure-master, and as such had to be trusted by all. Nolan retired from piracy in the following year under the terms of the pardons granted periodically by the British. Many ex-pirates soon gambled and drank their way into abject poverty, but Nolan was a clever man who managed to establish himself as a respectable citizen and, indeed, even served as a character witness at the trials of other pirates.

There were nine survivors from the two vessels which went down, in the form of two from the *Whydah* and seven from the *Mary Anne*, and some 130 crew from the two vessels were therefore lost. Probably appreciating the value of the cargo that might have been loaded on the *Whydah* and the *Mary Anne*, the governor of Massachusetts sent Captain Cyprian Southack to undertake an attempted salvage of the vessels, but the weather was unremittingly adverse and the men of the Cape Cod communities refused to co-operate, so after 12 days Southack gave up the salvage effort. The nine surviving pirates were brought to Boston where, on October 18 of the same year they were put on

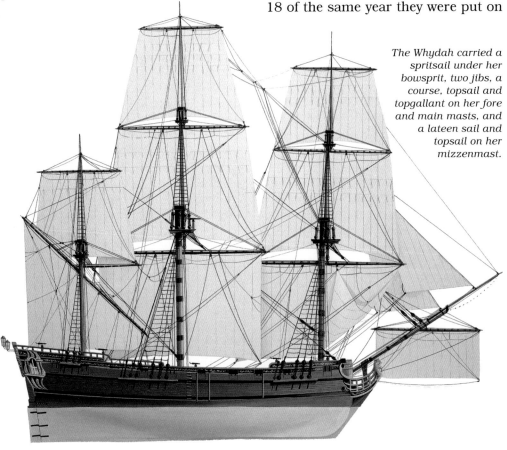

The Whydah carried a spritsail under her bowsprit, two jibs, a course, topsail and topgallant on her fore and main masts, and a lateen sail and topsail on her mizzenmast.

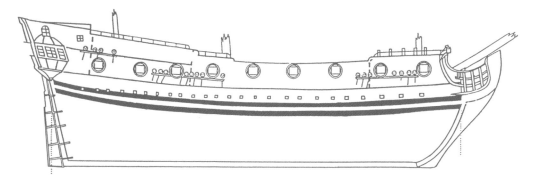

The lines of the Whydah's hull were typical of the time, and the hull included nine gun ports and 25 oar ports on each side.

trial for "Piracy, Robbery and Felony Committed on the High Sea ... To the high displeasure of Almighty God, in open Violation and Defyance of His Majesty's good and wholesome Laws." Seven of the men were found guilty of the charges against them and, after a month languishing in prison as a man of the cloth attempted to woo them back to God, they were hanged on November 15.

In 1982, the diver Barry Clifford began a search for the resting place of the wrecked *Whydah*, whose cargo he estimated might be worth anything between $80 and $400 million at the values of the time. On July 19, 1984 divers found a concentration of cannon and other artefacts from what were later found to be the remains of the *Whydah*, but it was September 1985 before Clifford finally received the permits he required to start the salvage effort in and round the wreck itself. This effort netted large numbers of artefacts and also many millions of dollars in gold coinage. By this time, though, Clifford's effort was attracting a considerable measure of disapproval, especially from historians and archaeologists who criticized an undertaking in which the profits of treasure hunting had been put before the needs of history and the preservation of as much of the wreck as possible. It is worth noting, though, that the *Whydah* undertaking was just one of several underwater efforts of the 1980s to raise the level of public disapproval and so pave the way for the Abandoned Shipwreck Act which the Congress enacted in 1987 to provide a measure of hard-hitting federal protection to historic shipwrecks.

Whydah

Type:	three-masted galleon/ship-rigged galley
Tonnage:	300 tons
Dimensions:	length about 100 ft 0 in (30.5 m); beam not available; draught not available
Speed:	not available
Armament:	28 cannon and a number of swivel guns
Complement:	50 men

113

Yacht Caroline 1729

From the 16th century the royal houses of Europe made extensive use, for regal transport purposes and also for state occasions such as fleet reviews, of vessels known as "royal yachts." These were more akin to the warships of the time than anything that would be regarded as a yacht in later periods of history. The English and later the British royal houses were no exception to this rule, and among these have been two vessels bearing the name *Royal Caroline*. The first of them was laid down in 1700 at Sheerness Dock Yard, and entered English naval service as the *Peregrine Galley* before be adapted and decoratively enhanced as the *Carolina*, which soon became the *Royal Caroline*.

almost single-handedly created the Russian navy and started to switch the attention of Russia out to the world at large. Lord Danby's design efforts did not at first meet with the approval of the Lords Commissioners of the Admiralty, who did finally order the *Peregrine Galley*. As the *Royal Caroline* this vessel remained the royal yacht until 1749, when she was replaced by a new vessel of the same name. The original vessel then resumed her original name and role, but was lost with all hands in the Bay of Biscay during 1761.

The Royal Caroline was a ship-rigged vessel resembling a small frigate, and was renowned for her very elegant lines and also for the extent and opulence of her gingerbread work.

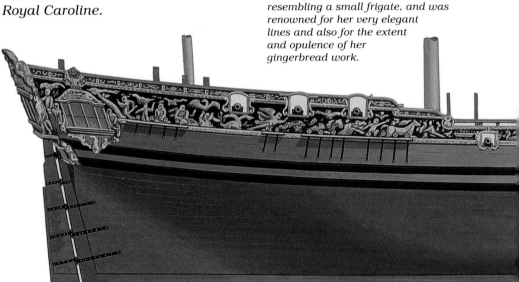

Ordered by King William III (1689-1702), this vessel was of somewhat unusual origins, for it was designed by Peregrine, Lord Danby, who was an English admiral responsible for the design of several vessels for Tsar Peter I the Great (1672-1725), the father of modern Russia and the far-sighted strategist who

The second *Royal Caroline* was in fact based on the lines of the *Peregrine Galley*, which had proved herself to be very successful. The second *Royal Caroline* was thus basically of the frigate type, but conceived as a very well appointed and extremely ornately decorated royal yacht for the use of King George II (1727-60) and his wife, Queen Caroline. In this period Britain was an established maritime power, a position which had been reaffirmed during the three Dutch Wars of the 17th century. The state of its shipbuilding capabilities, or art as it was termed at the time, was advanced, with most warships designed rather than just built by means of principles developed over the preceding century by master shipwrights such as Matthew Baker, Anthony Deane, and no fewer than seven members of the Pett family. The *Royal Caroline* was built in 1749-50 at Deptford Dock Yard under the supervision of Joshua Allin, her designer, and was in essence an adapted sixth-rate warship, which was a frigate-type vessel with up to 32 guns. The *Royal Caroline* was sailed for pleasure cruises by the royal family, and as a transport for members of court sailing between England and the Low Countries. On the latter route the vessel was normally escorted by as many as four frigates and, when the king was aboard, accompanied by the First Lord of the Admiralty. Her distinguished captains included Sir William Cornwallis and Sir Hyde Parker, both of whom became admirals.

After the accession of King George III (1760-1820), the vessel was very sumptuously fitted out and sent across the North Sea to Kiel in northern Germany to collect the Princess Sophie Charlotte of Mecklenburg-Strelitz, George III's queen consort-to-be. It was for this purpose that the vessel's name was changed from *Royal Caroline* to *Royal Charlotte*. The vessel was extensively used by the British royal family up to 1805, but then saw little more service before being broken up in 1821.

The validity of Lord Danby's design thinking is thus attested by the fact that the second *Royal Caroline* was based on the first vessel of this name, and also by the fact that the second *Royal Caroline* herself formed the basis of long and successful series of 20-gun and 32-gun ships, including the "Richmond" class frigates, of which the last units were ordered as late as 1804 in the Napoleonic Wars.

Royal Caroline (later *Royal Charlotte*)

Type:	ship-rigged royal yacht
Tonnage:	232 tons burthen
Dimensions:	length 90 ft 1 in (27.4 m); beam 24 ft 0 in (7.3 m); draught: 12 ft 1 in (3.7 m)
Speed:	not available
Armament:	24 guns
Complement:	70 men

Muletta 1750

Known in English as a bean-cod, the *muleta* (a word of Spanish origin) was also known as the *muletta*, *moleta* and *mulet*, and was a Portuguese fishing boat used mainly for coastal and estuarine fishing purposes, but also as a pilot and despatch boat. The hull was of almost canoe-like shape with a notably high and sharp bow which was strongly curved in a line that extended round toward the rear at its top. The stern was also sharp and curved, and carried the rudder. This latter was operated not by a tiller, as might have been expected, but by a small spar set athwartships through the rudder head and operated by tackles coming in over the sides of the hull. On each beam was a leeboard that could be raised when required, and also helped to stabilize the vessel when it had been drawn up onto the beach by a coastal community lacking any harbor. The *muleta* had a single mast, and this was short and raked

well forward to carry a large lateen sail that extended over virtually the full length of the vessel. The basic sail plan made the *muleta* extremely well suited to the task of holding a course well up into the wind.

This was only the core of the sail plan, however, for the *muleta* also had a long bowsprit, a long outrigger spar extending well over the stern, and provision for one or two booms that were set almost vertical on the foredeck. The *muleta* generally cruised to and from its fishing ground under its lateen sail and a jib, but over the fishing ground could set an extraordinary array of differently sized and shaped head and stern sails.

Any particular setting of head or stern sails could be set or taken in to provide the maneuvrability required while the vessel was drifting with its net lowered into the water. As far as the head sails were concerned, in addition to the jib two spritsails could be set below the bowsprit and two or more additional triangular sails could be set, with their clews extended

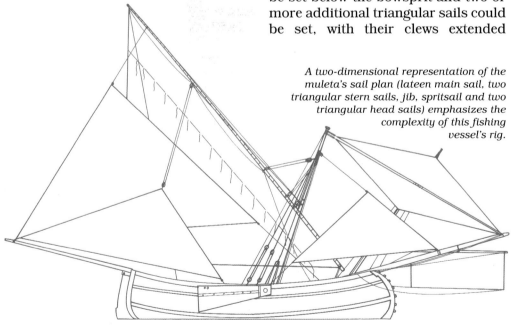

A two-dimensional representation of the muleta's sail plan (lateen main sail, two triangular stern sails, jib, spritsail and two triangular head sails) emphasizes the complexity of this fishing vessel's rig.

A muleta under way with head and stern sails set, and the starboard leeboard lowered.

upward or downward by one of the nearly vertical booms. This created what was in effect a primitive spinnaker, and was used to ease the task of keeping the bow of the drifting vessel in the desired position. As far as the stern sails were concerned, the key element was the long outrigger spar extending beyond the stern, and was used to spread the sheets of two more triangular sails which were hoisted by halyards to the outer part of the lateen sail's long yard.

Though undoubtedly strange and complicated, this rig was the result not of academic theory but rather of practical experience by generations of coastal fishermen working in the water of the Tajos estuary, and as such as admirably well suited for the work undertaken as a matter of local livelihoods by the *muleta*. It is worth noting that Spanish fishing boats of the Catalonian coast, on the other side of the Iberian peninsula from the Tajos estuary, had a generally similarly arrangement of their masts and lateen sail, but unlike the Portuguese craft carried no bowsprit and jib.

Muleta	
Type:	Portuguese coastal and estuarine fishing vessel
Tonnage:	not available
Dimensions:	(typical) length 50 ft 0 in (15.2 m); beam 11 ft 6 in (3.5 m); draught 4 ft 6 in (1.4 m)
Speed:	not available
Armament:	none
Complement:	5 men

Skerry Boat 1768

Though generally characterized by a fore-and-aft schooner rig on two masts, the skerry-boat was also built to what is believed to be a Norwegian variation, known as early as 1768, with three masts square-rigged on the fore and main masts, and carrying a small boomed gaff sail on the mizzenmast. The boat had a comparatively long bowsprit, and this allowed two jibs to be set in the fore triangle. The main elements of the square-rigged skerry-boat were very simple, for there was no provision at all for topsails on any of the masts. The pole masts were short and were not designed to support topmasts or flagpoles, and the courses set on the fore and main masts were cut to the trapezoidal shape that was characteristic of Norwegian sails of this type. The sails were carried by simple yards controlled by two braces, and carried two sets of reefing points high on the sail rather than toward their bottoms.

A similar rig was proposed in Great Britain in the very last years of the 18th century for battery transport vessels in a form only slightly revised from this Norwegian pattern through the use of a leg-of-mutton or sliding gunter sail rather than a spanker on the mizzenmast.

The skerry-boat was also used by the Swedes, one of whose descriptions of this type of *skaerbaat* vessel as a "small armed vessel, several of which patrol between the skerries of Stockholm to protect the harbor entrance." The use of the skerry-boat in an armed force for the protection of vital inshore waters and their associated facilities was also typical of other Scandinavian countries, who appreciated that the skerry-boat, as a result of its shallow draught and agility (especially in coming about), was ideally suited for construction and operation as the core of a numerous force of patrol and protection vessels limited to inshore service as they had a freeboard of only some 3 ft (0.9 m).

In this capacity the skerry-boat was the successor, in the fleets of the

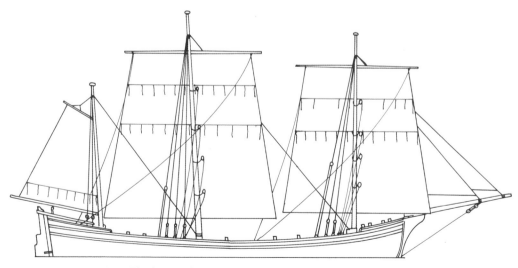

The key to the skerry-boat's sail plan was simplicity.

Despite its basic simplicity, the skerry-boat's sail plan provided good performance both on and off the wind.

Baltic nations, to the Mediterranean type of oared galley. These had operated galleys for at least 100 years up to the end of the 18th century, although in the latter part of this period the galleys had been relegated mainly to defensive operations.

The early development of the skerry-boat can be dated to the 1760s, and the type that emerged from this process was not dissimilar to the fast brigantines of the Levantine coastal powers. Through the vessels were designed to sail, the vessels also carried 10 to 12 pairs of sweeps providing the ability to move when the wind was absent or contrary. Although it has been suggested that the skerry-boat did not appear until the mid-1780s, the type of Danish vessel on which this suggestion was based was a gun boat rather than a skerry-boat, and characterized by greater beam and an armament of two 18-pdr guns.

Skerry-boat

Type:	three-masted coastal patrol and defence vessel
Tonnage:	not available
Dimensions:	length 54 to 66 ft (16.45 to 20.1 m); beam not available; draught not available
Speed:	not available
Armament:	eight to 10 swivel guns and howitzers
Complement:	50 men

HMS Endeavour 1770

It was in the course of 1768 that Lieutenant James Cook of the Royal Navy was invited to command a scientific expedition to the South Seas under the sponsorship of that eminent body, the Royal Society. The society had wanted the appointment to go to Alexander Dalrymple, who had made his name as a cartographer of eastern waters when working for the East India Company, and later became the first Hydrographer of the Navy when the relevant department was created in 1795. The Admiralty preferred Cook, however, to lead an expedition which had a double mission. The first of these was a visit to Tahiti so that an observation could be made of the transit of Venus across the sun on June 3, 1769, deemed to be "a phenomenon that must...contribute greatly to the improvement of astronomy, on which navigation so much depends." The second was to establish, positively or negatively, whether there was a great southern continent, then classified as Terra Australis, as had been suggested at earlier times by Portuguese and Dutch explorers.

The Admiralty's choice of ship for what would turn out to be the first of Captain Cook's three expeditions to the Pacific Ocean was not an adapted frigate, as had first been suggested with HMS *Rose* and *Tryal*, but at the suggestion of the Navy Board it was decided to use a North Sea "cat-built bark." The vessel selected was a bluff-bowed but notably sturdy vessel which had been built in 1764 at Fishburn near Whitby in Yorkshire as the collier *Earl of Pembroke*. Cook was well versed in the ways of such vessels as he had first gone to sea in such a type. Cook also knew that such as vessel, though not speedy, was sturdy, capacious, and agile enough to maneuvre safety in the waters of the South Pacific, where were known to abound with reefs.

Renamed as the *Endeavour* and re-rigged as a ship with square sails on all three masts, but always known as His Majesty's Bark *Endeavour* to distinguish her from another Royal Navy ship of the same name, the vessel sailed from Plymouth on August 25, 1768 with an extremely

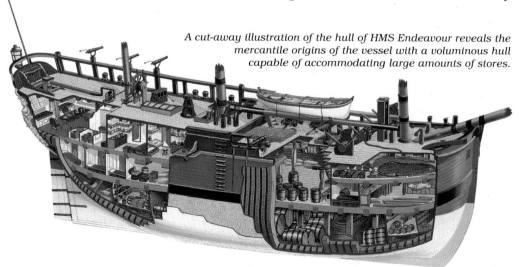

A cut-away illustration of the hull of HMS Endeavour reveals the mercantile origins of the vessel with a voluminous hull capable of accommodating large amounts of stores.

capable scientific party including the naturalists Joseph Banks and Daniel Solander, and a crew among whom were Lieutenants John Gore and Charles Clerke, both veterans of HMS *Dolphin*, which had made two voyages of exploration round Cape Horn into the Pacific. The *Endeavour* proceeded via Madeira, Rio de Janeiro, and the Bay of Good Success in Le Maire Strait to enter the Pacific and reach Tahiti on April 13, 1769 Cook's crew established good relations with the Tahitians, who had welcomed the crews of two French exploring ships, *La Boudeuse* and *L'Etoile* under the Compte Louis Antoine de Bougainville, in the previous year, and stayed on the island for three months. When the British ship sailed, its complement had been swollen by two persons, in the form of a Tahitian named Tupaia and Taiata, his servant. After calling elsewhere in the what were called the Society Islands at that time as a result of the fact that they lay close together, the *Endeavour* proceeded south and then west, reaching the North Island of New Zealand on October 9. In the course of a six-month cruise, the *Endeavour* established that New Zealand consisted of two main islands, round each of which the ship sailed, divided by the Cook Strait, a named suggested by Banks. with the search for Terra Australis now abandoned, the

ST. HELENA £1.50

HMS ENDEAVOUR AT ANCHOR 1771

A stamp of St. Helena records the visit of HMS Endeavour to the island during her circumnavigation of the world.

Endeavour departed New Zealand on March 31, 1770 and directed her course due west across the Tasman Sea as Cook hoped to enter the Indian Ocean via Van Diemen's Land (now Tasmania).

The *Endeavour* was driven off course by the arrival of adverse winter weather conditions, and on April 19, reached the coast of New Holland (now Australia). Nine days later the *Endeavour* entered a bay, just to the south of what is now Sydney, to which the name Botany Bay was given in reflection of the mass of unknown plants which the botanists collected there in the following week.

HMS Endeavour *continued*

The *Endeavour* weighed anchor on May 6th and followed the Australian coast until June 10th, when the ship struck the Great Barrier Reef near Cape Tribulation and was holed. It took the crew two days to get the ship off the reef, and the leak could be stopped only by fothering (drawing a sail closely thrummed with yarn or oakum) the hole. Nine days after this, the *Endeavour* reached land at what is now Cooktown, and here Cook began repairs that occupied the next six weeks. Cook claimed New Holland in the name of King George III, and then sailed through the Torres Strait, stopping at Savu Island to the west of Timor, and then reaching the Dutch trading center at Batavia (now Jakarta).

An interesting and successful experiment carried out at Batavia involved what was termed an "electrical chain," a lightning conductor which allowed the *Endeavour* to survive a lightning strike during a storm in which Dutch East Indiaman was severely damaged by another strike. All in all, however, the *Endeavour's* stay in Batavia was unhappy, for the ship's hull needed more repairs and the crew was struck by disease and suffered the loss of seven men, including the two Tahitians. The *Endeavour* therefore left Batavia only on December 26, 1770. Even so, the ship did not leave the legacy of her stay in the East Indies behind her, for during the voyage across the Indian Ocean another 23 of the crew died from disease.

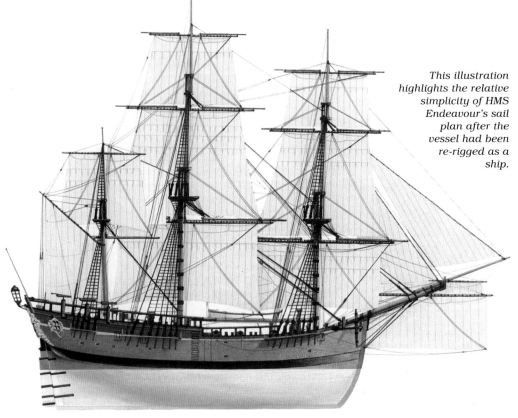

This illustration highlights the relative simplicity of HMS Endeavour's sail plan after the vessel had been re-rigged as a ship.

HMS Endeavour is a popular subject for stamps of South Pacific nations, reflecting the importance of the ship in the history of this vast region.

The *Endeavour* reached Cape Town near the southern tip of Africa on March 15, 1771 and remained there until April 14 before sailing for the island of St. Helena, where she remained for three days until May 4, and finally reached the Downs, in the outer estuary of the River Thames on July 12, 1771. The ship had completed her circumnavigation of the world in two years, nine months and 14 days.

Cook did not long remain at home. Leaving the voyage's "curiosities" in the hands of Joseph Banks, who later left them to the British Museum, Cook sailed once more for the Pacific in July 1772. By this time he had been promoted to commander, and now commanded HMS *Resolution* and had HMS *Adventure* in company.

The *Endeavour* was now refitted at Woolwich Dockyard, and undertook three voyages to and from the Falkland Islands before finally being paid off in September 1774. The ship was sold out of naval service on March 7 of the following year, and returned to her original task as a North Sea collier for 15 years. In 1790 the vessel was sold to French owners and was renamed as *La Liberté*, which operated in the whale trade until 1793. In that year the ship went aground off Newport, Rhode Island, and was later broken up.

Given the importance of the *Endeavour* in Australian history, it is hardly surprising that a replica of the ship was commissioned at Fremantle in 1994.

HMS *Endeavour* (formerly *Earl of Pembroke* and later *La Liberté*)

Type:	three-masted collier cat-bark and later ship-rigged exploratory vessel
Tonnage:	369 tons
Dimensions:	length 97 ft 8 in (29.7 m); beam 29 ft 4 in (8.9 m); depth in hold 11 ft 4 in (3.4 m)
Speed:	8 kt
Armament:	six 4-pdr guns and eight swivel guns
Complement:	85-94 men

Hector 1773

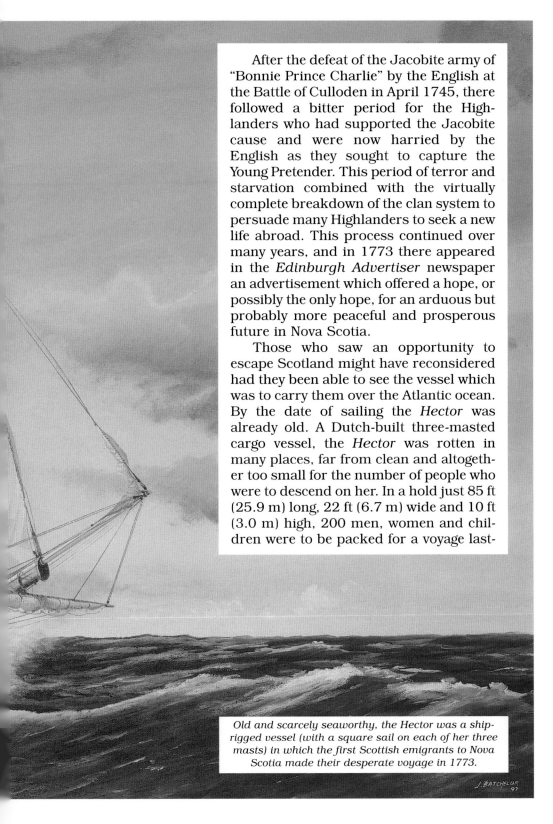

After the defeat of the Jacobite army of "Bonnie Prince Charlie" by the English at the Battle of Culloden in April 1745, there followed a bitter period for the Highlanders who had supported the Jacobite cause and were now harried by the English as they sought to capture the Young Pretender. This period of terror and starvation combined with the virtually complete breakdown of the clan system to persuade many Highlanders to seek a new life abroad. This process continued over many years, and in 1773 there appeared in the *Edinburgh Advertiser* newspaper an advertisement which offered a hope, or possibly the only hope, for an arduous but probably more peaceful and prosperous future in Nova Scotia.

Those who saw an opportunity to escape Scotland might have reconsidered had they been able to see the vessel which was to carry them over the Atlantic ocean. By the date of sailing the *Hector* was already old. A Dutch-built three-masted cargo vessel, the *Hector* was rotten in many places, far from clean and altogether too small for the number of people who were to descend on her. In a hold just 85 ft (25.9 m) long, 22 ft (6.7 m) wide and 10 ft (3.0 m) high, 200 men, women and children were to be packed for a voyage last-

Old and scarcely seaworthy, the Hector was a ship-rigged vessel (with a square sail on each of her three masts) in which the first Scottish emigrants to Nova Scotia made their desperate voyage in 1773.

The Hector was small, poorly provisioned and equipped for the transport of bulk freight rather than passengers.

ing many weeks. The vessel's crew was 14 men, and most of the little spaces that could otherwise have provided accommodation were full when the passengers started to pour into the hold, whose only lavatory and sickness facilities were canvas-covered wooden buckets.

There were no drying facilities, so anyone who took a soaking on deck had to endure wet clothing for some time. Feeding 200 passengers on a ship the size of the *Hector* had its own problems. Each day the passengers lined up on deck as the mates measured out a pint of water for each adult and less for each child. This pint (0.5 l) had to do for all purposes. Each week every adult received 3 lb (1.4 kg) of salt beef, 3 lb (1.4 kg) of bread and 4 lb (1.8 kg) of oatmeal, which had to be stored and guarded from theft. Families or consenting groups were

allowed on deck to cook their food over small sandbox fires. Life was hard even while the weather was pleasant and much advantage was taken of the sunshine at the beginning of the voyage.

It is thought that the *Hector* sailed from Loch Broom on the west coast of Ross-shire on July 10, 1773, and it is hardly surprising that illness soon appeared. First dysentery, but then many people developed the symptoms of smallpox; 20 children and three adults died. When the leadsman hit bottom on the Grand Banks, off Newfoundland, all thought that the voyage would last only another two weeks or so. But then a northwesterly storm drove the *Hector* southeast, back toward Europe. It was six weeks before the storm blew itself out. During the vast majority of this time the hapless emigrants had been bat-

Gary Bannerman, a direct descendant of the only MacDonald on the Hector's voyage, stands on deck of the reconstruction of this ship at Pictou. (Photo: Patricia Bannerman).

tened down in the reeking hold with only a few oil lamps in appalling conditions: some died from prolonged seasickness, dehydration and exhaustion. In the storm the *Hector's* timbers worked, and the worse the storm became the more water she took through faulty seams. The miseries of life battened down in the hold was thus worsened by the stench of bilge water further contaminated by the excrement and vomit poured through cracks in the hold's deck.

At the end of the storm the *Hector* was nearly back to Scotland, and some of the passengers wished to get off the vessel. But the captain had been paid to deliver his human cargo to Nova Scotia, and headed west once more. The ship's bread had been spoiled by the storm water, and its water was green with scum and algae, being drinkable only with drops of vinegar added. Thirst was the passengers' greatest problem, and the fact that there was little more than salt beef to eat worsened matters.

The would-be emigrants had set off in high hopes in mid-May. Now it was September and they had been four months in the ship's ghastly hold. Then finally on September 15 the *Hector* sailed over the bar and dropped anchor in the lovely little harbor of Pictou, Nova Scotia.

Hector	
Type:	ship-rigged merchant vessel of the Dutch *fluyt* type
Tonnage:	200 tons burthen
Dimensions:	length 110 ft 0 in (33.5 m) between perpendiculars; beam 22 ft 0 in (6.7 m); draught 11 ft 6 in (3.5 m)
Speed:	not available
Armament:	none
Complement:	14 men and provision for 200 passengers

Nile Boats

The River Nile of northeastern Africa is the longest river in the world. From Lake Victoria in east central Africa, it flows generally north through Uganda, Sudan and Egypt to debouch into the Mediterranean Sea via a vast delta after a run of some 3,470 miles (5585 km). From its farthest headstream, the Kagera river in Burundi somewhat to the south of the equator, the river is some 4,160 miles (6695 km) long, and its basin covers some 1.29 million square miles (3.35 million km²) draining about one tenth of the African continent in parts of modern Tanzania, Burundi, Rwanda, Congo (Kinshasa), Kenya, Uganda, and Ethiopia, most of Sudan and the cultivated part of Egypt, and the average flow is 682,000 Imp gal (3.1 million liter) per second. The basin is bordered in the north by the Mediterranean Sea, in the east by the Red Sea Hills and the Ethiopian Plateau, in the south by the East African Highlands including Lake Victoria, and in the west by the somewhat less well defined watershed between the Nile, Chad and Congo basins, extending northwest to include the Marrah mountains of Sudan, the Al-Jilf al-Kabir Plateau of Egypt, and the Libyan Desert, which is part of the Sahara. The upper part of this vast river system is known as the White Nile, and the River Nile proper is created by the confluence, at Khartoum in Sudan, of the White Nile and the Blue Nile. The latter originates in Lake Tana in Ethiopia, and is some 950 miles (1530 km) long. Another major contributor to the Nile is the River Atbara, which flows into it some 200 miles (320 km) downstream from Khartoum, and is the source of much of the silt that makes the Nile so vital to Egypt.

Unlike the other great rivers known to the Egyptians and Greeks, the Nile flows from south to north, and this fact was as perplexing to them as the other manifest oddity that

Nile boats at Sahil Atar el Nahi, Old Cairo. The high stems of these craft resemble those of the vessels built by the ancient Egyptians, but the lateen sails are derived from Arab practice. The very long yard of the lateen sail is notably useful in raising the peak high enough to catch the wind even when the felucca is sailing close to a high bank of the Nile river.

the river is also in flood at the warmest season of the year, when the water in the other great rivers of their experience was decreasing. Together with the Tigris and Euphrates in modern Iraq, and the Indus in modern Pakistan, the Nile was thus ideally placed to birth one of the world's earliest civilizations, dating back to the sixth millennium BC and including people who were among the first to embark on agriculture and the use of the plough. Carrying rich silt from its three precursor rivers, the Nile floods annually, depositing the silt to create the fertile plains upon which the people of ancient Egypt depended, and its size and course led to the use of the river as the primary social and economic artery of the Egyptian civilization. Indeed, the Egyptian civilization came into existence because of the fertility offered by the alluvial flood plains along the river's course, and then developed as the river came to be exploited for the movement of raw materials and the development of trade.

With its tack close to the centerline, the lateen sail allows the felucca to sail well up into the wind, while with its tack moved up to windward the sail operates well as the craft runs before the wind.

The classic river transport vessel of Egypt is the flat-bottomed *felucca*. This came into being as a trading vessel of the Mediterranean coasts, but now survives almost exclusively on the Nile and a few other Middle and Near Eastern rivers. The larger *feluccas* are decked galley-built vessels of narrow beam and propelled by lateen sails on one or two masts, supplemented occasionally by a small mizzenmast which is also lateen-rigged. The smaller *feluccas* are propelled by four to six oars, but many are also fitted with one or two masts, and are on occasion seen with oars and sails being used together.

Felucca (typical)

Type:	lateen-rigged riverine trading vessel
Tonnage:	14 to 30 tons displacement
Dimensions:	length 50 to 75 ft (15.2 to 22.9 m); beam 15 to 25 ft (4.6 to 7.6 m); draught not available
Speed:	not available
Complement:	three to five men

HMS Resolution 1775

After his first voyage of discovery in HMS *Endeavour*, Commander James Cook was given two ships to search for the supposed great southern continent. Cook's vessel was HMS *Resolution* launched in 1770, while Commander Tobias Furneaux had HMS *Adventure*. These barque-rigged North Sea colliers were re-rigged as full ships, and sailed in July 1772. After a stay at Cape Town, during November they headed south to become the first ships known to have crossed the Antarctic Circle, reaching as far south as 67° 15' S. The ships became separated in fog and Cook sailed east along the edge of the pack ice until March 17, when he altered course to New Zealand. The *Resolution* reached Dusky Sound on South Island and later met

the *Adventure* at Ship Cove in Queen Charlotte Sound on May 18.

A month later the ships sailed east, looking for land, then turned for Tahiti. Sailing west, the ships put in to Tonga before heading again to New Zealand, which they reached at the end of October. The ships lost touch again in a storm and, after waiting in the Cook Strait until November 26, Cook headed south. The ship crossed the Antarctic Circle and reached 71° 10' S. After calling at Easter Island, Cook headed via the

Captain James Cook was one of the master mariners of sailing history, and as notable for the care of his men as for his navigation and sailing skills.

Celebrated as the ship in which Captain James Cook undertook his second and third great voyages of discovery, HMS Resolution was a converted collier of sturdy construction and the volume to carry a mass of stores. The ship is seen here in Antarctic waters.

Marquesas Islands to Tahiti, where he remained six weeks. Cook later surveyed Espiritu Santo, New Caledonia and Norfolk Island before reaching the Cook Strait. On November 9th Cook sailed for Cape Horn, and explored Tierra del Fuego and Staten Island before sailing east and discovering South Georgia Island and the South Sandwich Islands. Cook then sailed via Cape Town to Spithead, where the Resolution anchored on July 29.

Now a post-captain, Cook was instructed to find a North-west Passage. Partnered by HMS *Discovery* under Captain Charles Clerke, the *Resolution* had a crew including Lieutenant John Gore and, as master, William Bligh. The *Resolution* sailed in July 1776 and met the *Discovery* at Cape Town. The ships continued to Tahiti, then sailed north and, after touching the Sandwich (Hawaiian) Islands in January 1778, headed toward North America, reaching Nootka Sound on March 29. Here the *Resolution* was overhauled before the ships passed northwest along the Alaskan coast, anchoring in Prince William Sound on May 12 and Cook Inlet a fortnight later. Rounding the Alaska peninsula, the ships entered the Bering Sea, passed round Cape Prince of Wales on the eastern side of the Bering Strait, and sailed north and west as far as Icy Cape. On August 29 the ships reached the Chukotski peninsula, and between October 3 and 26

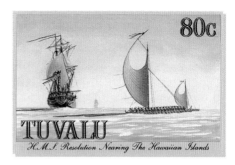

Nearing the Hawaiian Islands with HMS Adventure astern, HMS Resolution is greeted by a large two-masted war canoe of the islands' Polynesian inhabitants.

remained at the Russian settlement of Unalaska before turning back to the Sandwich Islands. The ships wintered here and sailed again on February 4, 1779, but had to turn back a week later after the *Resolution* had sprung her foremast. On February 14, after an argument between Hawaiians and a shore party, Cook and four marines died in a skirmish.

Command now passed to Clerke, with Gore in the *Discovery*. The ships sailed from the Sandwich Islands in March for Petropavlovsk on the Kamchatka peninsula and, after a second foray past Icy Cape to 71° 56' N, Clerke abandoned the effort to find a northern passage to the Atlantic. Clerke died on August 22, and command now fell to Gore. The ships sailed to Macao and Cape Town, and thence the Atlantic. The ships reached the Nore on October 4th after a voyage of 4 years 2 months and 22 days.

HMS *Resolution*

Type:	ship-rigged sloop
Tonnage:	461 tons
Dimensions:	length 110 ft 7 in (33.7 m); beam 30 ft 5 in (9.3 m); depth of hold 13 ft 2 in (4.0 m)
Speed:	not available
Armament:	12 6 pdr and 12 swivel guns
Complement:	112 men and 12 civilians

Philadelphia 1776

During the American War of Independence (1775-83), one of Britain's first strategic aims was the isolation of New England from the rest of the colonies so that this revolutionary heartland could be retaken more easily. After the failure of the 1775-76 American invasion of Canada, this strategy was seen as all the more important, but was hampered by the poor north/south communications of the area except by water up the Richelieu river from Canada to Lake Champlain, where the American fort at Ticonderoga blocked access to Albany and the Hudson river valley extending south to New York. Realising the significance of Lake Champlain, General Benedict Arnold assembled a small force of soldiers and shipbuilders at Skenesborough, New York, to build a flotilla of three schooners, one sloop, five galleys and eight gunboats including the *Philadelphia*. Arnold referred to these gunboats as gondolas, but the more correct name was gundalow or gundelo, a type of river barge. At St. John's on the Richelieu river, the British built a force of five small warships, 20 gunboats and 28 longboats.

Armed with a single 12-pdr gun in the bows, two 9-pdr guns athwartships and eight light swivel guns along each beam, the flat-bottomed gundalow set two square sails on a single mast, but its primary propulsion was probably the eight large oars on each side. After four weeks of cruising at the northern end of Lake Champlain as the British prepared for their advance to the south, Arnold moved his flotilla south. On October 11, 1776 the American flotilla was moored off the southwestern side of Valcour Island, between the island and the mainland shore, some 55 miles (89 km) north of Ticonderoga.

The Philadelphia was extremely sturdily built, and needed to be so as she carried heavy armament for a craft of her size. In her bows she mounted one 12-pdr gun, and athwartships were two 9-pdr guns, with additional firepower provided by eight light swivel guns.

The British flotilla rounded the southern tip of Valcour Island to tackle the American force. In this six-hour engagement the greater size and weight of fire of the British vessels, manned by sailors rather than ill-trained landsmen, generally prevailed, although the Americans managed to stand firm in their crescent formation for some time. Arnold's flagship, the 12-gun schooner *Royal Savage*, ran aground before being boarded and burned, the two-masted eight-gun galleys *Congress* and *Washington* were run aground and captured, and at dusk the gundalow *Philadelphia*, already badly damaged, was sunk by a single 24-pdr ball. In the dark the surviving American vessels managed to evade the British and head south. However, the British caught the Americans again on October 13 at Crown Point, and effectively destroyed the remnants of the American flotilla. The three-day battle was a tactical defeat for the Americans, but also a strategic victory as the British, their ammunition depleted and winter weather threatening, halted and then pulled back into Canada, with fateful consequences for the British in the War of American Independence.

In 1934, the remains of the *Philadelphia* were located in some 60 ft (18.3 m) of water, her mast still standing. Remarkably preserved in the cold, fresh water, the hull was raised on August 1, 1935, and the *Philadelphia* is now the oldest "warship" on exhibit in North America, in this case as one of the most prized exhibits of the Smithsonian Institution.

Philadelphia

Type:	single-masted gundalow
Tonnage:	not available
Dimensions:	length 53 ft 3 in (16.3 m); beam 15 ft 6 in (4,7 m); depth of hold 3 ft 9 in (1.15 m)
Speed:	not available
Armament:	one 12-pdr, two 9-pdr and eight light swivel guns
Complement:	45 men

Ranger 1777

On 13 February 1778 the Ranger had the honor
of receiving the first foreign salute to the "Stars
and Stripes" when the American vessel entered Quiberon Bay.

One of the most important figures in the early days of what later became the US Navy, John Paul Jones (1747-92) was born John Paul at Kirkbean in the Scottish county of Galloway, and between 1761 and 1773 served in the British merchant marine. In 1773 he killed a mutinous but locally popular sailor in Tobago, and then changed his name to John Jones and fled to Virginia. When the 13 North American colonies rebelled against British rule in 1775 and the Congress authorized the establishment of the Continental Navy, John Paul Jones (as he now styled himself) was commissioned as a first lieutenant. On June 14, 1777, he was appointed to command the sloop of war *Ranger*,

Ranger *continued*

John Paul was born in 1747 in Galloway, Scotland, and began his seafaring life in the British merchant marine. After killing a mutinous but locally popular seaman in Tobago, John Paul fled in 1773 to Virginia in the American colonies and changed his name to John Jones. After the outbreak of the War of American Independence, John Jones was commissioned as a lieutenant in the Continental Navy, and soon rose to command the Ranger.

American sailors, of whom several hundreds were incarcerated in British prisons facing trials for treason. Selkirk was absent, though, and the American seamen, still scenting the possibility of profit, took the family silver. Coming to know of the theft, Jones offered his apologies, bought the silver from his men, and returned it to the Selkirk family.

laid down in January 1777 at the Langdon Shipyard across the Piscataqua River from Portsmouth, New Hampshire.

After reaching Nantes on the Atlantic seaboard of France on December 2, 1777 and taking two prizes en route, Jones visited Paris, where Benjamin Franklin, the American commissioner, sized him up as a great fighting seaman. Ordered to cruise about the British Isles, Jones concentrated his efforts on shore raids. After taking or burning four British vessels, on the night of April 22-23, 1778 the Ranger raided Whitehaven in the hope of burning the many ships in that harbor. However, the landing was poorly executed and little destruction was achieved. On the morning of April 23 Jones landed with a boat's crew on St. Mary's Isle, intending to take the 4th Earl of Selkirk as a hostage to obtain the release of

Altogether more important was the April 24 battle between the Ranger and the 20-gun HMS Drake, off Belfast Lough. The two vessels were similar in size and armament, and there followed a one-hour close action before the Drake, her rigging shot to pieces and her commander killed, surrendered. Initially towing his prize and then sailing her under jury rig, Jones reached the French port of Brest, and an exchange was then arranged for 200 British prisoners and American seamen in British prisons.

The Ranger returned to America under Lieutenant Thomas Simpson in company with the Boston and Providence, arriving at Portsmouth with three prizes on October 15, 1778. Between February and November 1779 the Ranger sailed with the Queen of France and, variously Warren or Providence, capturing

18 prizes of which three were later retaken. On November 23, 1779 the *Ranger* joined Commodore Abraham Whipple's squadron bound for Charleston, South Carolina. On January 24, 1780 the *Ranger* and *Providence* captured three supply transports off Tybee Island before returning to the defence of the port. When Charleston fell on May 11, 1780, the *Ranger, Providence* and *Boston* were captured and commissioned into the Royal Navy, HMS *Halifax* (ex-*Ranger*) being sold out of the service in the following year.

Jones was next promoted to command of a squadron centred on a 900 ton East Indiaman which the French government purchased for him and renamed *Bonhomme Richard* as a compliment to Franklin. The rest of the squadron consisted of the new *Alliance*, commanded by a more than eccentric Frenchman named Pierre Landais, the French frigate *Pallas*, and a French corvette and cutter, all flying the American flag. With huge difficulty Jones got the *Bonhomme Richard* adapted as a warship and manned. The squadron sailed from Lorient on August 14, 1779. The cutter became separated and never rejoined, and the *Alliance* went off prize-hunting for most of the voyage. Passing between Orkney and Shetland, Jones sailed south with the intention of extracting money from Edinburgh, but his notion failed and Jones continued south, intercepting a Baltic convoy of 44 vessels escorted by the frigate HMS *Serapis*, under Captain Richard Pearson, and HMS *Countess of Scarborough*.

There followed an extremely hard-fought battle on September 23, 1779. Pearson's first concern was for the safety of the convoy, whose northward escape he covered by holding the American squadron at bay. Having made sure of the convoy's safe departure, the *Serapis* turned to engage the *Bonhomme Richard* while the *Countess of Scarborough* tackled the much larger *Pallas*. After raking the *Bonhomme Richard* with gun fire, the *Serapis* grappled her in preparation for a boarding attempt but in the face of very determined American opposition could not get a foothold on the *Bonhomme Richard*. The two ships fought at muzzle-to-muzzle range for some two hours, the *Bonhomme Richard* having all but two of her guns knocked out of action before a fire erupted on the *Serapis* and Pearson was forced to surrender. The *Bonhomme Richard* was more damaged than the *Serapis*, and sank two days later. Jones transferred his command to the captured *Serapis*. The losses suffered by both ships' crews was high, the *Serapis* and *Bonhomme Richard* suffering 128 and 150 casualties respectively.

Ranger

Type:	three-masted ship-rigged sloop of war
Tonnage:	308 tons
Dimensions:	length 116 ft 0 in (35.4 m) on the gun deck; beam 34 ft 0 in (10.4 m); depth of hold 13 ft 6 in (4.1 m)
Speed:	not available
Armament:	18 6 pdr guns
Complement:	140 men

Carolina/Georgia Periauger 1780

The type of craft most commonly associated with the coasts and waterways of the Carolinas and Georgia in the 18th and 19th centuries, when roads were few and poor, is the periauger, sometimes called the petiauger in colonial Georgia. People living and working in these areas opted for waterborne transport of persons and freight through the maze of shallow rivers and streams constituting an inland waterway system.

The periauger was developed for such conditions, and was apparently very successful. Despite this fact, little of any precise nature is known about the periauger, which is frequently mentioned in the writings of the period but only in the sketchiest of manners. The first mention of the periauger is by John Lawson, the co-founder of Bath, North Carolina.

Writing of his travels in 1701, Lawson records that "Ciprus-Trees, of which the French make Canoes, will carry fifty or sixty Barrels. After the Tree is moulded and dug, they saw it in two pieces, and so put a Plank between, and a small Keel, to preserve them from the Oyster-Banks, which are innumerable in the Creeks and Bays betwixt the French Settlement and Charles-Town. They carry two Masts, and Bermudas Sails ... to transport Goods and Lumber from one River to another. Some are so large, as to carry thirty Barrels, tho' of one entire Piece of Timber. Others, that are split down the Bottom, and a piece added thereto, will carry eighty, or a hundred."

The periauger was in effect a large canoe split down the middle to permit a shaped keel log to be

*This illustration reveals periaugers with gaff and Bermudian rigs
(foreground and background respectively).*

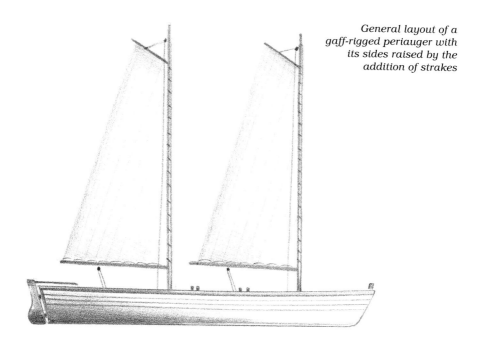

spliced between the two halves. This increased the volume available for cargo, improved stability and, through the addition of a keel extending below the bottom of the rest of the craft, helped to reduce the chances of damage from passage over oyster beds and other such obstructions. Lawson and slightly later travellers speak of periaugers as being "long, flat-bottomed boats, carrying from 20 to 35 Tons. They have a kind of a Forecastle and a Cabin; but the rest open, and no deck. There have two masts, which they can strike, and Sails like Schooners. They row generally with two Oars only." Later references indicate another rig with two gaff-rigged masts carrying a pair of four-sided fore-and-aft sails as an alternative to two Bermudian-rigged masts carrying a pair of three-sided fore-and-aft sails, in each case without any head sail. Almost certainly, the larger craft were also propelled, when the wind was not suitable, by as many as six or eight oars.

The periauger was thus a split-dugout craft with a log backbone inserted between the divided halves, sometimes with strakes added to increase the freeboard, partially decked, propelled by oars and having provision for two masts to be stepped when there was a suitable breeze. The periauger ranged in size between 3.5 to 7 tons burthen, with a length of no more than 30 ft (9.1 m), on the north-eastern part of North Carolina, but ranging up to 20 or even 35 tons, with a length in excess of 40 ft (12.2 m), on the Savannah River and the Gulf Coast. It is likely that these larger craft were plank-built rather than of the split-canoe type.

In 2003-04, the Perqimans County Restoration Association sponsored a periauger reconstruction of 5 tons burthen with a length of 30 ft 0 in (9.1 m), beam of 7 ft 0 in (2.1 m) and two gaff-rigged masts for a loose-footed foresail and a boomed mainsail. Much experimental sailing was undertaken, and this served to confirm the general utility of the periauger.

HMS Bounty 1789

In 1787 the Royal Navy decided to buy a merchant ship for the purpose of sailing to the Society Islands, as Captain James Cook had named the Tahiti group, to collect breadfruit saplings for shipment to the West Indies, where they would become a staple food for slaves. The vessel was the *Bethia*, built in 1784 at Hull. At Deptford Dock Yard the ship was refitted as HMS *Bounty* to carry 300 breadfruit trees on an upper deck rebuilt with additional scuttles to admit more air and light. Half the trees were to be delivered to Jamaica, and the other half to the Royal Botanical Garden at St. Vincent. Command was given to Lieutenant William Bligh, who had proved himself a superb navigator as master of HMS *Resolution* during Cook's last voyage.

The Admiralty ordered the ship's hull to be sheathed in copper for greater survivability against attacks by the teredo worm, and supplied three boats.

The *Bounty* sailed from Portsmouth in December 1787 and reached Tahiti on October 16, 1788. After five months in this island paradise, marred only by Bligh's harsh discipline, the *Bounty* departed on April 16, 1789 with more than 1,000 breadfruit trees. Just 22 days later, five of the 43-man crew seized the ship in a bloodless mutiny led by Fletcher Christian, a protégé whom Bligh had elevated from masters mate to acting lieutenant and the ship's second in command. Christian had Bligh and 19 of his supporters put overboard into the ship's 23-ft (7-m) launch, which

Small but very seaworthy, HMS Bounty was admirably suited to the task of circumnavigating the world.

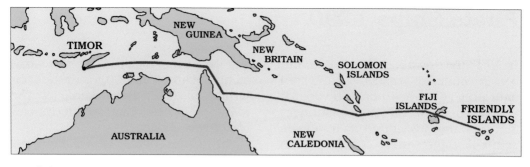

Bligh's voyage between the Friendly Islands and Timor in an overloaded and under-equipped open boat represents a monumental feat of navigation and seamanship.

Bligh sailed to Timor. The voyage of more than 4,150 miles (6680 km) with virtually no provisions or equipment is a classic of seamanship, navigation and leadership.

Christian tried to land on Tubuai, some 400 miles (645 km) south of Tahiti, but was poorly received and returned to Tahiti. Here the *Bounty* remained 10 days while the men loaded 460 hogs and 50 goats, and also embarked 28 Tahitians. Tubuai again proved inhospitable, and after a pitched battle the mutineers and their Tahitian shipmates sailed once more on September 17 with 16 friendly Tubuaians. The mutineers arrived back at Tahiti on September 20. Sixteen of the British sailors remained on the island, and on the following day Christian sailed with the Tubuaians, a few Tahitians, and eight of the crew, reaching Pitcairn Island early in 1790. On the very next day the mutineers set fire to the ship and prepared to settle the island.

Eighteen years later the Nantucket sealer *Topaz* visited Pitcairn, where the sole survivor of the original settlers was discovered to be one Alexander Smith, renamed as John Adams to lessen his chance of arrest should the island be visited by a British warship. Following the publication of Captain Frederick William Beechey's report of his visit aboard HMS *Blossom* 13 years later, Pitcairn came under the protection of the British crown in 1825. Fourteen mutineers were eventually arrested in Tahiti by the men of HMS *Pandora*, dispatched to capture the mutineers. On August 28, 1791, the *Pandora* ran aground on the Great Barrier Reef and sank, four of the mutineers being drowned. The *Pandora's* survivors sailed to Timor and the 10 surviving mutineers finally reached England and trial, three of them being hanged. Bligh finally completed his original task in 1792 in HMS *Providence*.

HMS *Bounty*

Type:	three-masted ship
Tonnage:	200 tons burthen
Dimensions:	length 91 ft 0 in (27.7 m); beam 24 ft 3 in (7.4 m); depth in hold 11 ft 3 in (3.4 m)
Speed:	not available
Armament:	4 4 pdr guns and 10 swivel guns
Complement:	46 men

Pirate Ships 1790

Pirates used small, fast, nimble and heavily manned vessels to overhaul their prey at sea and take it by boarding, and then, as naval gunnery matured, they also fitted their vessels with a sizeable battery of lighter guns to cut away rigging and sails and so slow their victims, rather than hull and possibly sink them. Between the later mediaeval period and the start of the 18th century organized piracy was the national industry for the North African cities, Tunis and Algiers being the primary centers. These Barbary pirates operated as far distant as the English Channel as they looked for ships to seize and crews to sells as slaves. The growing strength of European navies in the 18th century reduced the scale of Barbary depredations, though it was

not until the Anglo-Dutch bombardment of Algiers in 1816, and the subsequent French occupation of the whole of Algeria, that Mediterranean piracy was ended.

In British waters, Devon and Kent vessels were infamous for their piratical activities in the English Channel, and Fife and Berwickshire vessels for similar activities in the Firth of Forth. It only when these waters were swept by the navy of King Henry VIII in the first half of the 16th century that shipping was rendered safer. The "classic" period of piracy was that between the late 17th and early 18th centuries, when large numbers of the privateers working the West Indies and Indian Ocean turned to piracy. These pirates included John Avery, who operated from Madagascar,

When operating as a pirate vessel, a galleass such as this would have carried a crew of some 300 or more men. A galleass such as this was used by William Kidd, and with three men at each of the 46 oars the vessel could reach 8 kt in calm conditions.

A type of vessel much favored by pirates for its speed, agility and ability to carry a large and tactically decisive crew on short piratical raiding voyages, was the brigantine.

Edward Teach ("Blackbeard"), who scourged the coasts of Carolina, Bartholomew Roberts, who sailed the western coast of Africa, Anne Bonny and Mary Read the female pirates, and perhaps most notorious of all, William Kidd, who ranged between the Indian Ocean and the Caribbean. These and many other were finally killed, captured or driven from the seas by a major British effort using frigates that could match the speed and agility of the pirate ships but carry heavier firepower.

It was standard practice to hang convicted pirates in chains on headlands as a warning visible to passing ships or, in England, staked to the ground at Execution Dock in Wapping to be drowned by the rising tide. The last pirate was executed in England in 1840, in the USA during 1862. Though the worst types of piracy have been eliminated, it is worth noting that there still exist some parts of the world where piracy still continues on a limited, but rising, scale.

Queen Anne's Revenge (formerly *Concorde* built in Britain about 1710 and, after capture in 1717, Edward Teach's vessel)

Type:	three-masted ship
Tonnage:	200 tons
Dimensions:	length 103 ft 0 in (31.4 m); beam 24 ft 6 in (7.5 m); draught 13 ft 4 in (4.1 m)
Speed:	not available
Armament:	between 20 and 40 guns
Complement:	125 men

Sloops 1780-1800

Like many other nautical terms, the word "sloop" is not precisely defined, but in general was a type of single-masted sailing vessel which was fore-and-aft rigged and setting, so far as European sailors were concerned, only a single headsail. However, in the USA the term came to embrace vessels with two headsails. The sloop and the cutter were the result of parallel development for much the same basic task and in basically the same period, from about 1740 but especially later in the 18th century, and as a result there is considerable overlap between the sloop and the cutter. Both the sloop and the cutter were designed for comparatively short-endurance work such as scouting for the fleet, undertaking inshore patrols and, when these types were adopted for the purposes of piracy and smuggling, the interception and capture of destruction of these vessels.

The sloop was based on a comparatively short but deep hull, was fully decked, and carried a large area of canvas on a mast comprising a lower mast and a topmast supported at their overlap by lateral shrouds. The main elements of the sail plan were a large fore-and-aft gaff mainsail whose boom extended well past the stern, two square sails in the form of a course and a topsail, and a single staysail or jib. However, in the quest to wring the maximum speed out of such craft, many cutters were characterized by an exceptionally long bowsprit that allowed another two headsails, namely a pair of jibs to be set. This allowed the sloop, now a cutter in all but name, to point up well into the wind, and in favorable conditions to reel off a speed of 11 kt or more. Perhaps just as importantly, the area and disposition of this huge sail plan made the sloop as agile, or more so, than the schooner or brigantine that was the naval vessel most commonly used to attempt an interception.

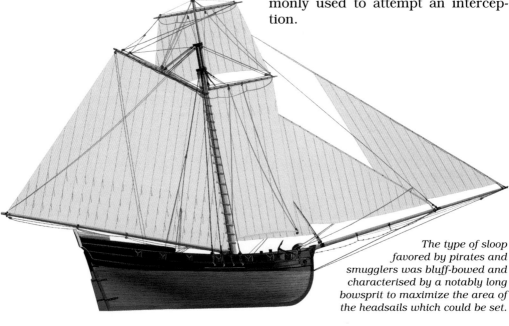

The type of sloop favored by pirates and smugglers was bluff-bowed and characterised by a notably long bowsprit to maximize the area of the headsails which could be set.

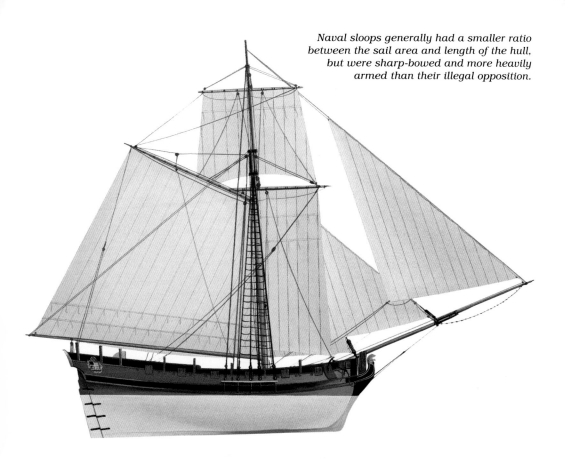

Naval sloops generally had a smaller ratio between the sail area and length of the hull, but were sharp-bowed and more heavily armed than their illegal opposition.

The type of sloop used by pirates was generally of some 100 or so tons and drew some 8 ft (2.4 m) of water, and with a complement of about 75 men was armed with some 14 light cannon. The response of the navy in attempting to defeat the pirates was generally another sloop, but in this instance of somewhat larger size and with a sharp rather than bluff bow line for greater speed. The sloop also had seven pairs of oars so that she could make way when the wind had dropped or was in the wrong quarter. The vessel was armed with guns slightly heavier than those of pirate vessels, and a well trained crew could get off two rounds every three minutes.

Naval sloop (typical)

Type:	single-masted light warship
Tonnage:	113 tons
Dimensions:	length 65 ft 0 in (19.8 m); beam not available; draught not available
Speed:	11 kt
Armament:	12 9-pdr guns
Complement:	70 men

Bomb Ketch

Created by a French designer in the last quarter of the 17th century for bombardment of targets along the Barbary coast of North Africa, and otherwise known as a bomb vessel, the bomb ketch was a vessel armed with one or sometimes two heavy howitzers or, more typically, mortars. As indicated above, this type of vessel was created specifically for use in amphibious assaults or when conventional land-based artillery bombardment was impossible. The weapons in such vessels were normally of the mortar type, with a notably short barrel firing a large-caliber explosive-filled shell whose detonation was initiated by a fuse that had to be very carefully cut so that its burning time corresponded most exactly with the shell's ballistic flight. As such, the

bomb ketch was best suited to the task of firing their shells over obstacles, such as high shorelines or fortifications, to plunge into the target just as they detonated.

The mortars were generally mounted in a vessel of the two-masted ketch type. A particular feature of the bomb ketch was that the mainmast was stepped well aft, in the position it would have occupied in a three-masted vessel, thereby leaving the foredeck as clear as possible for the operation of the main weapon(s). Bomb ketches were either constructed specially for the task, or otherwise converted from small three-masted standard by the removal of the fore mast to provide the required large deck area forward. The bomb ketch still had a long bowsprit to anchor the

A bomb ketch in action with anchors out for and aft with provision for springs if required. With her sails furled and the main stays removed, the bomb ketch had a clear field of fire over her forward half.

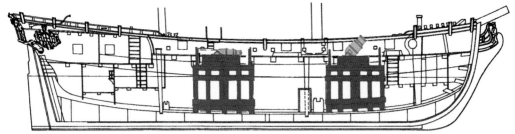

The bomb ketch was specially strengthened internally.

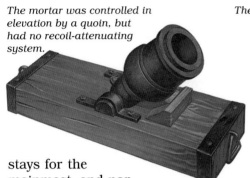

The mortar was controlled in elevation by a quoin, but had no recoil-attenuating system.

stays for the mainmast, and normally carried large headsails to balance the square sails carried by the main and mizzenmasts. Even so, the bomb ketch was always known to be a poor sailer.

When employed in the bombardment role, the bomb ketch was moored in position with springs on its cables. The use of the springs meant that the whole vessel could be trained in azimuth so that the mortar(s) fired on precisely the intended bearing. Range was varied by careful selection of size of the black powder charge which fired the shell, and also by alteration of the mortar's angle of elevation.

Up to 1804 the mortars in bomb vessels of the British navy were manned and worked by the Royal Artillery; and after that date by the Royal Marine Artillery established in that year. The development of naval guns which could be trained and elevated regardless of the ship's course later rendered the bomb vessel effectively obsolete, especially after the appearance of a more modern counterpart in the form of the monitor. It is worth noting that in the later part of the 18th and early part of the 19th centuries, the bomb ketch saw extensive ancillary service in arctic exploration toward the north and south poles. The vessels were well suited to this task as they were always very sturdily constructed, with their decks reinforced with heavy beam bridges and other structures to support the massive downward and rearward shock of the heavy mortars' recoil forces, and so were ideally suited to cope with the pressure of ice when moving through pack icc or fiozen in over the winter.

"Hecla" class bomb ketch (British, mid-1820s)

Type: three-masted bomb vessel

Tonnage: 272 tons

Dimensions:	length 105 ft 0 in (32.0 m); beam 28 ft 6 in (8.7 m); draught: 13 ft 9 in (4.2 m)
Speed:	not available
Armament:	one 13 in (330 mm) mortar, one 10 in (254 mm) mortar, eight 24 pdr guns, and two 6 pdr guns
Complement:	67 men

HMS Discovery 1792

By the end of the 1780s, the British and Spanish were in dispute about the ownership of the admittedly little mapped lands on the Pacific northwest of the North American continent. The lands were already known to be rich sources of the furs that were so important in European trade interest, would almost certainly prove to be good sources of other trading materials, and would in the longer term prove highly suitable for colonization. The British, believing that they would secure success in the conflict that had started in 1789, when Spanish

HMS Discovery lies to with some of her sails backed as a small party puts off in one of the ship's boats.

Revenue Cutter 1792

The term revenue cutter was used for the type of single-masted craft of notably fine lines designed, built and operated specifically for the tasks of preventing smuggling and enforcing customs regulations. The primary requirements in such a craft were the maximum possible speed so that any possible offender could be caught, considerable agility so that the chase could be brought to an end as rapidly as possible, and the ability to carry a crew and armament larger and heavier than those of any possible opponent so that this later could be halted and, if necessary, boarded.

The type of vessel selected for this role was the cutter, which was a small but decked vessel with one mast and a bowsprit, and carrying gaff mainsail on a boom, a topsail on a square-rugged yard, and one or two headsails (a staysail and jib, or two jibs). This type of cutter was introduced in about 1740, and proved itself to be relatively fast on the wind, to point up well

into the wind, and to be able to carry up to 22 4-pdr guns or sometimes 10 long 9-pdr guns designed to cripple an opponent at a range greater than that of the weapons habitually carried by smuggling vessels, as well as a comparatively sizeable crew as there was no need to carry a mass of provisions, powder and shot in a vessel created basically for short-endurance missions.

The heyday of the revenue cutter was during the later part of the 18th century and earlier part of the 19th century, and most especially during the French Revolutionary Wars (1792-1800) and Napoleonic Wars (1800-15). The prohibition of trade in certain goods and the levying of his import duties on others made it commercially feasible for smugglers to run dutiable goods into many countries, especially Great Britain. The general absence of coastguard stations left many parts of the coast free for the landing of smuggled

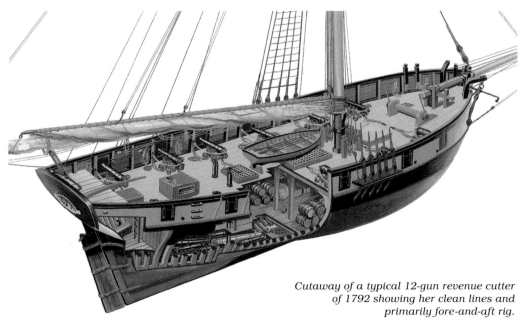

Cutaway of a typical 12-gun revenue cutter of 1792 showing her clean lines and primarily fore-and-aft rig.

goods, and the only realistic way to intercept this trade was to combine intelligence with a force of cutters fast enough to catch the luggers most commonly used by the smugglers. These luggers were sometimes two- but often three-masted vessels notable for their great weatherliness and useful speed, and were often well armed. North Sea smugglers also had a penchant for schooners. A larger example of the smuggling craft was the *Ranger*, which operated from southwest England, and was a 250-ton vessel mounting 22 guns and carrying a crew of 100. This opened the possibility of the vessel giving a good account of herself against a revenue cutter, of which the largest was the Colchester-based *Repulse*, which was a 210 ton vessel carrying only 33 men. Next largest were the *Tartar*, *Speedwell* and *Rose*, which were 190 ton vessels with about 12 guns and 30 men: these were based at Dover, Weymouth and Southampton.

A revenue cutter under way with a gaff mainsail, topsail, staysail and jib.

Many cutters were small 40 to 55 tons craft.

An example of a typical load is provided by the French-owned *Iris*, which was abandoned by her crew in 1819 as the cutter *Badger* closed on her off Boulogne. When boarded, the deserted smuggling vessel was found to be carrying 382 Imp gal (1736 liters) of brandy, 545 Imp gal (2478 liters) of gin, 55 bags of tea, and 355 lb 161 kg) of tobacco.

Revenue cutter (typical)	
Type:	single-masted smuggler interception craft
Tonnage:	130 tons
Dimensions:	length 85 ft 0 in (25.9 m); beam 24 ft 0 in (7.3 m); draught 11 ft 0 in (3,4 m)
Speed:	8 kt or more
Armament:	12 x 9-pdr guns
Complement:	25-30 men

Building a Wooden Ship

The process of building a wooden warship began in the mould loft, for it was here that the plan specifications of the designer were transferred into full-size wooden patterns. These were the templates used in the fashioning of the hull timbers, and in the United States of America the two most favored types of timber were white oak and live oak, which combined strength and durability with a comparatively high level of "workability" in the construction process. The amount of timber required was prodigious: for example, a 74-gun line-of-battle ship required some 2,000 trees for its structure, and wherever possible shapes that had grown into the living tree, by accident or design, were preferred as these offered the greatest strength. With the patterns being made and the timber selected, joiners moved onto the building way, which was angled down slightly toward the water, to lay the keel that was the spine of the hull, and then to raise the stem and stern post before adding the frames. These last were the hull's ribs, and their careful shaping created the contours of the hull. Together with horizontal deck beams and vertical stanchions, this constituted the basic skeleton of the ship. Up to 1829 the members of the structure were secured by wooden treenails, but then bolts and spikes of iron and copper became standard. Over the skeleton were laid the hori-

The growing interest of the USA in the Pacific was reflected in the 1825 authorization by the Congress for the construction of a new class of sloops for war. These three ships were built between 1825 and 1827 on the Charlestown Navy Yard. The work force of Charlestown Navy Yard in 1825 included 138 carpenters, 56 ropemakers, 40 laborers, 37 joiners, 34 blacksmiths, 25 sailmakers, 19 riggers, 18 coopers, 7 plumbers, 16 boatbuilders, 14 sparmakers, 12 blockmakers, 11 painters, 6 caulkers, 6 masons and 6 sawyers.

Picture Courtesy National Park Service, U.S. Department of the Interior, artist John Batchelor.

zontal deck and vertical hull planking. The rudder was hung from the rear of the stern post, the hull was caulked to make it watertight, and the area beneath the waterline was sheathed with copper to defeat the efforts of teredo worms to eat their way into the wood.

After the hull had been launched, the riggers moved in to step the masts on the keelson, which was a long and notably sturdy horizontal beam bolt-ed onto the upper side of the keel. The next step was the setting up of the standing rigging to support the masts, the crossing of the yards and the setting of the sails. The final stage in the construction of the ship was the setting up of the running rigging used to control all of the complexity of the moving elements (yards and sails) dependant on the masts. At this stage the ship was ready for her final outfitting.

Schooners 1800

In its pure form, the schooner was a two-masted sailing vessel with the main mast taller than the foremast, and each rigged with a fore-and-aft gaff sail which was of the boomed type on the main mast and sometimes of the loose-footed type on the foremast. The fore mast also carried one or two square topsails, but as the development of the schooner continued, these were often replaced by a jib-headed or jackyard topsail of the type that was also set above the gaff sail on the main mast. The schooner generally had a long bowsprit and/or jib-boom, allowing several jibs to be set.

Words similar to schooner are used in Dutch, German, Portuguese and Spanish, but it is believed that the origins of the name are to be found in the Scots word 'scoon', a verb describing the skipping progress of a stone skimmed over the water. Whatever the origins of the name, the schooner was certainly created in the British colonies of North America, probably as a development of a Dutch design of the 17th century, and the first

known schooner was one launched in 1713 at Gloucester, Massachusetts, from the yard of Andrew Robinson. The need for such a type, which can tack much more quickly than a square-rigged vessel, was very evident along the eastern seaboard of North America, where inlets, reefs and shoals abound. While square-rigged vessels were effective while sailing before the wind, they were not as useful in such coastal waters, where the situation also demanded the ability to sail well and hold a course with the wind in any quarter. The schooner handled better in variable winds, had the shallower draught which facilitated safe passage in coastal waters, and on a size-by-size basis required a smaller crew as fore-and-aft sails are more easily handled that square sails.

By the end of the 18th century the schooner had become the most important type of coastal vessel in North American waters, where it was widely used for coastal trading, and also for cod fishing over the Grand Banks, off Newfoundland. By the end of the 18th century the capabilities of the schooner had caught the attentions of European traders and shipwrights, who started to built similar vessels with the changes that optimized them for service in European waters. Soon after the start of the 19th century, the schooner was to be

The typical schooner of the pirates of North America and the Caribbean was two-masted and had her fore mast stepped well forward. Such craft were easily handled and agile, and could readily be concealed from searchers.

The schooner later became popular with private owners for cruising and racing. This is the 128-ton Livonia, the unsuccessful British contender for the 1871 America's Cup races.

found in the waters of virtually every part of the world.

With its good turn of speed, great agility, and the ability to carry a small but useful payload, the schooner also commended itself both to pirates and to the naval forces who sought to wipe them out. The schooner was also used by naval forces for scouting, despatch carrying, and the movement of equipment and officers urgently required in other waters.

It is also worth noting that in the USA, where speed became a key element in trade with China and California gold industry in the middle of the 19th century, the hull design of the schooner was combined with the square-rigged three-masted upper works of the ship to create the clipper.

A stamp of St. Helena depicts the Royal Navy schooner HMS St. Helena of 1815.

Pirate schooner (typical)

Type:	two-masted schooner
Tonnage:	100 tons
Dimensions:	length not available; beam not available; draught 5 ft 0 in (1.5 m)
Speed:	11 kt
Armament:	eight cannon and four swivel guns
Complement:	75 men

Transit 1800

Built in 1800, the *Transit* was unlike any other sailing vessel before or since, and was a design patented by Captain R.H. Gower, formerly of the Honourable East India Company's marine, and constructed by him using his own as well as investors' funds. The vessel was a five-masted (later reduced to four-masted) barquentine, square-rigged on the foremast and fore-and-aft rigged on the other masts. The hull was of notably great length/beam ratio, and was of V-section between the keel and the rails. This last meant that the hull's skeleton could be built by ordinary carpenters as the framing was simple and there were no curves above the waterline, meaning that shipwrights were needed only for the planking.

Although the hull was novel, it was the vessel's rig which was unique, inasmuch as each of the masts was a self-supporting unit entirely independent from its neighbors in terms of standing rigging. Each mast was therefore rigged in flag pole fashion, i.e. stayed to four points (one on each side fore and aft of the mast) with wires rather than the otherwise conventional arrangement of rope shrouds. On the foremast the forestay was attached to the mast above the lowest yard, requiring the fore course to embody a triangular hold through which the stay passed, and the foot of this sail was laced to a boom, and the reef points were tied round this boom rather than the yard. Above the course, the topsail and topgallant sail were basically orthodox.

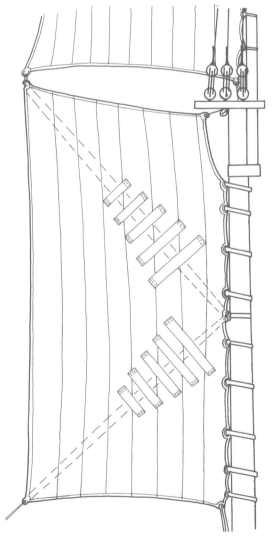

The course on each of the Transit's fore-and-aft rigged masts was very neatly conceived for ease of control and also for efficiency, with canvas strap "pockets" on each side of the sail for the two sprits that served as battens and kept them extended and also as flat as possible. Note also that the doubling of the lower mast and the topmast was reversed by comparison with that of other vessels to allow the topmast to be struck down on deck without disturbing the course.

There are suggestions that Gower intended the Transit to be entirely fore-and-aft rigged, but as an economy used a square-rigged foremast he had been given.

The other masts each carried three fore-and-aft sails described by Gower as the course, topsail and topgallant. The courses and topsails were of rectangular shape, the former extending from the lower mast cap almost down to the deck, and the latter from cap to the topmast hounds. On each mast these two sails were laced to the mast along their luffs, and the course was extended by two spars or sprits whose forward jaws fitted round the mast. The sprits were designed to hold the sail flat as well as support the peak and clew, and were therefore held against the sail by canvas straps sewn to the sail at regular intervals and at right angles to the sprits. The sprits therefore extended diagonally across the upper and lower halves of the sail to the peak and the clew respectively. The topsail was similar except for its use of a single sprit extending diagonally from the tack to the peak, and

was provided with brails so that it could be brailed back to the mast with the sprit extending vertically behind the mast. The topgallant sail also had a single diagonal sprit, but was not quite rectangular. The sail plan was completed by the headsails, which comprised two jibs.

Gower tried to interest both the Admiralty and the HEIC in the value of his novel hull, rigging and sail plan, but to no avail. He was permitted to undertake a comparative trial against a naval sloop, and the *Transit* proved altogether superior on every point of sailing. But nothing came of this, and Gower used his vessel for commercial purposes, constantly outsailing the other vessels of the convoys to which his vessel was allocated.

Frigates 1770-1810

The term frigate reached its definitive meaning, in the era of sail, during the Seven Years' War (1756-63). It was now generally agreed that the frigate was a vessel smaller than a multi-decked line-of-battle ship but still possessing considerable firepower. By general consensus the frigate was a three-masted ship of the square-rigged type with its main armament carried on a single gun deck and more guns on the poop and forecastle. The number of guns ranged from 24 to 56, but averaged 30 to 40. Frigates lacked the size and strength to stand in the line of battle in any fleet engagement, but had greater speed and agility than the line-of-battle ships and thus could scout for the fleets, or stand off and repeat flag signals from commanders so that every ship in the line could see them. A role independent of the fleet was escorting merchant convoys against the depredations of the enemy's frigates and privateers, or conversely as a commerce raider preying on the enemy's shipping.

Faster than the line-of-battle ship, and both larger and more heavily armed than the sloop-of-war and other smaller naval vessels, the frigate was classified by the British in the period between 1640 and 1860 as a fourth-, fifth- or sixth-rate warship, and was the smallest warships commanded by a post-captain. Because it was smaller and lighter, a frigate could be built more quickly and more cheaply than a line-of-battle ship, and was therefore constructed in larger numbers. The frigate thus became probably the hardest-worked of warship types during the age of sail. While line-of-battle ships were commonly used for tasks such as blockading an enemy's coasts and ports, frigates were pushed far and wide in any and all weather and geographical conditions on a host of tasks that demanded that the vessels be driven as hard as possible and their captains taxed in their skill and capacity for independent command.

Frigates usually fought in small numbers or singly against other frigates and, unlike the larger ships that were placed in ordinary (laid up in a dockyard or harbor without their

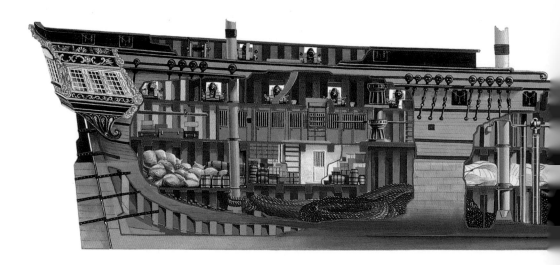

guns, masts, yards, rigging and sails), frigates remained in service during times of peace to undertake more cheaply the role that would probably have been performed in war by a line-of-battle ship, to provide the naval links still required in peace as much as in war, and to provide the means whereby officers (commissioned and warrant) could gain and exercise the experience which would make them all the more valuable in war.

Though the term frigate reached its classic meaning in the middle of the 18th century, the word had first been used in the previous century, usually for a warship which was faster than most others. The master ship-wright Peter Pett, whose greatest success was the *Sovereign of the Seas*, also created what is generally conceded to have been the first frigate, the *Constant Warwick*, which paved the way for the type of 17th century frigate that was later developed into the two-decked line-of-battle ship carrying 60 to 74 guns as epitomized by the "74" that was the workhorse of the battle fleets. In the 17th century the frigate became a masterpiece of design and construction. The British added more sails and weapons, the Dutch reduced

the draught, and the French added bow and stern weapons as well as a mass of useless but nonetheless magnificent decoration. During this period the term frigate was steadily extended in scope to cover large vessels carrying 70 or more guns on two decks right down to small vessels mounting only 22 guns on one deck.

The direct origin of the classic frigate of the Napoleonic Wars (1800-1815) can be found in French developments in the second quarter of the 18th century when the frigate matured

This cut-away illustration depicts the interior of a typical light frigate's hull, with the main armament carried high and all the stores, magazine as cables, as well as much of the accommodation, deeper in the hull.

Frigates *continued*

The frigate always had the appearance of elegance as she sailed, especially with her courses brailed up.

as a warship with its main guns on a single deck, which had been the upper gun deck on earlier two-deck warships of similar size. The deck which had been the lower gun deck of these two-deckers now became the orlop deck providing storage, the magazine and cabin space for the junior officers. This deck was in fact placed below the waterline of the definitive frigate as this began to come off the slips.

With its single gun deck located comparatively high above the water, the new frigate was able to fight effectively even in a sea rough enough the compel the two-deck ship to keep her lower deck's gun ports closed. Like the larger 74-gun line-of-battle ship which was developed over much the same period, the new frigate was both a good sailer and a good fighting vessel as a result of its combination of a long hull and low upper works. Impressed with the capabilities. especially for inshore work, of the small number of the new French frigate type it captured during the early stages of the Seven Years' War, the Royal Navy

placed these in British service, began to build copies, and finally worked to adapt the type to its own particular requirement. The success of this British development of the French starting point set the standard which most other maritime powers son started to emulate.

Early frigates were armed with 9-pdr guns, but inevitable escalation meant that the standard cannon was soon the 12-pdr and

Key features of the frigate (right the 40-gun HMS Horatio, and above right) included the rated armament on a single deck sufficiently high above the water that the guns could be worked in most sea conditions, and a tall ship rig.

The British 36-gun frigate HMS Amazon under way with her courses brailed up. This was the normal practice in action so that there was less chance of a sail catching fire from a spark from one of the guns.

then the 18-pdr weapon. By the end of the 18th century the largest frigates were equipped with 24-pdr cannon. The most common armament scheme was based on 32 to 44 such long guns. As demand for more ships and heavier firepower continued to increase, the frigate increasingly adopted the carronade, which was a light-barrelled weapon firing a heavy ball over short range. Not being cannon, such weapons were not reckoned in the ship's rating.

Royal Navy frigates of the late 18th century were based on the 1780-vintage "Perseverance" class frigate with a displacement of some 900 tons and carrying 36 guns. This class was notably successful, and was succeeded from 1801 by the 15 ships of the "Tribune" class, which displaced more than 1,000 tons and carried 38 guns. During the wars against France (1793-1815), the British introduced a class of 44-gun frigates, rated as fourth-rate warships, carrying guns on two decks, but this was not successful. Among many famous frigate names of the sailing navy era are the USS *Constitution*, which fought a notable action against the frigate HMS *Java*; HMS *Shannon*, which defeated the USS *Chesapeake* in an action lasting merely 15 minutes; HMS Euryalus which shadowed and reported the Franco-Spanish fleet during the two days and nights before the Battle of Trafalgar; and HMS *Pallas*, commanded by Captain Lord Cochrane, which captured a number of very valuable prizes.

HMS *Cyane* (built by Bass at Topsham and launched in 1806)

Type:	three-masted sixth-rate frigate
Tonnage:	539 tons
Dimensions:	length 110 ft 0 in (33.5 m); beam 31 ft 6 in (9.6 m); depth in hold 17 ft 4 in (5.3 m)
Speed:	not available
Armament:	22 x 32-pdr, 10 18-pdr and two 12-pdr guns
Complement:	180 men

HMS Victory 1805

The seventh ship and the third first-rate line-of-battle ship of this name, HMS *Victory* is the world's oldest warship still theoretically in commission. The ship was designed by Sir Thomas Slade, laid down at Chatham Dock Yard in 1759 and launched in 1765, but the uncompleted ship was then put into reserve and not commissioned until 1778, after France's alliance with the rebellious American colonies in the War of American Independence (1775-83). The *Victory* was flagship of the Channel Fleet, and on July 23 of that year fought in the inconclusive Battle of Ushant. She remained with the Channel Fleet over the following two years, and for a short time was assigned to the North Sea convoy squadron. In 1780 the ship had the underside of her hull covered with 3,923 copper sheets weighing some 37,500 lb (17010 kg), and on December 12 of the following year captured a French America-bound convoy off Ushant. In 1782, the *Victory* was Admiral Lord Howe's flagship in the relief of Gibraltar from a Franco-Spanish siege, but with the end of the American war in 1783 was paid off at Portsmouth, and remained in ordinary for eight years.

In 1792 the *Victory* was flagship of the Mediterranean Fleet, which occupied Toulon after its surrender by French loyalists, and also took Bastia and Calvi on Corsica as British bases in 1794. In 1795 she became the flagship of Admiral Sir John Jervis, and on February 14, 1797 Jervis sailed with 15 British line-of-battle ships to

HMS Victory was a large but perfectly conventional first-rate ship by the standards of the time of her design in the middle of the 18th century.

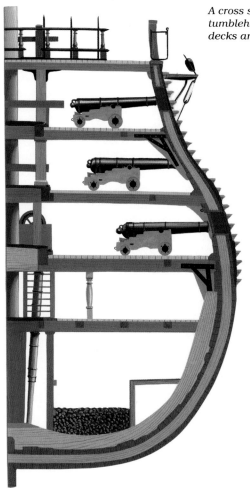

A cross section of HMS Victory's hull reveals the strong tumblehome of the sailing warship as well as the three gun decks and considerable storage on the ship's lowest decks.

1798 the *Victory* returned to Portsmouth, where she was surveyed and rated as fit only for use a prison hospital ship at Chatham.

In 1800 the Admiralty decided to have the *Victory* rebuilt, which took three years. On May 16, 1803 the revitalized ship, under Captain Thomas Hardy, became flagship of Vice Admiral Lord Nelson's Mediterranean Fleet. With Napoleon now laying obvious plans for an invasion of England, Nelson was ordered to contain Vice Admiral Pierre Villeneuve's squadron at Toulon. Villeneuve managed to slip out in January 1805, however, but then returned before departing once more on March 30. After linking with Admiral Federico Carlos Gravina's Spanish fleet at Cadiz, Villeneuve sailed for a rendezvous with other French forces off Martinique in the West Indies. Nelson pursued the Franco-Spanish fleet across the Atlantic and in June, discovering that Nelson was on his heels, Villeneuve headed back to Europe with Nelson in pursuit Nelson arrived off southern Spain four days before the Franco-Spanish fleet fought a tactically unsuccessful action with Vice Admiral Sir Robert Calder's squadron of 18 line-of-battle ships off El Ferrol.

Villeneuve arrived at Cadiz on August 21 and remained there, blockaded first by Vice Admiral Sir Cuthbert Collingwood and then, in

intercept a large Spanish convoy guarded by 27 line-of-battle ships. There followed the Battle of Cape St. Vincent, in which the British broke the Spanish line and inflicted terrible damage on the Spanish flagship, the 112-gun *Principe de Asturias*, before forcing the 122-gun *Salvador del Mundo* to strike her colors. The *Victory* lost only nine killed and wounded in the battle. The British also captured the first-rate *San Josef* and the two-deckers *San Nicolás* and *San Ysidro* in a battle whose successful outcome was the result, to a large extent, of the efforts of Captain Horatio Nelson of HMS *Captain*. In

One of the 200th anniversary stamps designed by John Batchelor.

HMS Victory *continued*

October, by Nelson. The French admiral refused to sail until he learned that Napoleon was replacing him, and on October 19 the 18 French and 15 Spanish line-of-battle ships set sail: the news was almost immediately relayed to Nelson, cruising 50 miles (80 km) to the southwest. The Franco-Spanish fleet took two days to straggle out of Cadiz, and while it seemed initially that he was going to make a run for the Mediterranean, on October 21 Villeneuve turned back to face Nelson.

In a move that might well have failed if tried by any other commander, Nelson divided his fleet into two divisions, the weather division headed by the *Victory* and Collingwood's lee division by HMS *Royal Sovereign*. As the two British columns neared the Franco-Spanish fleet, Nelson ordered his most famous signal run up *Victory's* masts: "England expects that every man will do his duty." The *Victory* failed to cut off Villeneuve's flagship, the *Bucentaure*, but came under all but unchallenged broadsides from the *Redoutable* for 45 minutes. The *Victory* finally maneuvred under the French ship's stern and raked her, though she herself was soon enfiladed by three French ships, the *Bucentaure*, *Redoutable* and *Neptune*. Nelson had insisted on wearing his full allotment of medals and decorations, and early in the afternoon he was wounded by a French sharpshooter. In the meantime, the *Redoutable* and *Victory* exchanged side-by-side salvoes until the *Redoutable* drifted into HMS *Téméraire*. Now fast between the unrelenting broadsides of two British ships, the *Redoutable* finally surrendered and the *Victory* was out of the battle.

The British flagship's mizzen topmast had been shot away, many of the other masts had been acutely weakened, and her bulwarks and hull were badly damaged by shot of all sizes. Nelson had been taken below and, after being told of the capture of 15 of the Franco-Spanish ships, died. In overall terms the British took more than nine French and 10 Spanish ships. Two of these escaped, four were scuttled, and eight sank in a storm that struck after the battle's conclusion. The Franco-Spanish

A cutaway illustration highlights the internal arrangement of HMS Victory.

HMS Victory breaks the Franco-Spanish line at the Battle of Trafalgar. By kind permission of Nigel Fordham.

Slide mounted, the carronade could be used effectively as a "smasher" in the type of short-range fighting in which the British sailors excelled.

losses were 6,953 men, while those of the British were 448 dead and 1,241 wounded including 57 dead and 102 wounded in the *Victory*. First towed to Gibraltar by the *Neptune*, the *Victory* received short-term repairs and then sailed for England, reaching Sheerness on December 22. From Sheerness Nelson's body was carried to St. Paul's Cathedral for a state funeral. Trafalgar had destroyed any real threat of a French invasion of England, and set the scene for a British naval domination of 100 years.

HMS *Victory*

Type:	three-masted first-rate line-of-battle ship
Tonnage:	2,162 tons
Dimensions:	length 226 ft 5 in (69.0 m); beam 52 ft 0 in (15.8 m); depth in hold 21 ft 6 in (6.6 m)
Speed:	not available
Armament:	two 68-pdr, 28 x 42-pdr, 28 x 24-pdr, 28 x 12-pdr and 16 6-pdr guns
Complement:	850 men

Chasse-marée and Lugger

Chasse-marée (tide chaser) was the French designation of the type of tide-working coastal vessel that was known to the British as a lugger. The vessel commonly used from the 16th century by the French, as well as by other northern European nations with a coastal trade, was a small three-masted vessel square-rigged on the fore and main masts, and lateen-rigged on the mizzenmast, together with a main topsail and a spritsail below the bowsprit. This rig was moderately effective, but during the 18th century was steadily replaced by the more easily controlled lug rig that had first been evolved on fishing vessels probably in the later part of the 16th century. The lug sail was a four-sided sail similar to a gaff sail except for its wider throat, and was set on a lug or yard about two-thirds of the length of the sail's foot.

The chasse-marée and lugger were generally two-masted fully decked vessels, although a small mizzenmast was sometimes stepped by the largest such vessels, with a length of some 75 ft (22.9 m), intended for tasks such as privateering and smuggling, in which the greatest possible speed was desired. The mizzen mast was stepped hard up against the vessel's flat transom stern, and its sail's clew was controlled via a bumpkin or bumkin, which was a short spar extending directly over the stern and carrying a block through which the sail's sheet was led inboard. With speed and weatherliness both seen as factors of the utmost importance, the chasse-marée and lugger had provision for a long bowsprit that allowed a large jib to be set. All three masts carried a standing lug sail, and on some of the larger chasse-marée and lugger vessels

The best point of sailing for a chasse-marée and lugger was close to the wind, the vessels being able to point up into the wind far better than any square-rigged vessel.

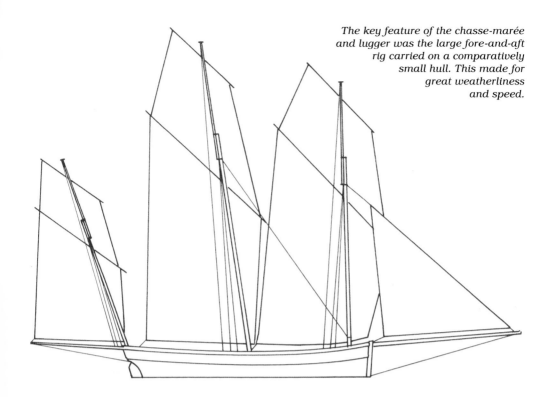

The key feature of the chasse-marée and lugger was the large fore-and-aft rig carried on a comparatively small hull. This made for great weatherliness and speed.

there was also provision for lug top-sails.

The chasse-marée and lugger saw extensive use during the period of the French Revolutionary War (1792-1800 and Napoleonic Wars (1800-1815) in naval as well as commercial service, the latter being taken to include priva-teering (largely by the French) and smuggling. The pressures of these wars saw development in the rig of these vessels for improved speed, the masts generally be raked back and the maximum possible sail areas being employed. It is also interesting to note that the French believed British luggers to have better lines than their own coastal traders, and the first chasse-marée for French naval service, built in 1773, was *l'Espiegle*, was based on lines drawn from an English lugger.

Experience revealed to the French operating the chasse-marée in the privateering role, mainly along the southern coast of the English Channel between Calais and the Breton peninsula, was the need for a large crew to extract the maximum benefit from the vessel's large sail area, and also to man the guns. This demanded the embarkation of larg-er quantities of stores even on short sorties from port, and also had an adverse effect on the economics of privateering as there were more men entitled to a share of the profits that were, after all, the primary reason for undertaking this way of life. Moreover, privateers and smugglers alike to came to appreciate that while the chasse-marée and lugger might have the advantage over square-rigged vessels in up-wind opera-tions, the reverse was true in down-wind chases, when the square-rigged vessel had a decided advantage over the chasse-marée or lugger it was pursuing.

Fijian Ndrua 1810

Beginning in the islands of Southeast Asia and reaching the Tongan and Samoan island groups, in all probability about 1000 BC, the Polynesians started to look farther out into the Pacific Ocean's vast open reaches. The first step was east to the Society Islands and then to the Tuamoto and Marquesas Islands, the second southeast to Easter Island and northwest to the Hawaiian Islands, and third southwest to reach New Zealand and the Chatham Islands. The long-range voyaging, probably undertaken as a search for new land in the face of increasing population growth, was achieved in voyaging canoes, which were mostly double canoes in Polynesia and outrigger canoes in Micronesia. The size of these vessels seems to have been in the region of 50 to 75 ft (15.2 to 22.9 m), a length that provided the greatest possible seaworthiness available with the region's materials and technology. Although it has often been stated that these Micronesian and Polynesian vessels were based on hollowed-out tree trunks, they were in fact generally based on a type of planked construction, with broad strakes stitched or lashed to each other and to the ribs

The Fijian ndrua was an ocean-going outrigger canoe of considerable size and a speed of up to 15 kt.

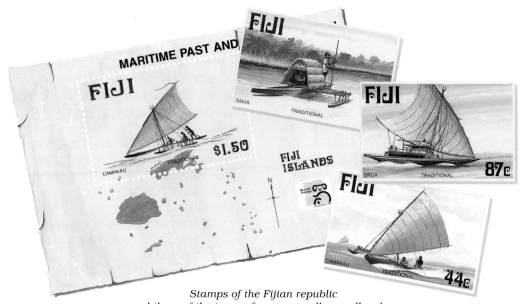

*Stamps of the Fijian republic
reveal three of the types of canoe, small as well as large,
which were traditionally the means of communication between the islands
and with neighboring island groups.*

and keel with coconut fibre. The keel was adzed out from solid log and was composed of several sections fastened together to create a V-shaped cross section everywhere except Fiji, where the round-bilged Melanesian hull form was apparently retained when numerous Micronesian features were adopted.

The *pahi* was the ocean-going vessel of the Tahitian and Tuamotuan archipelago, and was a twin-hulled two-masted type up to 70 ft (21.3 m) long. The *tongiaki* was the definitive Tongan double canoe analogous to Samoan craft and, like the *pahi*, had equal-length hulls bridged by a sizeable platform. The *ndrua* was the Fijian double canoe with a length of 115 ft (35.0 m) or more, and differed greatly from the *tongiaki* and *pahi* in its unequal-length hulls, the smaller serving rather like an outrigger, and a mast stepped on the larger hull rather than on the connecting bridge structure. It offered a greater level of agility than the *tongiaki*, and started to

replace the older twin-hulled canoes in western Polynesia shortly after the arrival of the first white explorers. The *baurua* was the voyaging canoe of the Gilbert and Marshall Islands, and was an outrigger vessel with a length of up to 100 ft (30.5 m). The most significant difference in the various sailing canoes of Oceania was concerned with tacking, i.e. those which tacked by moving the head of the vessel though the wind and those which altered the direction of the apparent wind by changing ends. Tacking canoes had distinctive and permanent bows and sterns like western craft, while the Micronesian canoes had identical bows and sterns so that they could sail either end foremost. The outrigger was always kept to windward, where it served as a balance weight, and to go onto the opposite tack, the mast was raked toward the "new" bow, the sail was swung round behind the mast, and the steering paddle was moved to the "new" stern.

HMS Pickle 1805

One of the most celebrated schooners to have served with the Royal Navy was HMS *Pickle*, which was built at Plymouth as the *Sting* for the civil role but was bought by the Admiralty in 1800 and then adapted as a fast despatch and scout vessel with the light armament of 10 guns. During 1803 the *Pickle* was attached to Admiral Sir William Cornwallis' Inshore Squadron, for which she undertook the close reconnaissance of French harbors during the blockades of Brest, Rochefort and L'Orient. On March 25, 1804, in company three other British ships of the Inshore Squadron and under the command of Lieutenant John Lapenotiere, the *Pickle* went to the assistance of HMS *Magnificent*, which had struck a shoal off the Black Rocks, and rescued the 650 men of the line-of-battle ship's crew.

On October 9, 1805, the *Pickle* and HMS *Weazle* were sent to aid Captain Henry Blackwood in the all-important task of keeping watch of the coast around Cadiz and so providing Vice Admiral Lord Nelson with timely tactical information about any movement of the Franco-Spanish combined fleet. During this time, just before the climactic Battle of Trafalgar, the *Pickle* was able to capture a Portuguese settee (lateen-rigged two-masted vessel) which had sailed from Tangier with a cargo of fresh meat, and also managed to see and report that there were 33 line-of-battle ships in Cadiz. During the Battle of Trafalgar on October 21, 1805, the *Pickle* was the second smallest of the vessels potentially available to Nelson, and was one of the British fleet's minor vessels kept back from the

HMS PICKLE   JOHN BATCHELOR

fighting. The *Pickle* was thus stationed to the northwest of the windward division of British ships, which Nelson was leading in HMS *Victory*. In the latter stages of the battle, the *Pickle* and three other vessels approached the French line-of-battle ship *Achille*, which was blazing fiercely, to take off the surviving members of her crew.

After the British victory, Vice Admiral Sir Cuthbert Collingwood wrote the despatch that would inform the Admiralty of the victory and also of the death of Nelson. Collingwood chose the *Pickle*, one of the "fast advice" vessels, to carry this despatch back to England, with a copy following in the 26-gun HMS *Nautilus*, a 443-ton sloop of war, under the command Captain Sykes. The schooner left the fleet on October 26 and reached Britain in a mere nine days despite having had to weather a gale off Cape Finisterre. In this gale the *Pickle* was blown well off her course, and Lapenotiere ordered that four carronades should be jettisoned to lighten the schooner's load. At 9.45 a.m. on November 4th the *Pickle* anchored in Falmouth Bay, and by mid-day Lapenotiere was on his way to London in a hired post-chaise coach, which was flying a Union flag over a tattered Tricolor on a broomstick. The *Nautilus* anchored off Plymouth just under 12 hours after Lapenotiere had left Falmouth by road. The journey from Falmouth to London normally took a week, but in 37 hours and after 19 horse changes, Lapenotiere arrived at the Admiralty at 1.00 a.m. on November 6. He was shown through to the First Secretary of the Admiralty, Mr. Marsden, and Admiral Lord Barham, First Lord of the Admiralty, was then raised from his sleep to receive the news. The prime minister, William Pitt, was informed of the news two hours after Lapenotiere had reached the Admiralty, and King George III and Queen Charlotte were informed four hours later. Lapenotiere was later given an audience with the king and queen, who presented him with a silver cruet that was the first thing that came to the king's hand, and was later promoted to commander.

The *Pickle* then returned to normal service, and on January 3, 1807 captured a French privateer of 18 guns off the Lizard. On July 28, 1808 the *Pickle* went aground on a shoal as she entered Cadiz harbor when carrying despatches, and was wrecked. Lapenotiere went on to further sea service before being badly injured in an explosion. He then moved to a desk job, and died in 1834. The significance of the *Pickle* in British naval history is perpetuated by a celebration for warrant officers of the Royal Navy on November 5th, known as *Pickle* Night, similar to the Trafalgar Night whose celebration is reserved for commissioned officers.

HMS *Pickle*

Type:	two-masted despatch and close reconnaissance schooner
Tonnage:	127 tons displacement
Dimensions:	length 73 ft 0 in (22.25 m) on the gun deck; beam 20 ft 0 in (6.1 m); draught not available
Speed:	not available
Armament:	eight 12-pdr carronades
Complement:	40 men

Periagua Gunboat 1810

Otherwise known as the pirogue and piragua, the periaugua was a sea-going canoe fashioned from the trunks of two trees (often cedar) which were hollowed and fastened together to create a comparatively large hull. The periagua was a common form of transport among the Spanish merchants trading on the west coast of South America and in the Gulf of Mexico during the 16th and 17th centuries, and its sturdiness and capability meant that its use gradually spread to the southern coast of North America and then up the Mississippi River and along the seaboard of the original 13 English colonies at least as far to the north as New York, where the type was known as a perry-auger. In the north the periagua became a somewhat different craft with a flat bottom, leeboards instead of a keel, decked bow and stern sections, provision for a 25-ton load, and propulsion by sweeps or gaff sails on two masts which could be struck.

Early in the 19th century, the new US Navy required a costal and estuarine gunboat type, and the periagua was adapted to meet this requirement, which resulted in the commissioning of 14 gunboats. Designed by Christian

The periagua gunboat sailed well despite its unusual appearance, and the lack of a bowsprit and its associated rigging was a decided boon to operations in the increasingly crowded waters around New York and in the estuary of the Hudson River.

Bergh in 1806, the gunboats were optimised for propulsion by sails rather than sweeps, and had an easily managed rig based on a foremast located well forward in the bows and raked forward, and a mainmast that was raked backward at the same angle. The fore mast carried a loose-footed gaff sail, while the main mast carried a schooner-type gaff sail with a boom. As if the fore-and-aft rake of the masts was not sufficient in itself to create something of a stir, there was provision for a flying staysail to be set between the two mast heads. The standing and running rigging were made as simple as possible. The objections of several captains, who were unimpressed by the gunboats' proved sailing capability, were met by revizing some of the gunboats with a standard schooner rig.

The armament was centered on a single 24-pdr gun on a pivoted mounting, and to optimize this weapon's capabilities the hull was deliberately made low and wide, although still well able to cope with the weight of the armament. The secondary armament was a pair of 18-pdr carronades mounted one on each side. The latter were son believed to offer no useful

The sail plan of the periagua gunboat was simple yet effective, and was a decided asset to the vessel's ability to maneuver swiftly and precisely in crowded waters.

additional to the gunboats' fighting capability and were removed, which had the useful side effect of increasing the volume available for accommodation, which had been very cramped up to this time.

Periagua gunboat

Type:	local defence gunboat
Tonnage:	not available
Dimensions:	length 48 ft 3 in (14.7 m); beam 18 ft 0 in (5.5 m); depth in hold 5 ft 6 in (1.7 m)
Speed:	not available
Armament:	one 24-pdr (occasionally 32-pdr) gun and two 18-pdr (occasionally 12-pdr) carronades
Complement:	10

USS Essex 1812

One of the most celebrated of all frigates was the USS *Essex*, which reflected the desire of the Americans to offset a numerical inferiority by building frigates which were qualitatively superior to the individual frigates of potential enemies. Thus the Americans created a navy based on capable frigates including a few large vessels carrying greater numbers of heavier guns than was typical of their British and French counterparts. Designed by William Hackett and built by Enos Briggs of Salem, Massachusetts, for launch on September 30, 1799, the *Essex* was a heavy frigate constructed to the order of the citizens of Essex County, Massachusetts, who presented her to the US government. The ship was commissioned, under the command of Captain Edward Preble, into the US Navy, which had come into existence as successor to the Continental Navy as a result of legislation enacted by the Congress in 1794. On her first voyage in 1800, during the Quasi-War with France (1798-1800), the *Essex* helped convoy a fleet of Dutch East Indiamen through the Indian Ocean. In 1801, she was one of several ships sent to the Mediterranean to contain the Barbary corsairs attacking American shipping, under the command first of William Bainbridge and then James Barron, and was laid up from 1806 to 1809.

At the start of the War of 1812 (1812-15) with the British, the *Essex* was restored to service under the command of Captain David Porter, and took 10 prizes, including an 18-gun sloop of war, HMS *Alert*, between

The USS Essex was too slab-sided and tall to be truly effective as a fighting frigate, and was further hampered by the fact that her armament was centered on carronades, which fired a heavy weight of metal but were essentially short-range weapons.

July and September. On October 28, 1812, the *Essex* sailed from the Delaware River to rendezvous with the USS *Constitution* and the USS *Hornet* for a cruise into the South Pacific. After waiting on the coast of Brazil for the arrival of the two others vessels, which did not arrive, Porter decided in January 1813 to press on into the Pacific. The voyage round the southern tip of the Americas was dismal in the extreme, but then during 1813 the *Essex* effectively terminated the British whaling industry in the South Pacific and in the process seized 15 prizes, including the whaling vessel *Atlantic*, which was armed with 10 6-pdr long cannon and 10 18-pdr carronades. Porter saw in this ship the making of a useful auxiliary, and converted her for this task as the *Essex Junior*. In October, the *Essex* and the *Essex Junior* sailed to Nuka Hiva in the Marquesas Islands, where the *Essex* completed a major refit after having been at sea for 11 months.

On February 3, 1814, the two ships reached Valparaiso on the coast of Chile, and here the American ships were blockaded by the 26-gun frigate HMS *Phoebe* under the command of Captain James Hillyard, and the 18-gun sloop of war HMS *Cherub*, which had been dispatched to the Pacific for the task of destroying the American fur industry in the Pacific Northwest and now chanced on the American ships. Porter realised that the *Essex*, despite her heavier broadside, was at something of a tactical disadvantage to the *Phoebe* as the British vessel was more nimble than the American frigate, and carried 18-pdr long cannon which considerably outranged the American ship's 32-pdr carronades. Porter decided to wait in the neutral port of Valparaiso until reinforcement arrived, but on March 28 the *Essex* was driven from her anchors by a gale and Porter decided to use this opportunity to evade the British blockade. Unfortunately for the Americans, however, the *Essex* lost her main topmast in a squall and Porter headed back toward the neutral cost. Disregarding Chilean neutrality, Hillyard attacked and, taking advantage of his guns' longer range, slowly but steadily reduced the hapless *Essex*. After three hours Porter felt himself compelled to surrender to avoid further senseless loss of life. The butcher's bill after the fighting had ceased revealed that 58 men had been killed, 31 drowned and 70 wounded, while the British casualties had amounted to no more than five men killed and another 10 wounded. The *Essex* was repaired and taken into the Royal Navy as a 42-gun frigate. In 1823 she became a convict ship, and in 1837 the vessel was sold out of the service. The *Essex Junior* was allowed to depart, and sailed with paroled American seamen to New York, where she was sold.

USS *Essex*

Type:	three-masted frigate
Tonnage:	850 tons
Dimensions:	length 140 ft 0 in (42.7 m) between perpendiculars; beam 37 ft 0 in (11.3 m); depth in hold 12 ft 3 in (3.7 m)
Speed:	not available
Armament:	40 32 pdr carronades and six 18 pdr guns
Complement:	319 men

USS Constitution 1812

The USS *Constitution* was one of the US Navy's "six original frigates" (with the USS *United States, President, Chesapeake, Constellation* and *Congress*) authorized by the Congress to provide the new American service with the means to tackle the Barbary pirates of the Mediterranean. The ship was designed by Joshua Humphreys, Josiah Fox and William Doughty, and built in Boston, Massachusetts at the yard of Edmund Hartt for launch on October 21, 1797. All six frigates were fast, heavily built ships. The *United States, Constitution* and *President* were rated as 44-gun frigates but actually carried 30 24-pdr and 20 or 22 12-pdr long guns, replaced at a later stage by 42-pdr short-range carronades. The *Constellation, Chesapeake* and *Congress* were slightly smaller and rated as 38-gun frigates with 28 long guns and 18/20 carronades.

A temporary peace with the Barbary states was agreed before the *Constitution* was completed, but the frigate was commissioned in time for service in the Quasi-War with France (1798-1800), in which she took a number of smaller ships and privateers. Returning to the Charlestown Navy Yard in 1801, she was placed in ordinary (laid up with her guns, masts, yards, sails and rigging stored ashore). The USA's next conflict was with Algiers, Morocco, Tripoli and Tunis, and in 1803 the *Constitution* was despatched to the Mediterranean as flagship of Commodore Edward Preble's Mediterranean Squadron, and the rulers of Algiers and Tunis finally felt themselves compelled to sign agreements exempting US shipping from paying "tribute."

After a refit in New York, the *Constitution* joined the North Atlantic Squadron of Commodore John Rodgers in 1809, and in the

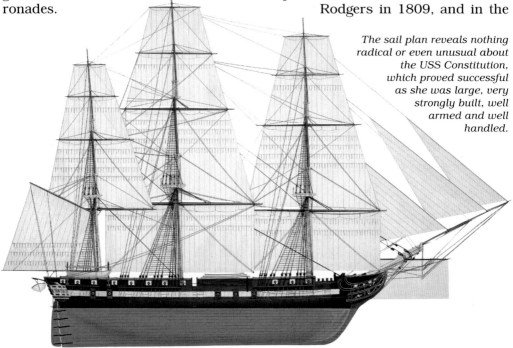

The sail plan reveals nothing radical or even unusual about the USS Constitution, which proved successful as she was large, very strongly built, well armed and well handled.

The USS Constitution fights HMS Guerrière into submission.

next year Isaac Hull became her captain. On the outbreak of the War of 1812 (1812-15) against Britain, the *Constitution* put to sea on July 5 and patrolled off the coast of New Jersey coast. Here on July 17 she spotted ships that were initially though to be the North Atlantic Squadron but were in fact HMS *Africa* (64) and the frigates HMS *Shannon* (38), HMS *Guerrière* (38), HMS *Belvedira* (36) and HMS *Aeolus* (32) as well as the recently captured US brig *Nautilus* (12), under the command of Captain Sir Philip Broke. There followed a 66-hour chase which started in light airs, but the *Constitution* kept out of range of the British ships by kedging, towing with the ship's boats and finally, after the wind had strengthened, what Broke later said was "very superior sailing."

On August 19 the *Constitution* was near the Grand Banks, off Newfoundland, and once against met the *Guerrière* commanded by Captain James Dacres, who only recently sent Rodgers an invitation to meet "U. States frigate President...or any other American frigate of equal force for the purpose of having a few minutes tête-à-tête." The *Guerrière* opened fire at long range at 5 o'clock in the afternoon, and the *Constitution* steadily closed the range until giving the order to open fire at 6.05, when the two frigates were very close to each other. In this sort of engagement the American frigate's heavier firepower, ably served, inevitably prevailed, and only 25 minutes later the *Guerrière* had been dismasted and beaten. The *Constitution* had suffered seven men killed and another seven wounded, while the *Guerrière* had 78 dead and wounded, and was so badly damaged that on the following day Hull ordered the wrecked frigate to be blown up. It was during this battle that the *Constitution* earned her nickname

USS Constitution *continued*

"Old Ironsides" after British cannon balls failed to penetrate her hull. The *Constitution* returned to Boston.

The need to attend to family problems now forced Hull to leave the *Constitution*, and command passed to Captain William Bainbridge. Off the coast of Brazil while on passage to join the frigate USS *Essex* and the sloop-of-war USS *Hornet* in the South Pacific, on December 29, 1812 the *Constitution* met another British frigate, HMS *Java* (38) under Captain Henry Lambert. Though the British warship initially had the better of a combat which started early in the afternoon, the heavier firepower and excellent gunnery of the American frigate soon began to tell, and by 5:25 in the afternoon the *Constitution* had turned the *Java* into a dismasted wreck with 124 of her crew killed or wounded, including Captain Lambert. The *Constitution* suffered only 34, or 52 according to the British, casualties. Like the *Guerrière*, the *Java* had been so badly damaged by the American frigate's gunnery that she too had to be blown up. However, the damage the *Constitution* had suffered in the fight was so grave that Bainbridge decided not to continue the voyage.

The USS Constitution is depicted with one of her victims in this Bhutanese stamp.

The *Constitution* therefore returned to Boston where Bainbridge, wounded in the Java fight, was replaced by Captain Charles Stewart. The *Constitution* now completed a short foray into the Caribbean early in 1814, and then remained at Boston until December 1814, when

The USS Constitution now lies in Boston harbor, and on July 4th every year is turned round so that one side of the frigate does not become more weathered than the other.

182

she slipped out through the British blockade. One week after the war had ended, a fact unknown to the oceanic combatants, on February 20, 1815 the American frigate entered combat with two British vessels, the frigate HMS *Cyane* (32) and HMS *Levant* (20) off Madeira, compelling both to surrender, although the *Levant* was retaken by a British squadron early in March. The *Constitution* arrived in New York on May 15 as the US Navy's most famous ship.

The US Navy's 44-gun frigates, which actually carried 56 to 60 guns, were very powerful and also of very great structural strength. These ships were so well-respected that they were often seen as equal to fourth-rate ships, and the Royal Navy's fighting instructions ordered British frigates, most of which carried 32 or fewer guns, never to engage American frigates unless they had at least a 2/1 numerical advantage.

The *Constitution* returned to commission in 1821 and operated in the Mediterranean up to 1828. Two years later she was saved from the breaker by public outcry. The ship was rebuilt and re-entered service in 1835, and her career after this date included service with the Home and Mediterranean Squadrons, service in the South Pacific, and a 29-month circumnavigation of the world ending in 1846. During the Civil War (1861-65) she was a navy training ship. Rebuilt in the 1870s, she was a training ship until 1881, after which she became a receiving ship in New Hampshire. In 1897, she was brought to Boston for preservation. She made a goodwill tour in 1931-34, being towed to 76 ports along the Atlantic, Gulf and Pacific coasts. Now Maintained as a museum ship at Boston, USS *Constitution* is the is the oldest commissioned warship afloat anywhere in the world, for the first-rate line-of-battle ship HMS *Victory*, though older, is dry-docked.

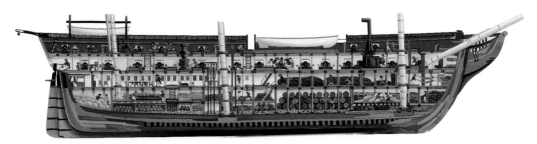

A cut-away illustration reveals the interior details of the USS Constitution's hull.

USS *Constitution*

Type:	three-masted heavy frigate
Tonnage:	2,200 tons
Dimensions:	length overall 204 ft 0 in (62.2 m); length on the gun deck 175 ft 0 in (53.3 m); beam 43 ft 6 in (13.25 m); draught 22 ft 6 in (6.9 m); depth in hold 14 ft 3 in (4.3 m)
Speed:	not available
Armament:	32 24-pdr, 20 32-pdr and two 24-pdr guns
Complement:	450 men

Norwegian "Jekta"

The jekta (yacht) was a small trading vessel which evolved to meet the specific needs of the Norwegian coastal trade. The vessel had a high bow with a strongly curved stem that provided excellent anchorages for the tall mast's forestay, and was characterized by a decked-in bow an open central part of the hull, and a notably small enclosed cabin at the stern. The jekta varied in size quite considerably, and some of the larger examples could carry up to 120 tons of cargo. Unlike most of the other vessels used for trading purposes round the North Sea and in the Baltic sea, the jekta was square-rather than gaff-rigged on a single mast. The

original practice was for this mast to carry a single sail with as many as three bonnets, which were additional strips of canvas that could be laced to the sail's foot to increase its area under good sailing conditions, but it later became standard for the sail to be made larger and incorporate as many as four lines of reef points to that the area of the sail could be reduced by reefing under adverse sailing conditions. It should be noted, though, that some of the later examples of the jekta carried a somewhat smaller mainsail with a topsail above it.

The original practice was for the vessel to have provision for two additional planks to be fitted over the bows as a washboard. This was designed to reduce the amount of spray and water breaking over the bow and entering the vessel's open waist, where the cargo was often perishable goods such a grain or non-perishable goods such as baled wool that

The jekta was a mainstay of the Norwegian coastal trade, offering a reasonable cargo capacity in a vessel that could be handled by a small crew and possessed a sturdy hull optimized for the conditions typical of Norwegian waters.

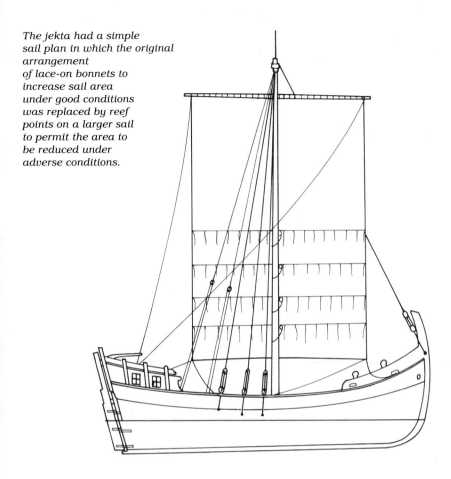

The jekta had a simple sail plan in which the original arrangement of lace-on bonnets to increase sail area under good conditions was replaced by reef points on a larger sail to permit the area to be reduced under adverse conditions.

would be damaged by being wetted with salt water. There was also provision for a large but bulky load, such as hay, to be loaded into the open waist of the vessel, where it was protected from the worst of any flying water by a "superstructure" of lashed planks fitted inside light vertical beams.

Build in moderately large numbers, the jekta was admirably suited to the particular demands of the Norwegian coastal trade, and the last examples did not disappear from service until well into the 20th century.

Jekta (typical)

Type:	coastal trading vessel
Tonnage:	not available
Dimensions:	length 38 ft 0 in (11.6 m); beam 11 ft 3 in (3.4 m); draught 5 ft 6 in (1.7 m)
Speed:	not available
Armament:	none
Complement:	5 men

Chesapeake and Shannon 1813

At the start of the War of 1812 (1812-15) in June 1812 the US Navy had only 14 seaworthy vessels to face a well established Royal Navy with 1,048 warships, but in the first six months of the war did remarkably well, its small ships besting no fewer than four British warships in single-ship actions. But then the balance of the naval war began to swing in favor of the British. Though on February 13 the first of 1813's single-ship actions, fought between two sloops off the coast of Brazil, saw victory for the USS *Hornet* over HMS *Peacock*, on June 1 the boot was on the other foot in the clash between a pair of frigates, the USS *Chesapeake*

and HMS *Shannon*, the latter a member of the "Leda" class which was the largest frigate class ever constructed by the British. The *Shannon* had been laid down in September 1804 at Brindley's Yard in Frindsbury, and launched in April 1806. The last and least fortunate of the original six frigates ordered by the Congress in 1794, the *Chesapeake* was designed by Josiah Fox and laid down in 1795 at Gosport Navy Yard, Norfolk, Virginia, and completed only after the start of the Quasi-War with France (1798-80). The ship was rated as 38-gun frigate and designed to carry 28 24-pdr and 18 to 20 12-pdr guns. The *Chesapeake* sailed from Norfolk on

In a short and very sharp action in which the excellent training of the British allowed them completely to outshoot their American counterparts, the Shannon crippled, boarded and captured the Chesapeake.

June 6 1800 under Captain Samuel Barron to patrol the West Indies during the Quasi-War with France, and captured one French privateer before the end of the war. In April 1802 the *Chesapeake* was flagship of the Mediterranean Squadron under Commodore Richard V. Morris, but was laid up at Washington from mid-1803 to 1807, when she was readied for a two-year assignment as the flagship of Commodore Barron in the Mediterranean.

With the outbreak of the War of 1812 the *Chesapeake*, now under the command of Captain Samuel Evans, cruised against British shipping between December 1812 and April 1813 from the West Indies to Africa, taking five British prizes. Back at Boston, the ship was taken over by Captain James Lawrence, and on June 1st put to sea to meet the *Shannon*, a crack Royal Navy vessel under the command of Captain Philip Bowes Vere Broke. Accepting an implicit challenge from Broke, the *Chesapeake* met the *Shannon* soon after 4.00 p.m. Highly trained for such an action, the *Shannon's* crew fired accurately and fast, killing or fatally wounding most of the *Chesapeake's* officers, including Lawrence, and shooting away her head sails before boarding her and hauling down the American flag. In the bloodiest naval action of the war, and also one of the shortest as it lasted a mere 15 minutes, the *Chesapeake* and *Shannon* lost 48 and 30 men killed as well as 98 and 56 men wounded respectively.

The *Chesapeake* was taken to Halifax for repair, and was bought into the Royal Navy. In the second half of 1814 the *Chesapeake* sailed for England and ran aground off Plymouth. By mid-1815 she was at Cape Town, where she learned that Great Britain and the USA were no longer at war. She was sold at Portsmouth and broken up in 1820. The *Shannon* was hulked in 1831.

USS *Chesapeake*

Type:	three-masted frigate
Tonnage:	1,244 tons
Dimensions:	length 152 ft 6 in (46.5 m) between perpendiculars; beam 40 ft 11 in (12.5 m); depth in hold 13 ft 10 in (4.2 m)
Speed:	not available
Armament:	20 32 pdr guns and 28 18-pdr guns
Complement:	340 men

HMS *Shannon*

Type:	three-masted frigate
Tonnage:	1,052 tons displacement
Dimensions:	150 ft 1.5 in (45.8 m); beam 39 ft 9 in (12.1 m); draught 13 ft 9 in (4.2 m)
Speed:	not available
Armament:	two 32-pdr carronades and two 9-pdr guns on the forecastle, 28 18-pdr guns on the upper deck, and six 32 pdr carronades and eight 9-pdr guns on the quarterdeck
Complement:	284 (normal)

Crab Claw Boat

For more than 1,000 years right into the 20th century, the Maoris, best known as the first inhabitants of New Zealand since about 800 to 1000 AD but also a people living in the Cook Islands, sailed *tainui* double-hulled canoes, some 70 ft (21.3 m) long, across many vast stretches of the Pacific Ocean. The Maoris are of mixed Polynesian and Melanesian origin, and reached the Cook Islands at an uncertain time in the millennium following 1000 BC. This was just one event in a series of migrations that extended the colonization of the Pacific to the east of New Guinea and Australia from Southeast Asia to Melanesia and island groups such as Vanuatu, Fiji, Tonga and Samoa between 1500 and 1000 BC, and then the areas as far to the east as the Cook, Society, Tahiti and Marquesas island groups by the dawn of the Christian era.

The people of the Cook Islands made their transpacific migration and subsequent inter-island and regional trading voyages in apparently fragile wooden craft propelled by sails shaped like giant crab claws. These craft were double canoes based on a side-by-side pair of hulls at whose bows and sterns were decorative elevations some 20 ft (6.1 m) tall, shaped like blades and covered with highly ornamented decoration based on the Maoris' spiral motif. Carvings of this type of intricate nature were a high form of the peoples' art, and inlays of tridacna (bivalve mollusc such as the giant clam) shell and mother of pearl decorated these imposing double canoes.

The two hulls were connected by large crossbeams which also constituted the structural platform on which was erected a large cabin for the chief and his most important supporters. The women were quartered in one of the hulls, which was also laden with food

The tainui double-hull canoe was a masterpiece of concept and execution, readily created by a low-technology culture but wholly suited to the task required of it.

80c

TUVALU

H.M.S. Resolution Nearing The Hawaiian Islands

A stamp of Tuvalu illustrates the arrival of Captain James Cook's HMS Resolution off the Sandwich (Hawaiian) Islands, where she was greeted by a canoe driven by paddles and also two oceanic lateen sails, related to the crab claw sail but set directly on their masts.

and supplies for long voyages, or with livestock if a migratory voyage was envisaged. Additional planking, sewn onto the upper sides of the two canoe hulls with a twine of palm-fibre, gave the *tainui* the greater freeboard that offered a better level of cargo-carrying capacity and safety in the open ocean.

Sometimes but wrongly named as a catamaran, the double canoe was a type of vessel which originated in the South Pacific. With its paired hulls, it offered a considerably greater degree of stability than a traditional mono-hull or outrigger canoe, and also possessed a much greater carrying capacity, with obvious advantages for peoples bent on long open-ocean voyages. The double canoe was therefore of inestimable importance for long-distance voyages of colonization or trade across the open sea. The double-hull canoe was also of notably shallow draught, a fact that was of great importance in a region where virtually every speck of land is surrounded by a coral reef, and could also be drawn up onto the beach with little difficulty, thereby avoiding all the problems associated with anchoring in the lagoons of islands generally low lying and therefore offering little protection from any adverse wind which might spring up.

As well as its hull arrangement, the double canoe was characterized by its rig of one or two crab claw sails, so named for their likeness to the claws of these large crustaceans. The sail was of basically triangular shape and was common to many types of Polynesian canoe. The sail was of inverted triangular shape with a notably characteristic concave cut-out in the leach, which was the upper side of the sail. The sail was carried by two tall spars of flexible wood, often decorated with pennants on each side and with their upper ends drawn together for control and to give the sail the required belly. The sail or sails were set on centerline masts raked slightly forward and stepped on the crossbeams connecting the hulls, and the whole of the mast assembly (vertical mast, fore-and-aft stays and lateral shrouds) created a geometry in the form of one or more very stiff yet flexible trusses that supported the sail or sails with the minimum possible structural weight.

It is worth noting that the crab claw rig has been tested in a wind tunnel, revealing the fact that this Polynesian sail has a significant superiority to the triangular Bermuda sail at every point of sailing between the close-hauled and the run. This superiority is least when the sail in close-hauled, but as the angle to the wing is increased as the canoe bears to a reach, the driving force coefficient of the crab claw rig is about 1.7 by comparison with the Bermuda rig's coefficient of some 0.9. Translated into more easily assimilated form, this indicates that the crab claw rig delivers about 90% more driving power than the Bermudan rig.

Brig 1815

The brigantine was a two-masted vessel with a foremast that was square-rigged and a mainmast that carried a fore-and-aft rig. The name brigantine derived ultimately from the fact that it was a rig much favored by the pirates of the Mediterranean, although in that area primarily on an oared galley type of hull. The name was later and gradually abbreviated to brig, but further development then created the brig proper as a type of vessel somewhat different from the brigantine. The brig was widely built and operated, mainly for mercantile purposes on short and coastal routes, and the type also found favor later in its life among naval services as training vessels for boys destined for a naval career. In this capacity the brig lasted into the first decade of the 20th century, which was a period well into the days of steam power and even the replacement of the reciprocating steam engine by the steam turbine for warship propulsion purposes.

The brig proper was a two-masted vessel square-rigged on both her fore and mainmasts, and a variant on this theme was the hermaphrodite brig or brig-schooner, which was again a two-masted vessel but with a foremast that was square-rigged and a schooner's main mast setting a fore-and-aft main sail and square topsails. It is also worth noting that there was a Mediterranean variant of the brig, this being known as the polacre or alternatively as the polacca. The polacre was square-rigged on both of its masts, but these were pole masts formed by single spars, rather than masts each comprising two, three or even four sections stepped one above the other as required. The polacre's masts therefore lacked tops and crosstrees, and also footropes on

A snow just making way in harbor during a still day. The snow was a close relative of the brig.

their yards. The topmen therefore stood on a yard to loose, reef or furl the sail above, whose yard was lowered far enough for the men to accomplish their task.

It is worth noting that a type of vessel related to the brigantine and brig was the snow, which was the largest two-masted sailing vessel of its period between the 16th and 19th centuries, with a tonnage of up to 1,000 or so tons. Built and used solely in European waters, and most especially in northern European waters, the snow was brig-rigged with square sails on both masts, but also possessed a small trysail mast stepped immediately abaft the mainmast. On this trysail mast a trysail with a boom was set, the luff of this sail being hooped to the trysail mast. An alternative to the trysail mast was a horse on the mainmast, the luff of the trysail being attached to this hordes by rings. By about 1800 there was little difference between the brig and the snow other than the trysail mast.

With the end of the Napoleonic Wars in 1815 and the rapid rise in the demand for merchant shipping, there was great pressure to create mercantile vessels which could be sailed efficiently by smaller crews than had hitherto been standard. The result was the return to favor of the brigantine. As the type became fully re-established in the world's mercantile fleets, once again the name was steadily abbreviated to brig, which led to considerable confusion in following years.

Lady Washington (originally built in Massachusetts about 1750 and re-created as a replica in Gray's Harbor, Washington, during 1988-89)

Type:	brig-rigged trading vessel
Tonnage:	178 tons displacement
Dimensions:	sparred length 112 ft 0 in (34.1 m); length on deck 68 ft 0 in (20.7 m); length on waterline 58 ft 0 in (17.7 m); beam 22 ft 0 in (6.7 m); draught 11 ft 0 in (3.35 m)
Speed:	not available
Armament:	none
Complement:	not available

Snow 1817

The snow was a two-masted merchant vessel of the period right through from the 16th century to the 19th century, and with a tonnage of up to about 1,000 tons was the largest two-masted vessel of this period. Although developed primarily for mercantile purposes, the snow was on occasion used for naval purposes, such armed snows generally being designated as corvettes or sloops of war.

The snow was rigged as a brig, and therefore carried square sails on both her fore and main masts. However, the snow in its definitive form differed from the brig in several respects including the arrangement of the braces for the main topsail and topgallant sail, which were led forward rather than aft, the lack of any preventer stays, and the use of a snow or trysail mast.

This mast was stepped on deck immediately abaft the mainmast and with its head blocked and bolted between the aft parts of the mainmast trestle trees, or fastened with an iron band to the lower part of the mast

The snow was a merchant vessel of the brig type with an unusual small-diameter trysail mast immediately abaft the mainmast to carry the gaff sail.

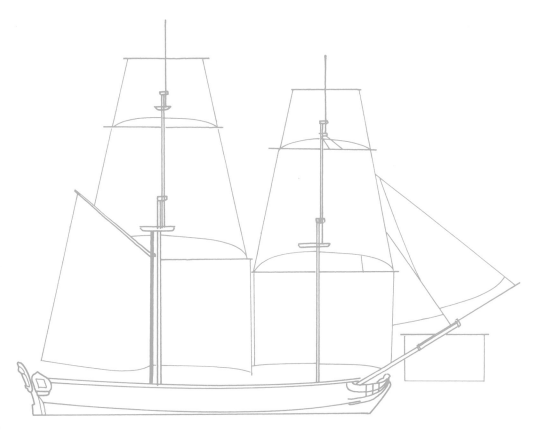

The key feature of the snow was the trysail mast immediately abaft the mainmast, allowing a four-sided trysail to be set. This is a snow of the period before 1800, when a boom became increasingly common on the staysail.

head. This arrangement added a small-diameter pole mast just to the rear of the mainmast, and at the head of the trysail mast was a gaff. The head of the four-sided trysail was bent onto the gaff, and its luff was seized to wooden hoops round the trysail mast, or laced directly to the trysail mast. This sail was loose-footed and extended aft to a point just inside the taffrail, where its sheets were led through blocks, but from about 1800 a boom was added to carry the foot of the trysail, allowing a larger sail to be set.

It is worth noting, however, that the trysail mast was sometimes replaced by a horse or jackstay on the main mast, especially on those snows for naval rather than mercantile service in which the trysail mast would have been very vulnerable. This horse or jackstay was spliced with an eye round the mast head and set up with deadeyes to an eyebolt on deck, and the trysail was then bent to thimbles or hanks on this horse or jackstay with the luff slung to the mast.

Snow-rigged vessels were at one time common around the coasts of the Great Britain, but it is believed that the last of these commercially important vessels was the Commerce, which was built in 1862 and operated from Newhaven. This vessel existed to a time as late as 1909.

Sailing Packets 1820

The packet boat was a vessel that operated between two ports for the carriage of mail and, when there was demand and space, passengers and light freight.

J.BATCHELOR

Beagle (Darwin) 1833

Best known of the several vessels of the name, HMS *Beagle* of Darwin fame was built by Woolwich Dockyard and launched in 1820 as one of 115 "Cherokee" class 10-gun brigs completed for the Royal Navy between 1807 and 1830. By the time of her first voyage the *Beagle* had been converted into a three-masted barque, or bark. The vessel's first major undertaking, between May 1826 and October 1830 in company with HMS *Adventure*, was the charting of the straits and passages of South America's southern tip. Captain Pringle Stokes committed suicide in August 1828, and the *Beagle* returned to Buenos Aires, where Lieutenant Robert FitzRoy assumed command for the voyage home.

FitzRoy commanded the vessel on her subsequent circumnavigation during which she was to complete the survey of Tierra del Fuego, the Chilean coast and a number of Pacific islands, and also to carry out chronometric observations. On board was a young botany student, Charles Darwin. The *Beagle* sailed from Devonport in December 1831 and reached Rio de Janeiro in April 1832. After three months surveying the Brazilian coast, the *Beagle* proceeded to Bahía Blanca in Argentina, where Darwin uncovered the fossils that persuaded him to look into the relationship of living and extinct species.

In January 1833, the *Beagle* arrived in Tierra del Fuego, and in the following month returned to Uruguay

His voyage on HMS Beagle provided Charles Darwin with the data from which he started to develop his theory of evolution.

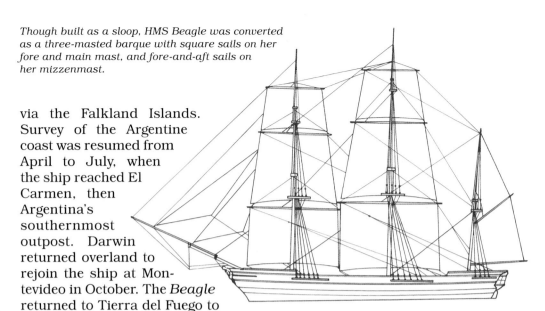

Though built as a sloop, HMS Beagle was converted as a three-masted barque with square sails on her fore and main mast, and fore-and-aft sails on her mizzenmast.

via the Falkland Islands. Survey of the Argentine coast was resumed from April to July, when the ship reached El Carmen, then Argentina's southernmost outpost. Darwin returned overland to rejoin the ship at Montevideo in October. The *Beagle* returned to Tierra del Fuego to complete her survey work in January, surveyed the Falkland Islands in March and April, passed through the Strait of Magellan into Chilean waters in June 1834, and reached Valparaiso in July. In the middle of 1835 the *Beagle* sailed for the Galápagos Islands, 600 miles (965 km) west of Ecuador, reaching the islands on September 17. It was here that Darwin made the observation that laid the foundation for his theory of natural selection. The *Beagle* left the Galápagos on October 20, and the main task of the rest of the voyage was chronometric observation. The *Beagle* called at New Zealand, Australia, Tasmania, the Cocos Islands, Mauritius, Cape Town, St. Helena and Ba-

hía, finally reaching Falmouth on October 2 1836.

Six months later the *Beagle* sailed for Australia. After surveying the western coast between the Swan and Fitzroy Rivers, she sailed around to the southeast corner of the continent. The *Beagle* conducted surveys along both shores of the Bass Strait, and then in May 1839 sailed to the shore of the Arafura Sea opposite Timor. Her work in Australia completed, the *Beagle* returned to Britain in 1843. Transferred out of the Royal Navy in 1845, the *Beagle* ended her days as the stationary *Beagle Watch Vessel* moored at Paglesham Pool on the Essex coast, and was sold and probably broken up in 1870.

HMS *Beagle*

Type:	three-masted barque
Tonnage:	235 tons burthen
Dimensions:	length 90 ft 4 in (27.5 m); beam 24 ft 6 in (7.5 m); draught 12 ft 6 in (3.8 m)
Speed:	not available
Armament:	two 9-pdr and five 6-pdr guns
Complement:	75 men

Whalers 1840

Whaler was the name for any type of sailing vessel, complete with its small whaleboats, which sailed to catch whales with hand-thrown harpoons before the introduction of the harpoon gun in 1865. The origins of whaling are lost in ancient history, and would have been confined to the smaller species which could successfully have been hunted from the shore or small boats. The hunting of larger species in European waters was undertaken by the Basques as early as the 10th century AD, reaching a peak in the 12th and 13th centuries, and concentrated on the Atlantic Right whale. These were generally harpooned from small

boats before being towed to the shore for processing. The whale fishery of the Bay of Biscay had entered a decline by the 17th century, but by this time the Basques had spread their efforts farther abroad with the whale fishery reaching the waters off Newfoundland by the latter half of the 16th century.

These pioneering long-endurance whaling voyages were quickly followed by an Arctic whale fishery off Spitsbergen (now Svalbard), discovered in 1596. The report of large numbers of whales round this northern island immediately drew the Basques, and the English learned the trade

Whalers such as the American Lagoda were based on capacious hulls to hold large quantities of stores, fuel and rendered oil, and also to carry the boats sent out to harpoon the whales.

Dead whales were towed alongside the whaler, where they were flensed and their blubber hoisted inboard, by means of a block and tackle depending from a yard, to be boiled down for the oil.

from the Basques from 1610. An English attempt to claim a monopoly in these waters was soon overtaken by the arrival of Danish and Dutch whalers. By the middle of the 17th century the Dutch had become predominant. The practice in the period when whaling in distant waters was becoming the norm involved the use of vessels of some 200 tons with a crew of some 50 men. The whale was pursued in small boats, harpooned, and towed back to the mother vessel for flensing, the blubber then being taken ashore to be rendered down. Each of the nations working the Spitsbergen whale fishery operated its own harbor, and it was here that gear was stored and the whale oil was extracted from the blubber by boiling. The extent of the Spitsbergen whale fishery is attest-

ed by the fact that in 1633 the Dutch whaling harbor of Smeerenburg (translating as Blubbertown) saw the arrival of more than 1,000 whaling vessels, and among its facilities included several shops, a bakery and a church.

Easily exploited whale fisheries such as that round Spitsbergen were soon brought to the point at which they were hardly profitable. Thus by the first part of the 18th century whales had become scarce off Spitsbergen, and the whaling vessels were perforce venturing into more distant waters, as far north as the Davis Strait between Greenland and the North American continent. Here the whalers, among whom the Dutch and Germans predominated, were based primarily on Disco Island. The Dutch remained

Whalers *continued*

the most significant of the whaling peoples into the middle of the 18th century. Then the British re-interested themselves, and whaling vessels were soon operating to Greenland waters out of ports such as Hull, London and Whitby. The waters round southern Greenland proved profitable into the first 30 years of the 19th century, but then the combination of over-exploitation and the introduction of coal gas steadily reduced their significance.

While the European countries had generally opted for the whaling grounds of the

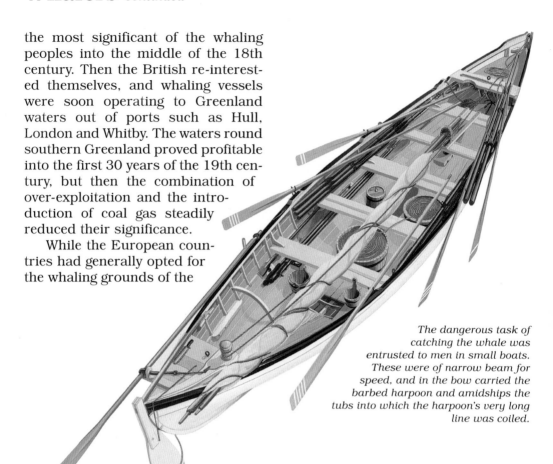

The dangerous task of catching the whale was entrusted to men in small boats. These were of narrow beam for speed, and in the bow carried the barbed harpoon and amidships the tubs into which the harpoon's very long line was coiled.

Arctic, a completely different and wholly independent whaling industry had emerged in the 18th century in the towns along the coasts of the British colonies in North America. This Southern Whale Fishery, as it was known, started in 1712 and gradually extended southward to Brazil by the middle of the century. Here the catch was the sperm whale. The American whalers' exploitation to the south was temporarily checked by the arrival of the British during and after the American Revolutionary War (1775-83), and 1787 was the year in which a British whaling vessel first sailed round Cape Horn into the Pacific Ocean. The Americans rapidly followed the British into the Pacific, and after the end of the War of 1812 (1812-15) grew steadily in number. By the third decade of the 19th century, American whaling vessels were to be found in every part of the Pacific and Indian Oceans, the first vessels reaching Japan in 1821 and the Seychelles and Zanzibar off the east coast of Africa just seven years later. By the 1840s American whalers were taking Right whales again in the North

Once the long strips of flensed blubber had been hoisted inboard, they were cut into manageable pieces and lowered into the large vats of the tryworks to be rendered.

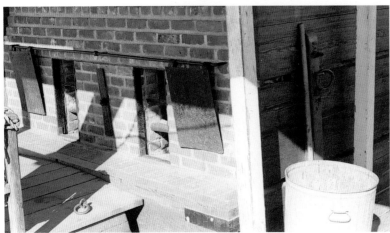

Fire was a constant hazard on ships with fabric sails as well as wooden hulls, masts and spars, so the tryworks of whaling vessels were permanent and sturdy brick-built units.

Pacific, off the coast of Kamchatka, and entering the Arctic Ocean by means of the Bering Strait. The Pacific whaling industry was based on San Francisco in California, but was curtailed by the Civil War (1861-65), started to grow once more, but received a huge blow during 1871, when the vast majority of the American whalers working the northern Pacific were caught in the ice and crushed.

Charles W. Morgan (built by Hillman Brothers, New Bedford, Massachusetts in 1841)

Type:	three-masted whaling ship
Tonnage:	314 gross registered tons
Dimensions:	length 111 ft 0 in (33.8 m); beam 27 ft 9 in (8.4 m); depth in hold 13 ft 9 in (4.2 m)
Speed:	not available
Armament:	none
Complement:	26 men

Dutch Hoy 1842

The smack was a type of light vessel of very poorly fixed characteristics, even if it had fixed characteristics at all, and was thus a very general term for a small coasting vessel of up to about 60 tons. In England the smack was also called the hoy, and was usually a single-masted craft with fore-and-aft sails including a gaff mainsail that was either loose-footed or laced to a boom. Basically a utility type able to undertake a variety of commercial tasks, the hoy was employed for any number of coastal roles, but its primary employment was the carriage of passengers from port to port.

Developed in the Netherlands but also used in Germany, on both its North Sea and Baltic Sea coasts, the Dutch hoy was a sea-going rather than riverine vessel employed largely in the coastal trade during the 18th and early 19th centuries typically to carry upward of 40 tons of cargo, but with the larger exam-

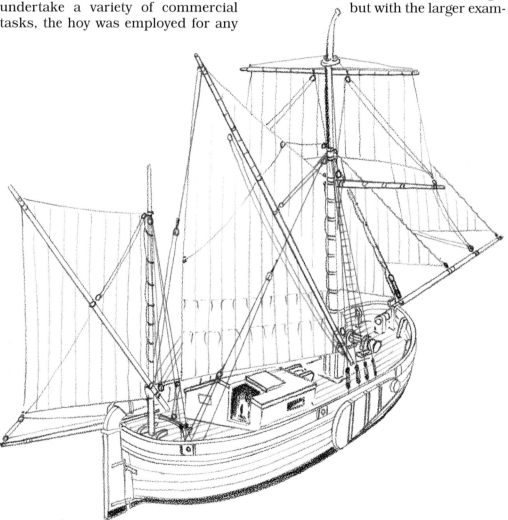

Sail plan of the Dutch hoy in its classic form with two spritsails, a main staysail, two jibs and a topsail.

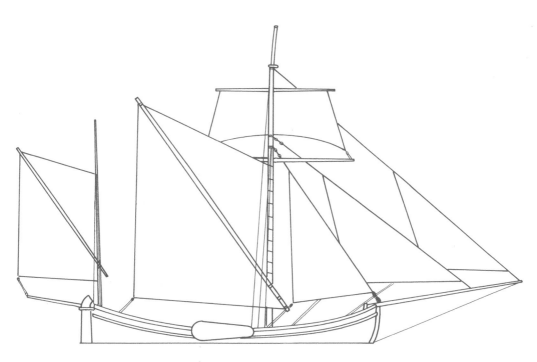

The Dutch hoy was conceived for practical trading purposes rather than elegance, and could be worked effectively by a small crew.

ples of this type of useful vessel carrying up to 200 tons of cargo the hoy was able to range as far afield from the Netherlands as the southern parts of Norway and the northern coast of the Iberian peninsula.

In overall terms the Dutch hoy was a 2 masted vessel with a large mainmast (often carrying a topmast) and a small mizzen mast stepped just before the sternpost. Both the main and mizzen masts initially carried a spritsail, that is a rectangular sail whose peak was supported by a sprit extending diagonally upward and rearward from a snotter (chain-attached fitting) just above deck level at the sail's tack. Later examples of the hoy were more conventionally gaff-rigged. The mainmast spritsail or gaff was usually loose-footed, while that of the mizzenmast sometimes had its clew attached to the outboard

end of a boom with its sheet rove through a block at the end of an outrigger to put the sail's leech abaft the stern. The other sails were a main staysail, one or two jibs set to the bowsprit, and a square main topsail that was very occasionally supplemented by a main topgallant. The hull was round-built fore and aft, had a flat bottom that facilitated settling on the bottom on an even keel as the tide receded from shallow waters, and like most Dutch coastal craft was fitted with leeboards that could be raised.

The Dutch hoy had a superstructure, which was always known as a roof, built up above deck level near the master's cabin, and this roof provided the volume (limited and cramped) that was required for the small galley and practical crew accommodation.

203

Erebus 1845

Designed by Sir Henry Peake and built at Pembroke Dockyard in Wales for launch in 1826, HMS *Erebus* was a square-rigged bomb vessel. She served two years in the Mediterranean before the strength of her hull commended her for conversion to work in polar waters. Adapted as a barque rig and strengthened structurally, she sailed to the Antarctic, and in 1839 came under the command of James Clark Ross, a veteran of Arctic expeditions and now entrusted with research into terrestrial magnetism as well as the location of the South Magnetic Pole and the completion of oceanographic, botanical, and zoological observations. Sailing in company with HMS *Terror* under Francis R. M. Crozier, the vessels departed on September 30, 1839, and reached Hobart in Tasmania during August 1840. The vessels departed for Antarctica on November 12, met ice two days after Christmas, and on New Year's Day 1841 crossed the Antarctic Circle. The vessels forced their way south through the pack ice until January 9, when they reached open water in what is now the Ross Sea.

A few days later, the crew landed on Victoria Land, which they claimed for Britain, and on February 1 reached an impenetrable ice barrier now known as the Ross Ice Shelf. The vessels remained in the Ross Sea until the end of February and returned to Hobart in April for a three-month refit.

On their second Antarctic expedition, the vessels entered the pack ice on December 18, 1841 and, held fast, drifted south at the mercy of the ice. On

HMS Erebus was a three-masted barque with a hull that was deemed suitable for polar navigation as it had been made especially string to cope with the recoil forces of the two large mortars which constituted her primary armament as a bomb vessel.

A stamp of St. Helena, which the vessel visited in 1826, reveals HMS Erebus in her original layout.

HMS Erebus and HMS Terror each had a steam locomotive lowered into its hold to power the propeller thought necessary for extra power in the high winds of the Arctic.

St. Helena

75p

HMS EREBUS 1826

January 18, 1842 both vessels' rudders were destroyed by ice, and the *Erebus* and *Terror* reached open water again only on February 1. Three weeks later the vessels again reached the Ross Ice Shelf. The vessels returned to the Falkland Islands and visited Tierra del Fuego in September before heading south once more in December, this time to the islands of the Antarctic peninsula. They were turned back by ice, and voyaged home to England, which they reached on September 4, 1843 after a voyage of four years and five months.

In 1844 the *Erebus* and *Terror* were each fitted with a propeller powered by a 20-hp (14.9-kW) steam engine, and committed to a search for the Northwest Passage under the command of Sir John Franklin with Crozier still commanding the *Terror*. The vessels sailed on May 19, 1845 with stores for two years, and supplies for another two years were delivered to the Whalefish Islands in the Davis Strait by a supply vessel. The *Erebus* and *Terror* were last seen in Baffin Bay near the entrance of Lancaster Sound in August 1845 before sailing though Lancaster Strait. The *Erebus* and *Terror* eventually became icebound in Victoria Strait between King William Island and Victoria Island. Here Franklin died of natural causes in June 1847, and by the following spring 23 members of the crew had died of starvation or scurvy.

On April 22, 1848, the 105 survivors abandoned their vessels for an overland journey to Fort Resolution, a Hudson's Bay Company outpost on Great Slave Lake, more than 600 miles (965 km) distant. In the next 12 years, many expeditions were launched to search for survivors. The vessels' fate was revealed only by the discovery of human remains, diaries, and relics.

HMS *Erebus*

Type:	"Hecla" class three-masted bomb vessel
Tonnage:	372 tons
Dimensions:	length 105 ft 0 in (32.0 m); beam 28 ft 6 in (8.7 m); draught 13 ft 9 in (4.2 m)
Speed:	8 kt
Armament:	one 13-in (330-mm) mortar, one 10-in (255-mm) mortar, eight 24-pdr gun and two 6-pdr guns
Complement:	67 men

Dunbrody 1847

The barque, or bark, was a vessel with three or more masts rigged with square sails on all but the mizzenmast, which carried fore-and-aft sails. Until the middle of the 19th century barques were comparatively small, but were then developed as vessels of up to 5,000 tons with four or even five masts. The large barques were employed mainly on the grain and nitrate trades from the west coast of South America round Cape Horn to the eastern USA and Europe, some of the vessels being jackass-barques with square and fore-and-aft sails respectively on their forward and after pairs of masts.

A classic example of the barque is the *Dunbrody*, which was built in Quebec in 1845 by Thomas Hamilton Oliver, an Irish emigrant from County Derry. The vessel was built in less than six months under the watchful eye of John Baldwin, her captain from 1845 to March 1848, and was one of eight commissioned by the Graves family of traders from New Ross in southeastern Ireland to carry cargo to and from the Americas, most notably timber

from Canada, cotton from the southern states of the USA, and guano from Peru. Carrying 10,100 sq ft (938.3 m^2) of canvas, the vessel was also outfitted for the carriage of passengers, mostly Irish emigrants. From 1845 to 1851, between April and September, she carried passengers on her outward journeys to Canada and the USA. The standard was 176 passengers, but on one crossing she carried 313.

Although the *Dunbrody* was detained at the quarantine station at

A modern replica of the barque Dunbrody, as outfitted for emigrant transport, is based at New Ross in Ireland.

Grosse Ile in Canada on several occasions, the vessel's onboard mortality rate was extremely low, mainly as a result of the care exercised by her captains, Baldwin and then John W. Williams. Emigrants writing back to Ireland often praised their dedication.

The *Dunbrody* remained with the Graves family for 24 years before being sold in 1869 and becoming a British-registered ship. In 1874, en route to Quebec from Cardiff, the *Dunbrody's* captain elected not to wait for a pilot to assist him in navigating his vessel's course up the St. Lawrence river, and ran the vessel aground. She was fortunate, however, to be bought by a salvage company, repaired and sold on. In 1875, she went aground for the second time and on this occasion was not so fortunate. Sailing home to Liverpool with a full cargo of timber, the vessel was blown dangerously off her normal course by a fierce gale, and was driven toward the shore of Labrador. The exact details are not known, but it is believed that if the now-elderly vessel grounded while

The Dunbrody is depicted running before a quartering breeze. She is carrying three jibs, a fore staysail, a course and lower and upper topsails on the foremast, the same sails as well as a topgallant sail on the mainmast, and a driver on the mizzenmast.

fully laden with a timber cargo, her hull would have been broken up beyond any possibility of economic repair.

There is a modern replica of the vessel based in Ireland.

Dunbrody

Type:	three-masted barque
Tonnage:	451 tons
Dimensions:	length overall 176 ft 0 in (53.6 m); length of hull 120 ft 0 in (36.6 m); beam 28 ft 0 in ((8.5 m); draught 11 ft 6 in (3.5 m)
Speed:	not available
Armament:	none
Complement:	not available

Jhelum 1849

The only surviving British vessel of her type, a workaday merchant vessel "that deserves to be famous for being ordinary," the *Jhelum* was built by Joseph Steel & Son of Liverpool in 1849 for general trading between India and England, as suggested by her name, which is that of a tributary of the Indus river and the site of a battle between English and Indian forces the year before her launch. The vessel was completed as a three-masted ship with a very conservative hull shape reminiscent of the vessels of the 17th century, but with modern constructional features including extensive use of iron fittings for reinforcement. It was only shortly after the completion of the *Jhelum* that builders switched almost entirely to iron hulls. The ship's builder was also her owner, but Joseph Steel kept her in that trade for only one voyage before he reallocated the ship to the South American trade. Carrying general cargo on the outbound leg, the *Jhelum* returned from South America with nitrate fertilizer in the form of guano (bird droppings). This was the first of 13 voyages undertaken by the *Jhelum* to Chile, Peru or Ecuador before Steel sold his interest in the ship in 1863.

In her original form, the Jhelum was ship - rather than barque- rigged, and therefore carried square sails on her mizzenmast.

It is worth recording that the *Jhelum's* European destination was always Liverpool, although she called one time each at Hamburg and Baltimore on her way to this great British port. Her average times were about 100 to 110 days between South America and England.

Cut down to a bark rig in 1858, probably to reduce manning requirements and so reduce the cost of operating the vessel, the *Jhelum* in 1863 was sold into the ownership of a consortium including John Widdicombe and Charles Bell, who kept her in the same trade between England and South America, though mostly with coal rather than general cargo in the outbound voyage. On August 18, 1870, after a rough passage round Cape Horn, Captain Beaglehole put his ship into the Falkland Islands in a leaking condition, probably the result of having been knocked about in a *pampero* (violent local squall of South American waters) on the outbound voyage. The guano cargo may also

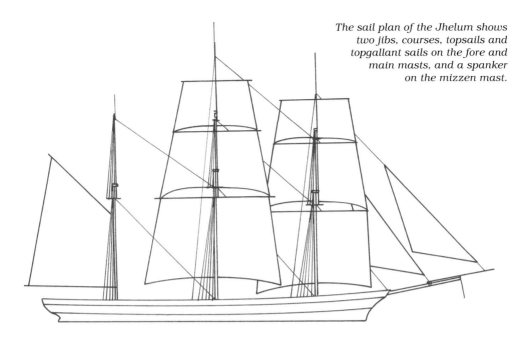

have become wet and shifted. Suffering from illness and having already revealed itself to include a number of malcontents, the crew refused to sail the *Jhelum* any farther, and in September of the same year a government survey found the vessel to be unfit for sea. Beaglehole had already changed the crew of his vessel twice, and reported that his final complement included two men who were "the most useless and ignorant men, of an able seaman's duty, fit only for an ordinary rating and scarcely deserving that."

The ship was abandoned at Stanley by her now-bankrupt owners, and was eventually transferred to J. M. Dean & Company but not before Beaglehole and the mate had spent almost nine months at Stanley before securing passage home in HMS *Charybdis*, which sailed from the Falkland Islands on May 27, 1871. The *Jhelum* was initially used as a floating warehouse for wool storage, as were many of the other ships condemned at Stanley, but was finally scuttled to serve as a jetty head and workshop area.

The *Jhelum's* remains are still visible, though rapidly deteriorating, and have been recorded and stabilized as far as is feasible, given the hulk's condition, by the Merseyside Maritime Museum.

Jhelum	
Type:	three-masted ship, or later barque
Tonnage:	428 gross registered tons
Dimensions:	length 123 ft 2 in (37.5 m); beam 27 ft 2 in (8.3 m); draught 18 ft 2 in (5.5 m)
Speed:	not available
Armament:	none
Complement:	14-21 men

Vicar of Bray 1849

Considered to represent a peak in the construction of wooden ocean-going merchant vessels in Britain, the *Vicar of Bray* was a three-masted barque built by Robert Hardy at Whitehaven in Cumberland during 1841. The vessel was framed in African oak, planked with African elm and African oak (lower and upper respectively). The vessel had oak floor and pine decks, and was fastened with treenails, copper bolts and forged iron knees.

The *Vicar of Bray* was built for the copper ore trade between Chile and Britain, the vessels employed in this vital trade carrying coal on the outbound leg of each voyage. The *Vicar of Bray* remained in this gainful employment until the late 1840s, when she was put into the general trading role between Britain and South America

and, later, Australia. In 1849 the vessel was chartered to carry two retorts, used to distil the quicksilver required for the process of extracting gold from its ore, to the New Almaden quicksilver mine in California. But even as the vessel was being prepared for this voyage, the discovery of massive gold deposits was being announced to the world, triggering the Californian "gold rush" as thousands of "49ers" made their way to California and the lure of riches. The *Vicar of Bray's* contract for this voyage probably had no direct involvement with the California gold strike, for at this time the Rothschild family had a near monopoly on Spanish quicksilver, and the New Almaden mines in California were owned by a British banking house, Baring Brothers.

The Vicar of Bray was involved in the great California "gold rush" of 1849, but probably as a result of existing commercial arrangements rather than the transport of men smitten by "gold fever."

THE CALIFORNIA GOLD RUSH

FALKLAND ISLANDS £1

THE BARQUE 'VICAR OF BRAY' IN SAN FRANCISCO HARBOUR DURING THE GOLD RUSH 1849

This stamp souvenir sheet shows the Vicar of Bray anchored in San Francisco harbor in 1849.

Between April 1848 and April 1849, only four vessels had put into San Francisco, but such was the impact of the gold strike that in the whole of 1849 no fewer than 777 vessels sailed from ports along the US eastern seaboard round Cape Horn to reach San Francisco. Reaching San Francisco, most crews deserted their ships, and this was true of the complement of the *Vicar of Bray*, which reached San Francisco on November 3, 1849 and almost immediately lost all of her crew. It took the captain several months to recruit enough seamen to depart San Francisco.

The *Vicar of Bray* continued in trade throughout the 1850s and 1860s. In 1870 the vessel, outward bound from Swansea to Valparaiso, put into Port Stanley in the Falkland Islands after suffering heavy damage in a Cape Horn storm. The vessel was condemned, but in 1873 was bought and refitted by the Falkland Islands Company to link the islands and Britain. In 1880 the vessel was moored in Port Stanley for use as a storage hulk. Some time between 1912 and 1917 the hulk was loaded with coal and towed by the company tug *Samson* to Goose Green, some 50 miles (80 km) west of Port Stanley. Here the hulk was promptly blown ashore by a gale, coming to rest a short distance from the head of the settlement's jetty. The jetty was then lengthened to meet the hulk, which became its pierhead.

In 1976 the Falklands Islands company sold the hulk to the National Maritime Historical Society for Preservation in San Francisco, which hopes eventually to salvage and restore the *Vicar of Bray*, the last surviving example of the vessels associated with the 1849 gold rush, for berthing in San Francisco.

A Falkland Islands stamp reveals the hulk of the Vicar of Bray at Goose Green in the Falklands in 1999.

Vicar of Bray

Type:	three-masted barque
Tonnage:	282 gross registered tons
Dimensions:	length 97 ft 0 in (29.6 m); beam 24 ft 3 in (7.4 m); draught 17 ft 0 in (5.2 m)
Speed:	not available
Armament:	none
Complement:	not available

FALKLAND ISLANDS

9p

VICAR OF BRAY, FALKLAND ISLANDS 1999

Challenge 1851

The term clipper was used to describe any merchant vessel in which high speed rather than cargo capacity was the key design parameter. The first vessels to be described with this term were the so-called "Baltimore clippers," which were in fact American schooners built in Maryland and Virginia, and used as blockade runners and privateers in the War of 1812 (1812-15) with Britain, and later as slavers. The key features of the clipper were a sharp-raked stem and an overhanging counter stern to keep waterline length to a minimum, and a draught deeper aft than forward. This type of hull was further enlarged to carry a three-masted ship rig, creating the true clipper whose first example was the New York-built *Rainbow* of

1845. The use of the clipper grew rapidly with the British opening of the China tea trade to all comers, and the discovery of gold in California and Australia in 1849 and 1850 respectively. Clippers seemed to fly out of US yards, followed belatedly by clippers from British yards.

Although the lead in American clipper building was soon assumed by Donald Mackay of Boston, New York shipbuilders were not far behind. One of the most celebrated, but infamous, of these was the *Challenge* designed and built in 1851 by William H. Webb for the N. L. & G. Griswold company's California trade. The largest merchant sailing ship yet completed when launched on May 24, 1851, the *Challenge* was designed to set the

The Challenge was a superb example of the "extreme clipper" that was profitable only when world conditions allowed premium prices to be demanded for very fast passages.

pace for the California trade. George Griswold persuaded Captain Robert Waterman to come out of retirement to skipper the *Challenge* round Cape Horn to San Francisco with a bonus of $10,000 if he could do so in 90 days or less. Waterman supervised the design of the clipper's very tall rig: the main truck was 230 ft (70.1 m) high, the main yard was 90 ft (27.4 m) long increasing to 160 ft (48.8 m) with the studding sails set, and the ship carried some 115,020 sq ft (10685 m²) of canvas.

The *Challenge* appeared in the period characterized by American domination of merchant sail through a combination of far-sighted designers working to the exacting requirement of hard-headed merchants, excellent yards, and ruthless captains. However, an item in notably short supply was experienced crew. Thus, as the *Challenge* departed from New York on July 13, 1851, Waterman described his 56-man complement as "the worst crew I ever saw." Half of the crew had never before been to sea, only six of the men had ever taken the helm, and the majority understood no English. Off Brazil on August 17, James Douglass, the first mate both hated and feared as a complete brute, was knifed by one of the crew in an attempted mutiny.

Waterman drove his ship ferociously to pass into the Pacific Ocean against the winter storms south of Cape Horn, driving as far south as 75° S as he sought the wind that would carry him past the Horn. The *Challenge* reached San Francisco on October 29 after a 108-day passage, and there learned that about two months earlier the *Sea Witch* had become the first clipper to break the 90-day "barrier" for a voyage between New York and Sam Francisco. Within days the *Challenge's* crew had spread accounts of the officers' brutal treatment of the men, 10 of whom had died of disease, harsh treatment and the elements. Now finally retiring, Waterman fought back with charges of mutiny, but the crew was exonerated and Douglass got off with a light sentence. The *Challenge* was now seen as a bad ship on which to serve, and her new skipper, Captain John Land, had to offer as much as $200 per man for the 40 crew he needed for a voyage to Shanghai in China.

Dismasted in the China Sea in 1859 while sailing to Hong Kong, the *Challenge* was sold in 1860 to Thomas Hunt, who renamed the clipper as the *Golden City* for service between China and India. In 1866, the London-based shipper Captain Joseph Wilson purchased the *Golden City* and sailed her in the Far Eastern trade for 10 years before she went aground on rocks off Ushant and sank after being towed off.

Challenge (later *Golden City*)

Type:	three-masted "extreme clipper"
Tonnage:	2,006 tons
Dimensions:	length 230 ft 6 in (70.25 m); beam 43 ft 2 in (13.2 m); draught 26 ft 0 in (7.9 m)
Speed:	not available
Armament:	none
Complement:	40-60 men

America 1851

During 1851 William H. Brown, a New York shipbuilder, decided to construct an ocean-going racing schooner to beat British yachts in British waters. So he suggested that his yard should build such a vessel on the understanding that a syndicate headed by John C. Stevens, the New York Yacht Club's commodore, would buy the schooner for $30,000 if she was faster than any American opposition, and that Brown would then buy her back if she lost to British yachts in British waters. Behind this arrangement was Brown's belief that he could create a vessel to sail as an unofficial yet wholly representative US contender in the great races organized in conjunction with the "Great Exhibition," which opened at the Crystal Palace in London on May 1, 1851, just two days before the *America* was launched into the East River.

The *America* was designed by the head of Brown's mould loft, George Steers. The new yacht was schemed as a schooner as Steers knew that this type of vessel was fast and handy with only a comparatively small crew, and he designed the *America* with an all-wood hull that marked a major shift from the type of bluff-bowed hull typical of the trading and fishing schooners of the USA's eastern seaboard. The *America* was schemed with a shallower wedge-shaped bow which tapered outward and downward to the vessel's widest point, which was located about midway along her length, before gradually tapering inward to a wide, rounded transom. The *America* was rigged with two backward-raked masts each carrying a gaff sail (boomed and loose-footed in the case of main and fore sails respectively), a topsail above the gaff mainsail, and a large jib in the fore triangle.

In the trial races in the USA, the *America* was beaten by the *Maria*, which was a centerboard sloop designed specifically for inshore racing, but the New York Yacht Club syndicate nonetheless offered Brown the reduced sum of $20,000 for the *America*, which sailed on June 21. Reaching Le Havre in northern France, the *America* was put into racing trim and tuned for the particular conditions of the English Channel, and sailed to her

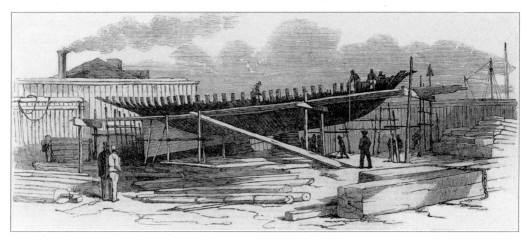

An engraving of the period reveals the very clean lines and the structure of the America's hull.

In her original form without a jib-boom, the America was notable for the large size of her head sail.

mooring off the Royal Yacht Squadron at Cowes on the northern side of the Isle of Wight on July 31.

The New York Yacht Club consortium hoped to recoup its expenditure in buying, equipping and sending the *America* across the Atlantic by betting on any match race to which its yacht was challenged, but the sleek appearance of the US vessel prevented any British gambling men from taking American bets. Thus Stevens decided to commit the *America* to an open race scheduled to take place on August 22 for the Royal Yacht Squadron's £100 Cup. The race was a circumnavigation of the Isle of Wight, without any form of handicapping. The *America* was the only non-English vessel in the 15-strong fleet (seven schooners and eight cutters). The race started at 10.00 a.m. in the easterly direction which would take the vessels clockwise round the island. The *America* made a poor start, but her speed through the water was excellent and within an hour the US schooner had climbed to fifth place. After the *America* had passed the Noman's Land buoy toward the eastern end of the Isle of Wight, the wind picked up and the American yacht was soon in the lead. Although her jib-boom, which had been added in England, broke, when she passed the Needles at just before 6.00 p.m., the *America* had a lead of 7.5 miles (12 km) over the smallest vessel in the race, the 57-ton cutter *Aurora*, which was lying in second place. Some 15 minutes later the *America* dipped her flag as she passed the royal yacht *Victoria and Albert*, an honor which was returned on the next day when Queen Victoria and the Prince Consort paid a visit to the victorious schooner, which had crossed the finish line at 8.53 p.m.

"America" (Cup) continued

The Royal Yacht Squadron's £100 Cup became the America's Cup after its ownership had passed to the New York Yacht Club, and is still the most prized trophy in yachting.

The victory of the *America* was much admired in Great Britain and greeted with enormous enthusiasm in the USA, but the unsentimental New York Yacht Club consortium decide to divest itself of the schooner, which was therefore sold to John de Blaquiere, an Anglo-Irishman who soon sailed in his new acquisition on a Mediterranean cruise. In a second race round the Isle of Wight, during 1852, the *America* was placed second. The yacht was then laid up, but in a series of transfers finally became the property of Henry Montagu Upton in 1856, Henry Sotheby Pitcher in 1858, and then Henry Edward Decie, who in April 1861 sailed her to Savannah, Georgia. Renamed *Camilla*,

she returned to England with Confederate government agents, and Decie then raced the yacht a few times in the Solent before sailing for France in August. By the end of October she was to be found at Jacksonville, Florida, and here she was sold to the Confederate government and, possibly renamed *Memphis*, used as a blockade runner. Scuttled in the St. John River, Florida, when Union forces took Jacksonville, she was salvaged by Lieutenant John Stevens, re-rigged and armed with three muzzle-loading guns in the form of one 12-pdr rifled and two 24-pdr smooth-bore weapons to become the USS *America*, which entered service with the South Atlantic Blockading Squadron. With this squadron, which was concerned mainly with the blockade of Charleston, South Carolina, the *America* was responsible for the Confederacy's loss of three vessels either captured or compelled to run themselves aground.

After a refit at New York in 1863, the *America* became a school ship for US Naval Academy cadets. The schooner was laid up at Annapolis in 1866, but was brought back into commission in 1870 to compete in the first race for the trophy now called the America's Cup in her honor. The America was placed fourth out of 24 competitors. On the grounds that her upkeep was too costly, in 1873 the America was sold to General Benjamin Butler, and Butler raced her for some 20 years.

The course of the race round the Isle of Wight. Starting at the northern tip, off Cowes, the 15 competitors sailed in a clockwise direction round the island.

The start at Cowes

ISLE OF WIGHT

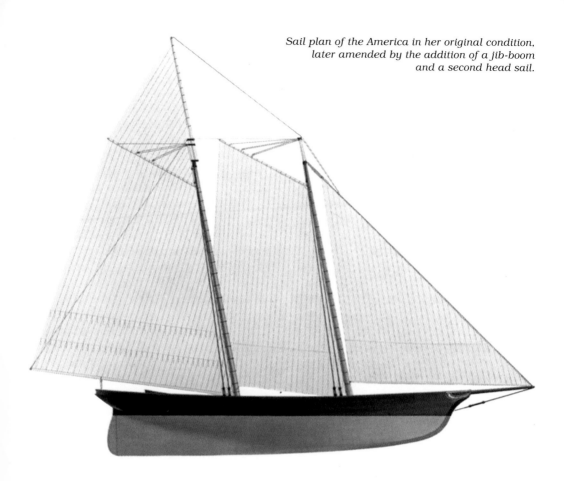

Sail plan of the America in her original condition, later amended by the addition of a jib-boom and a second head sail.

The schooner was an unofficial contestant in the 1876 America's Cup race. After Butler's death in 1893, the *America* passed to his grand-nephew Butler Ames, who raced her for the last time in 1901. Laid up for 15 years, the *America* was then donated to the Naval Academy. In 1940 the Schooner, now in poor condition, was placed in storage under a shed roof. When the shed collapsed in 1942 under the weight of snow, the *America's* fate was sealed, though it was not until 1945 that the US Navy ordered her to be broken up. Near replicas were built in 1967 and in 1995.

America (later *Camilla, Memphis* and *America*)

Type:	two-masted racing schooner
Tonnage:	180 tons displacement
Dimensions:	length overall 101 ft 3 in (30.9 m); waterline length 88 ft 7.5 in (27.0 m); beam 22 ft 10 in (7.0 m); draught 10 ft 11.5 in (3.35 m)
Speed:	not available
Armament:	none
Complement:	25 men

"Snow Squall" 1863

The *Snow Squall* was a clipper built in 1851 by Cornelius Butler of Cape Elizabeth, Maine, and after her maiden voyage to New York was bought by Charles R. Green, who remained the clipper's owner throughout the rest of her life at sea, when she was used to carry general cargo on her outward passengers from the USA to China before returning with high-value goods such as silk and tea. The *Snow Squall* averaged one return voyage each year from New York or, in 1858, Boston. The clipper made her outward voyage south and then west round Cape Horn on three occasions, but on every other voyage sailed south and east round the Cape of Good Hope, often calling at ports in Australia. The *Snow Squall* was an "extreme clipper" optimized for speed with a high-value cargo of only mod-

est size. At the time of her launch the ship was described as "very sharp at the bows, with a lean but handsomely graduated run, but from her great breadth of beam, will be enabled to carry well, while at the same time she cannot fail of being a fast sailor."

Nowhere was the *Snow Squall's* capacity for fast sailing more evident than in the time of a mere 94 days for the passage between Penang on the western side of the Malay peninsula and New York in 1863. On July 28, 1863, near the Cape of Good Hope, the ship approached the bark-rigged CSS *Tuscaloosa*, which closed the clipper flying the US flag as a *ruse de guerre* and, only when alongside, showed her true colors as a Confederate raider and opened fire. Captain Dillingham brought his vessel close onto the wind and pulled right ahead

The Snow Squall runs downwind with her studding sails set.

Carrying virtually all plain sail, the Snow Squall shows a clean pair of heels to the Confederate raider CSS Tuscaloosa on July 28, 1863.

of the *Tuscaloosa*, which abandoned the chase some four hours later. On her next voyage the *Snow Squall* sailed from New York for San Francisco, but on February 24, 1864, was becalmed in the Straits of Le Maire, east of Cape Horn, and drifted ashore on Tierra del Fuego. With her hull below the waterline damaged, the *Snow Squall* was taking on water and her captain decided to reverse course and make for Stanley in the Falkland Islands, where she was condemned.

In the Falkland Islands, the *Snow Squall* was incorporated into a makeshift jetty created by the Falkland Islands Company. This extemporized but in fact long-lived jetty later incorporated two other ships, the *Egeria* and the *William Shand*. Over the next 122 years, the *Snow Squall's* hull was filled with ballast stone, pierced for pilings, and generally hammered by the adverse conditions typical of the South Atlantic in these latitudes. Then, at a time early in the 1980s, the archaeologist Fred Yalouris, of Harvard University, began the Snow Squall Project to save what remained of this last surviving American clipper. The first of five visits for the documentation of the bow occurred during 1982, just two weeks before Argentine forces invaded this British colony. Four years later, and well after the British recapture of the islands, a large section of the bow was cut free and transported to the Spring Point Museum in South Portland, which was formerly called Cape Elizabeth, and then to the Maine Maritime Museum in Bath.

Snow Squall

Type:	three-masted "extreme clipper"
Tonnage:	742 tons
Dimensions:	length 157 ft 0 in (47.85 m) between perpendiculars; beam 32 ft 0 in (9.75 m); depth in hold 18 ft 6 in (5.6 m)
Speed:	not available
Armament:	none
Complement:	not available

Mumbles Oyster Boat 1865

One of the most important British areas for oyster dredging in the period up to the last quarter of the 19th century, and during much of the 18th century considered as providing oysters of the finest quality, was that in and around Swansea Bay, including the Mumbles headland in the parish of Oystermouth. For much of the "historical" period of oyster dredging in this area, the work was undertaken mainly from open boats, known as Oystermouth lug boats, which evolved into a type of vessel, also seen farther north in Wales and also in Swansea where its was used as a pilot boat,

shallop-rigged with two masts each supporting a gaff-headed sail. The oyster-dredging trade was both profitable and sustainable until the rich pickings of the area drew the attention of "foreign" oyster dredgers, the most predatory being those from Essex. The local response was the use of larger and more efficient craft. Thus, in the mid-19th century, men from the Mumbles and neighboring areas travelled to Colchester in Essex to order a number of smacks as successors to their existing but somewhat smaller craft. The first of these was named as the *Seven Sisters*, and such craft

The Mumbles oyster boat could carry much sail in light area, but the rig allowed for easy reduction in sail area should the wind become stronger.

became known as Mumbles oyster boats, the older, smaller craft being oyster skiffs.

The oyster boat had an almost straight, vertical stem and moderately high freeboard over its forward end, this freeboard declining farther aft to a short and square-off counter that facilitated the hauling of the dredges. The ballast, it should be noted, was generally copper dross from the smelters in Swansea. The long bowsprit allowed the oyster boat, generally rigged as a cutter, to spread a large area of canvas in light airs. The oyster men of Swansea Bay soon spread their boat orders to southwest England. Thus many Mumbles oyster boats were later built in the small yards of Appledore, which lies across from south Wales on the other side of the Bristol Channel, and still others, including the *Emmeline* 14SA built in 1865 and believed to have been the last of these specialized craft to survive into the period after the end of World War I (1914-18), came from William Paynter's St. Ives yard in Cornwall. Paynter was very well known as the builder of excellent craft, and his luggers were ordered from as far away as Campbeltown on the lower reaches

of the River Clyde, from which they were employed for herring and mackerel drifting.

Larger numbers of more capable oyster-dredging craft meant an initial increase in the profitability of the trade and then, inevitably, the trade's collapse. By 1871 there were 188 oyster boats owned by local men, and in 1873 the trade peaked with the landing of 6.6 million oysters: over-fishing and disease then intervened, and by 1878 the local fleet had dwindled to 47 boats, and by 1910 to just 14 including the *Emmeline* 14SA.

Emmeline 14SA

Type:	Mumbles oyster boat
Tonnage:	not available
Dimensions:	length 40 ft 0 in (12.2 m); beam 10 ft 7 in (3.2 m); depth in hold 5 ft 3 in (1.6 m)
Speed:	not available
Armament:	none
Complement:	2 or 3 men

Sobraon 1866

During November 1866, the Alexander Hall & Co. yard of Aberdeen in Scotland launched a ship which was soon to acquire an enviable record for herself on account of her unusual yet elegant looks and her excellent sailing qualities in terms of handling and speed. This full-rigged ship was the *Sobraon*, which was of composite hull construction with iron frames and beams but otherwise entirely of teak, and apparently the largest composite ship ever built. The ship was at first to have been a square-rigged passenger steamer for the Gellatly, Hankey and Sewell company, and was planked up with two stern posts forming the propeller aperture before it was decided to complete the ship without machinery. Thus this aperture was filled with solid dead-wood before the ship was launched. The *Sobraon* had iron lower masts, steel was employed for the topmasts and all yards up to the upper topsails, and the topgallant masts and yards above the upper topsails were of wood. The ship originally carried a course, lower and upper topsails, topgallants, royals and skysails on all her masts, but the skysails disappeared at an early stage as the ship proved tender. The bowsprit was notably short (possibly a carry-over from her steamship origins) but beyond this she carried a very long jib boom.

The Sobraon was a full-rigged ship of exceptional sailing capabilities, and made her name on the route linking Great Britain and Australia.

The *Sobraon's* most unusual feature was the layout of her hull. Despite the fact that she had been schemed for the carriage of passengers and emigrants to Australia, she had only a very short half-round poop which did not reach the mizzen rigging, a configuration possible because the passenger accommodation was in the after part of the tween-decks and not, as in all other ships of her class, below the poop. The forecastle was notably longer than normal, and was a topgallant unit extending as far aft as the fore backstays. The *Sobraon*, so named for a British victory in the 1st Sikh War (1845-46), was owned by Lowther, Maxton & Company but chartered to Devitt & Moore for passenger service to Sydney. The ship soon became extremely popular among passengers for her well appointed first-class accommodation. This extended from right aft to just forward of the mainmast, and had long saloons down the center flanked by some 12 or 13 passenger cabins each with a lavatory.

Devitt & More chartered the *Sobraon* from the time of her first voyage right through to 1870, when the company bought the ship and continued to sail her until 1891. In this period the ship was under the command of Captain J. A. Elmslie for all but her first voyage. In all of her voyages to and from Australia, the *Sobraon* carried passengers and emigrants as well as a limited amount of general cargo on the outward leg, and a smaller number of passengers and a larger volume of wool on the homeward leg. In 1891 Devitt & Moore sold the now elderly ship to the government of New South Wales, which converted the vessel to replace the reformatory school ship *Vernon* in Sydney harbor The *Sobraon* served 21 years in this role before, in 1912, becoming a stationary naval training ship at Berry's Bay as HMAS *Tingira* (an Aboriginal word meaning "open sea") for 16 years. In 1928 the ship was considered of no further use and sold to a shipbreaking company. But before work could be started on the task of destroying her, public agitation to save the ship led to a last lease of life as a rest home for unemployed men. Two years later the ship was sold with a view to her conversion as a museum, but this plan fell through and the *Tingira* was sold once again, this time to W. M. Ford, a boat builder who wanted the ship for sentimental reasons and kept her at anchor in Berry's Bay. It was only after Ford's death that the final process began. The executors of Ford's will sold the ship to breakers, who took delivery of the ship in 1936. The breaking process stalled soon after work began, however, and the task was not completed until 1941.

Sobraon (later HMAS *Tingira*)

Type:	three-masted ship
Tonnage:	2,131 net
Dimensions:	length 272 ft 0 in (82.9 m); beam 40 ft 0 in (12.2 m); draught 27 ft 0 in (8.2 m)
Speed:	not available
Armament:	none
Complement:	up to 250 passengers and a crew of between 60 and 70 men

"Cutty Sark" 1870

Certainly one of the most celebrated sailing ships still in existence, and the only complete example of a clipper, the *Cutty Sark* was one of the last such vessels built for the China tea trade between the 1840s and 1870s. Ordered by Captain John Willis of London, designed by Hercules Linton, and built by Scott, Linton & Co. of Dumbarton in Scotland for launch in November 1869, the *Cutty Sark* was based on a hull of composite construction with teak planking over iron frames. The ship's basic concept is believed to have been suggested by another of Willis's vessels, *The Tweed*, which had been constructed in Bombay as the paddle steamer *Punjaub* before being converted into a full-rigged ship. The name *Cutty Sark* (short shift, or shirt) was derived from *Tam O'Shanter* by Robert Burns, a poem in which Tam spies on the witch Nannie wearing a cutty sark.

The contract which Willis negotiated with the builder specified the use of only the finest materials, and the need to buy in these materials before the receipt of any payment led to the builder's bankruptcy before the ship was launched. The *Cutty Sark* was therefore completed by William Denny & Brothers, the company which took over Scott, Linton & Co.'s yard.

The initial years of the *Cutty Sark's* career were poor

in terms of operating profit, and were also disappointing inasmuch as the *Cutty Sark* never beat the *Thermopylae,* her main rival, on the all-important route from China to Great Britain. The two clippers were almost identical in size, and their most exciting race home took place in 1872. The clippers loaded their cargoes of tea in Shanghai, sailed on the same tide, and were virtually side by side south through the China Sea. About 400 miles (645 km) ahead of *Thermopylae* in the Indian Ocean, the *Cutty Sark* lost her rudder in a severe gale, but her crew managed to ship a rudder extemporized from spare spars. This too was lost, and a third rudder had to be made and shipped. It was with this that the *Cutty Sark* completed the 16,000-mile (25750-km) voyage to London. With a time of 119 days, the *Cutty Sark* had inevitably been beaten to port by the *Thermopylae,* but the determination and seamanship of her complement excited great admiration.

While there was intense rivalry between the individual clippers, there was an even more important battle between the clipper and the steamship. Independent of the wind, and from 1869 able to

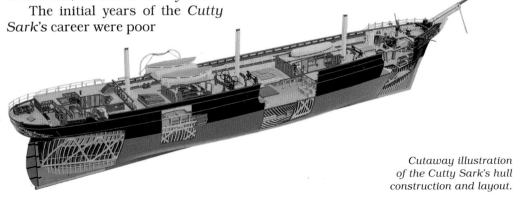

Cutaway illustration of the Cutty Sark's hull construction and layout.

use the Suez Canal to avoid the necessity of passing round the southern tip of Africa, the steamship could virtually guarantee a passage of only 60 days from Shanghai to London. Clippers could compete only by offering lower cargo rates. In the case of the *Cutty Sark*, this meant a rate more than 50% lower than had been typical in the period before 1869. The owners and captains of clippers hoped that this situation would prevail only with time-sensitive and premium cargoes such as tea, but the steamship quickly edged the clipper out of the market for general cargoes outward-bound from Great Britain. Thus the *Cutty Sark* was driven to the situation in which she had to sail with a general cargo from Britain to Australia, where she loaded coal for delivery to Shanghai, thereby carrying two paying cargoes on the outbound voyage before loading tea for the homebound voyage. This eased but could not solve the ship's financial problems, and by 1878 clippers had been driven out of the tea trade. The *Cutty Sark* was therefore relegated to workaday bulk cargoes such as coal, jute, hemp and wool, but even so was at a disadvantage even in the carriage of cargoes, in which volume rather than speed of delivery was the key factor, as less racy sailing vessels could carry considerably larger cargoes.

In 1878 the clipper was contracted to deliver coal from Wales to Shanghai for the US Navy, and thus embarked on one of her most unhappy voyages. The first mate killed a seaman and left the ship before he could be brought to trial: he was later caught, tried in London, and sentenced to seven years in jail for manslaughter before returning to sea and ending his career as a ship's master. The *Cutty Sark* was then becalmed in the South China Sea,

The restored Cutty Sark is now a prize exhibit at the National Maritime Museum at Greenwich. The clipper is notable for its high length/beam ratio, which was good for speed but reduced the cargo capacity.

her captain going mad and jumping overboard. It was almost as if the *Cutty Sark* was jinxed, and she had two more weak captains before coming under the more capable command of Captain W. Moore in 1882. Sailing from New York to Semarang with case oil, and then loading exotic Oriental goods in India, the clipper returned to Great Britain in 1883.

A stamp of Tristan da Cunha depicts the Cutty Sark under sail.

This marked the end of the indifferent second part of the *Cutty Sark's* career, and the clipper now began the last and most successful part, in part because her new standard cargo was wool, a time-critical commodity as it had to be loaded after the Australia clip and delivered in time for the British auctions, both of which took place at specific times of the year. On her first wool run, the *Cutty Sark* loaded a cargo of wool, and returned home via Cape Horn in the very impressive time of 79 days. On her second voyage she again made the return passage in 79 days. Moore left the ship and was succeeded by Captain Richard Woodgett, who became *Cutty Sark's* most famous master. Except for one more stab at the tea record, which came to naught as there was no tea, the *Cutty Sark* remained in the wool trade to 1893. Her fastest voyage from Sydney to England was 69 days in 1888, and the clipper's speed under the right conditions is attested by the fact that in 1893 she overhauled the P & O Line steamer *Britannia* near the Australian coast.

The *Cutty Sark* completed her last voyage to Australia in 1895, and was then sold to a Portuguese owner, J. A. Ferreira of Lisbon. Renamed *Ferreira*, she worked in general trade between Lisbon and Portugal's overseas possessions as well as Brazil, the Caribbean islands and sometimes British ports. In 1916 she was dismasted in a hurricane and re-rigged as a barquentine, and in 1920 passed into the ownership of another company, the Cia. de Navegacão de Portugal, which renamed the ship *Maria di Amparo*. In 1922 the vessel put into Falmouth as a result of a gale in the English Channel, and there was spotted by Captain Wilfred Dowman, who soon bought her and brought her back to England. Renamed *Cutty Sark* and

This sail plan shows the Cutty Sark with her full suit of sails including studding sails on the fore and main masts.

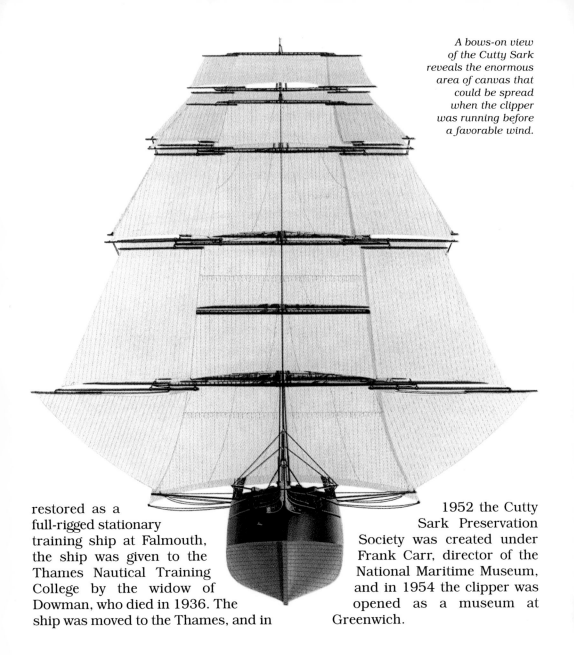

A bows-on view of the Cutty Sark reveals the enormous area of canvas that could be spread when the clipper was running before a favorable wind.

restored as a full-rigged stationary training ship at Falmouth, the ship was given to the Thames Nautical Training College by the widow of Dowman, who died in 1936. The ship was moved to the Thames, and in 1952 the Cutty Sark Preservation Society was created under Frank Carr, director of the National Maritime Museum, and in 1954 the clipper was opened as a museum at Greenwich.

Cutty Sark (later *Ferreira, Maria di Amparo* and *Cutty Sark*)

Type:	three-masted clipper
Tonnage:	963 gross registered tons
Dimensions:	212 ft 6 in (64.8 m); beam 36 ft 0 in (11.0 m); draught 21 ft 0 in (6.4 m)
Speed:	not available
Armament:	none
Complement:	19-28 men

Dutch Zomp 1885

A vessel that recorded its last commercial undertaking as late as 1939, the *zomp* was a Dutch type evolved to meet the particular needs of a low-lying country much intersected by navigable waterways but possessing only a rudimentary road network until the later 19th century, after which the importance of the *zomp* declined rapidly.

There were five basic sizes of *zompen* up to a load of 100 tons, and the most successful of these were the craft built at Enter, a small town at the head of the Regge river. The last Enter-built *zomp* was the *Recht door zee* (straight across the sea), which was completed in 1875. Given its use on rivers and canals, the *zomp* had to be light, flat-bottomed and narrow, but had also to

The zomp was optimized for the rapid delivery of substantial cargoes to destinations along the Netherlands' many inland waterways.

be strong so that a useful load could be carried, and a sharp sailer so that quick passages could be made on winding waterways. The hull of the *zomp* was built of oak planks each as long as the vessel, and this ensured strength despite the use of planks of only moderate thickness to keep weight down. The *zomp* was open, with a high decked bow and stern, and water was prevented from entering the hold over the low sides by the addition of large pine washboards along the edges of the hold. The *zomp* had a small two-person shelter in the bow, was steered with a tiller, and had two leeboards which could be raised and lowered as required. The single mast was stepped about 5 ft 0 in (1.5 m) abaft the bow section in a well-braced mast case that removed the need for shrouds, so the mast was supported only by a fore-stay, to which was hanked a jib or staysail. The mainsail was triangular and loose-footed, its leech being supported by a pair of diagonal sprits whose heels were secured to the mast by rope slings.

The zomp was perfectly conceived for its operating conditions, and was notably handy.

Recht door zee

Type:	single-masted *zomp*
Tonnage:	17 tons load
Dimensions:	length 40 ft 0 in (12.2 m); beam 8 ft 8 in (2.65 m); draught about 10 in (0.24 m)
Speed:	not available
Armament:	none
Complement:	2 men

Gaff-rigged "Koff" 1875

The *koff* reached the Netherlands, and also Denmark and Sweden, from the Frisian Islands in about the middle of the 18th century, and though initially used for the coastal trade along the north coast of Europe and into the Baltic and Norwegian Seas, the capabilities of the *koff* were soon reflected in voyages to destinations as far distant as the West Indies and Brazil.

The name *koff* was used for a number of different forms of the same basic type, but in general the *koff* was a decked cargo carrier with a wide bluff bow, a round stern, broad wales, a short tiller-operated rudder, a 1½-mast combined square and fore-and-

The koff was a comparatively small trading vessel typical of the northern coast of Europe, but proved very seaworthy and sometimes traded across the Atlantic.

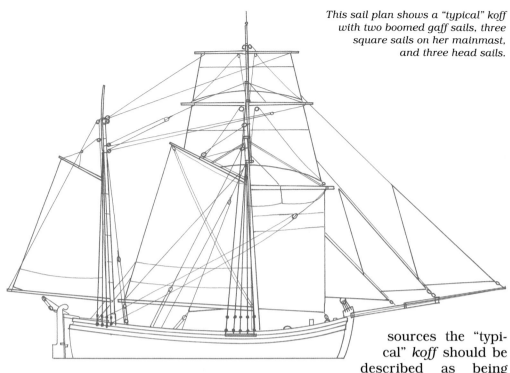

aft rig, and sometimes lee boards in vessels designed to operated in the shallow coastal waters of the Low Countries and similar areas. The masts comprised a mainmast with a topmast and possibly a topgallant mast, and a mizzenmast stepped on deck forward of the tiller, both sets of "sticks" being supported by shrouds. Although, as noted above, the *koff* was found in a wide assortment of subvariants. According to some sources, the *koff* carried a spritsail with bonnets as well as a topsail on each mast, together with the standard types of fore sails, while according to other sources the "typical" *koff* should be described as being rigged with a boomed gaff sail (with one or two rows of reef points) on each mast, a course, topsail and sometimes a topgallant sail on the mainmast, and a staysail as well as up to three jibs on the long bowsprit and jib boom. In either of these forms the *koff* was therefore well suited to downwind as well as upwind sailing.

The *koff* was also built in a number of sizes as well as a number of forms, and was typically credited with a tonnage between 100 and 300 tons, the larger size obviously being better suited to oceanic as opposed to merely coastal or seagoing passages.

Koff

Type:	1½-masted coastal and seagoing trading vessel
Tonnage:	generally between 100 and 300 tons
Dimensions:	not available
Speed:	not available
Armament:	none
Complement:	variable with size

Omani Dhow 1880

For many centuries, the peoples of the Oman region in the southwest corner of the Arabian peninsula were the core of a trade network extending north into Mesopotamia (now Iraq), east to India, south to Africa's east coast of Africa, and west into the Red Sea. Voyages took advantage of the region's regular, seasonal wind patterns, and the vessel on which this trade network was based was the *dhow*. This is a vessel of between 150 and 200 tons and lateen-rigged on a single forward-raked mast. The *dhow* is indigenous to the region, and over the centuries the concept was extended to encompass larger vessels, sometimes with two masts in the form of a larger mainmast and smaller mizzenmast, both of them lateen-rigged.

While the hull of the *dhow*, with its strongly raked stem and tall stern, combined with the lateen rig to produce good seagoing qualities, this was only one aspect of the ability of the Arabs to undertake long voyages. Another was the *kamal*, a navigating device that enabled them to fix latitude by gauging the height of the Pole Star above the horizon. The Arab seafarers could thus range far and wide, eventually establishing major trading posts (virtual colonies) along the East African coast.

A dhow puts out to sea from an Arab port. Note the long yard, bowsed down forward and controlled at its after end by a pair of braces.

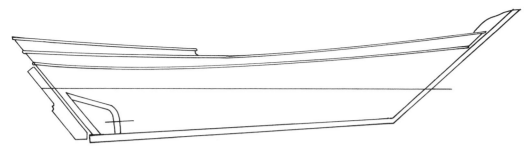

The modern Omani dhow lacks a mast and sail, propulsion being entrusted to a diesel engine powering a propeller.

The earliest *dhows* were shell-built craft, little more than dug-outs with planks sewn to their sides to form a hull. The size of the craft increased steadily as the builders introduced a keel to which planking was sewn and then braced in place by ribs or frames. It is worth noting that this shell-built construction was also used by early shipwrights in Europe, where it was gradually superseded by framed construction in which a solid frame (keel, ribs, beams, etc.) was built first and then planked. Shell-building made it possible for the shipwright to build his vessel at the rate of one plank at a time; if and when a change was required, the shipwright could easily alter the shape of a plank or its angle of attachment.

The *dhow* has a large number of variants indicating their hull shape and size. For example, the *ghanjah* is a large vessel with curved stem and a rearward-sloping transom which is often ornately decorated. No longer built, the *baghlah* was the traditional ocean-going *dhow* with a five-windowed transom and a poop deck. The *boom* is double-ended with stem and stern posts. Another type no longer built, the *battil* was characterized by a long stem surmounted by a large, club-shaped stem heads and a decorated stern post. The *badan* was a smaller type of dhow used in shallow waters. Iron nail fastenings began to supplant sewn planks after Portuguese and other European ships sailed into the Indian Ocean during the early part of the 16th century. The *dhow* is still very much alive, mainly for fishing and often with a diesel engine rather than a sail. While with their size and handsome decoration the great *baghlah* and *ghanjah* vessels are often considered to have been the classic *dhows*, it is the smaller, double-ended *battil* and *badan* vessels which should be regarded as the classic exemplars of the dhow tradition.

Baghlah

Type:	one- or two-masted ocean-going trading vessel of the *dhow* type
Tonnage:	up to 500 tons
Dimensions:	length up to 142 ft 0 in (43.3 m); beam and draught not available
Speed:	not available
Armament:	none
Complement:	variable according to size

Thistle 1887

After the *Mayflower* had beaten the *Galatea* in 1886 to ensure that the America's Cup remained in the hands of the New York Yacht Club, the next challenge was posted by the Royal Clyde Yacht Club with what was hoped to be an all-Scottish challenger, the cutter *Thistle* designed for James Bell by George Watson. In the event the yacht used English sails, with an area of 8,068 sq ft (749.5 m²), made by Ratsey and Lapthorn of Gosport and Cowes.

Watson was influenced by the lines of the yawl *Jullanar*, designed in 1875 by John Harvey and which had revealed excellent performance, and created the *Thistle's* hull on the concept of minimum wetted area with a clipper bow and a long counter to keep waterline length to a minimum as this was a major factor in determining the yacht's rating. Work on the construction of the yacht, which had a steel hull, started early in January 1887 in the yard of D. & W. Henderson, and the launch took place on April 26 of the same year. The all-Scottish crew, skippered by John Barr, extracted the best possible performance from the yacht, which surprised all with her good turn of speed

Though she lacked adequate windward performance, the Thistle was undoubtedly a very pleasing cutter in aesthetic terms.

in light conditions, but caused some consternation as she was at best indifferent when going to windward.

The *Thistle* sailed her first race on May 28, and before departing for the USA took part in 15 races, winning 11 of these. For the voyage across the Atlantic the *Thistle* was revised with a rig of more manageable proportions with a smaller topmast and shorter bowsprit. Departing from the west coast of Scotland on July 25, the *Thistle* crossed the Atlantic in 22 days to reach Tompkinsville, Staten Island, New York. Measurement here discovered the waterline length to be 86 ft 5 in (26.34 m) rather than the specified 85 ft 0 in (25.91 m), but even with her rating altered the *Thistle* received time from the larger defending yacht, Charles J. Paine's *Volunteer*, which had been designed only after the Americans had received initial details of the *Thistle's* dimensions.

There was enormous interest in the three-race series in both the USA and Great Britain, especially as virtually instant telegraphic communications added a real sense of immediacy to the proceedings. But the races failed to match the anticipation, for the *Volunteer* outmatched the *Thistle*. The first race was sailed on September 27 and resulted in an American victory by 19 minutes 24 seconds, while the second and deciding race was another US victory, this time by 11 minutes 49 seconds.

The *Thistle* sailed for home on October 14 even as post-mortem assessments of her performance continued. The consensus was that while the lack of underwater area might pay dividends in reducing drag, lack of adequate forefoot area inevitably resulted in poor windward performance. The *Thistle* raced for another year under Bell's leadership in Britain and was then sold. She raced for many more years, and was finally broken up only in 1911. Yet it must be said that while the *Thistle* may have been a disappointment for Bell, the interest in this yacht was one of the spurs for the great growth in the racing of large yachts, especially in Great Britain and Germany, and for the opportunities that now beckoned George Watson.

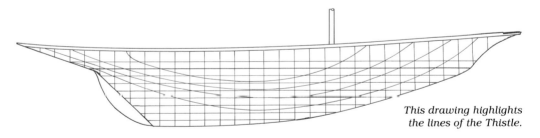

This drawing highlights the lines of the Thistle.

Thistle

Type:	single-masted racing cutter
Tonnage:	143.37 tons
Dimensions:	length overall 115 ft 1 in (35.1 m); beam 20 ft 4 in (6.2 m); draught 12 ft 11.5 in (3.95 m)
Speed:	not available
Armament:	none
Complement:	not available

Boomie Ketch 1887

A ketch is a two-masted vessel with its mizzenmast stepped before the rudder head, and the boomie ketch was typical of the craft of this type used for a multitude of practical purposes in the southeast of England during the second half of the 19th century. The boomie ketch was built at many yards between Great Yarmouth in Norfolk and Littlehampton in Sussex, and was in effect a flat-bottomed barge with straight sides that angled outward from the waterline, leeboards, and the ability to sail in coastal as well as purely tidal waters. The construction of the hull was entirely of wood, and as many of the yards which built these craft had previously constructed coasting schooners, many boomie ketches had hulls with lines more elegant than their workaday role strictly demanded. Among these elegant features were curved cutwater bows and counter sterns.

The trade most usually associated with the boomie ketch was the deliv-

The boomie ketch carried a gaff sail on each mast and a topsail on the mainmast, and as many as four headsails.

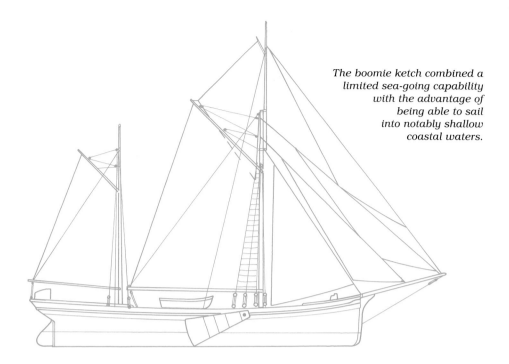

The boomie ketch combined a limited sea-going capability with the advantage of being able to sail into notably shallow coastal waters.

ery of coal to the southeast of England from the mining area of northeast England. The boomie ketch was nothing if not versatile, however, and in search of profit vessels of this type ranged as far afield as Norway and Spain as well as Germany, Ireland and the Netherlands. Boomie ketches were also built for South American purchasers and sailed out to their new homes. Though generally well suited to the task imposed on them, the boomie ketches had one primary failing, namely their inability to sail close to the wind. This was a failing that was most acute when the vessels had to sail up rivers, and attempts to mitigate the failing resulted in the use of vangs to reduce the tendency of the gaffs falling off to leeward.

The era of the boomie ketch effectively ended after World War I (1914-18), when the freeing of large numbers of coal-fired coasting vessels made the boomie ketches uneconomical to operate as they required a five-man crew, and many of them were therefore scrapped. The last of these interesting vessels to remain in trade was the 95-ft (29-m) *Martinet*, which had been built in Rye and sank in Hollesley Bay during 1941.

Boomie Ketch

Type:	two-masted "boomie ketch" barge
Tonnage:	not available
Dimensions:	length overall 101 ft 10 in (31.0 m); beam 23 ft 0 in (7.0 m); depth in hold 7 ft 6 in (2.3 m)
Speed:	not available
Armament:	none
Complement:	4 or 5 men

Norwegian Færing 1890

When, in about 900 AD, a Viking of great wealth and importance died, his body was buried with rich grave goods that included the now celebrated Gokstad dragonship and also three smaller boats. Of these latter, two were *færings* (four-oared boats) and the other was a *sixern* or *seksæring* (six-oared boat). Another classic type which in this instance was not represented, however, was the larger *åttring* (eight-oared boat). There are still *færings* on the coast of Norway, so this type of elegant little craft, eminently well suited to the fjords and inshore waters of that country's immensely long coast, has a history at least 1,100 years long and indeed

longer as the *færings* uncovered with the Gokstad dragonship are clearly craft fully developed in the light of lengthy experience from a time no later than the 4th century BC. While the modern *færing* is used mainly for pleasure, until recent times the *færing* was an everyday workboat built for fishing, passenger transport and the movement of goods.

Although primarily an open rowing boat, the *færing* can also be sailed with what is manifestly a direct descendant of the Viking longship's sail arrangement, namely a single almost rectangular sail carried by a yard hoisted on a shroud-supported mast and controlled with braces and sheets. In some

This færing from the west coast of Norway has the simpler of the two basic types of sail plan, namely a single square sail.

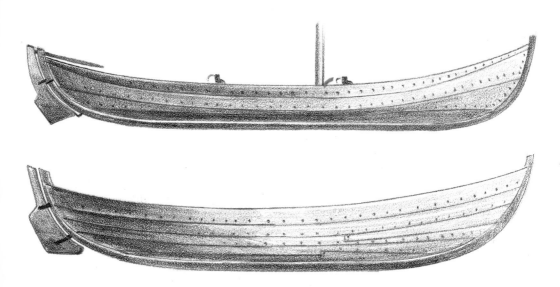

The færing was and indeed still is built in a number of sizes and forms with detail differences.

areas, however, a more advanced sailing arrangement, based on a spritsail and jib, is used. One of the key features of the sailing rig is the fact that it can be shipped and unshipped easily, a fact of singular importance in a region where the weather conditions can change radically and very swiftly. Just as evident is the relationship of the *færing* to the longship, for in the design and construction of the hull both types essentially identical. The one major change is the fact that the longship was steered with an oar, whereas the *færing* is steered by a tiller-operated rudder hinged to the stern post.

The *færing* is a double-ended boat based on a long keel which sweeps up at bow and stern into stem and stern post of a particular curved rake whose angles indicate the place at which the boat was built. The hull is low and wide, in the fashion of the long-ship, and also clinker built with five or six strakes on each side outside a varying number of ribs. The uppermost two or three of these are swept up strongly at bow and stern to meet the stem and stern posts. The

shape and construction of the hull, with its essentially flat bottom, makes the *færing* light and therefore able almost to "dance" over the surface of the water. But the hull would be too weak for sustained use were it not for the two rowing thwarts, which are interdependent with the primary structure and make the latter both stronger and more rigid. It was generally standard for the *færing* to be rowed by two or three persons, the latter with one person using two oars and the other two one oar each.

Norway has a very strong tradition of maintaining from the past what is still useful, and also what will serve to illustrate the country's history. The *færing* falls into both of these categories, so beside lovingly maintained *færings* a century of more old there are newly built craft whose detail differences highlight the ubiquity of the *færing* along the coast of Norway. It is worth noting that substantial numbers of *færings* were exported, mainly from the Hardanger region, to the Low Countries and Scotland in the Middle Ages.

239

Dutch Europa 1898

The *Europa* was arguably the finest clipper ever designed and built in the Netherlands, and the ship was without doubt a model of elegance which also set a number of passage records never bettered by another sailing ship.

Laid down in the Concordia yard of Huygens & Van Gelder in Amsterdam during 1897, the steel-hulled *Europa* was launched in the following year to the order of W. A. Huygens, and was the last of only five ships completed by that yard between 1886 and 1898 before the construction of a new railway station deprived the yard of access to the sea. The ship was square-rigged on three tall masts, her fore and mizzen masts carrying everything up to royals, and her mainmast everything up to a skysail. The ship's hull was characterized by a fine bow entry of the classic clipper type, rounded stern and magnificent bowsprit almost 100 ft (30 m) long,

supported by the standard dolphin striker and martingale stays, allowing the setting of a total of four triangular head sails. The height of the *Europa* to the truck of her main topgallant mast was some 188 ft (57.3 m), and she carried 21,927 sq ft (2037 m²) of sail with all canvas spread. This area of canvas could nonetheless be handled by only 25 men. Much of the credit for the sail plan and the ease with which it could be handled was owed to her first skipper, Captain Gunther Bona, who supervised every aspect of the ship's construction from the moment the keel was laid.

The *Europa's* intended role, at a time when steam had steadily eroded sail's commercial importance, was the rapid delivery of bulk cargo, but with a 44-ft (13.4-m) poop and a 24-ft (7.3-m) forecastle head she was also able to accommodate a small number of first-class passengers, and also carried four apprentices.

The Europa could sail very fast, but needed precisely the right handling to secure such a performance.

It took Bona some time to get the feel of his new ship, as indicated by the ship's very poor performance on her maiden voyage from the Netherlands to the East Indies, where Batavia was reached only in 99 days at a time when the record was 71 days. In the following year, once he had learned the ways of his ship and tuned the arrangement of the masts and rigging, Bona got fully into his stride with a series of truly remarkable passages. On March 9, 1899, for example, the *Europa* departed New York fully laden with casks of paraffin, and reached the Australian port city of Adelaide on May 19 after a passage of only 71 days, securing for her the inevitable soubriquet "The Flying Dutchman." Other notably fast passages were two voyages between New Zealand and Batavia by means of the Torres Straits in 42 and 44 days, Gravesend to New York in 36 days, New York to Melbourne in 90 days, Newcastle in New South Wales to Falmouth via San Francisco in 135 days, and Liverpool to Wellington in New Zealand in 95 days.

Then in 1904 Bona handed over the command of the ship to Captain Wiebes, who soon revealed the unfortunate fact that he could not extract the same performance from the *Europa*. The ship started her last voyage under the Dutch flag in 1906. Arriving at Frederikshald in Norway, Wiebes discharged the ship's ballast and took on a cargo of timber for Australia, and then made a good passage to Melbourne. Then things started to go wrong, and the planned circumnavigatory trading voyage that had been scheduled to last no more than 15 months eventually took 26 months as cargoes were carried from Melbourne to Newcastle in New South Wales in ballast, and from there to Chile with coal. Huygens had arranged for a cargo of saltpetre in Chile for the final leg home, but the ship missed the deadline and at a time of steadily declining saltpetre prices Huygens preferred to order the ship back to Australia in ballast, there to load grain for the British market. The grain cargo did not materialize, so Wiebes sailed to Port Pirie and there loaded nickel ore, which was another commodity whose price was falling steadily. After unloading the nickel ore at Dunkirk, the *Europa* finally returned to the Netherlands late in 1908, and Huygens then put the ship up for sale. The buyer was J. A. Henschien of Lillesand in Norway, who renamed her *Lotos*. Henschien sold her in 1916 to Heiskein & Son of Kristiansand, who changed her name again, this time to *Asra*. It was under this name that the ship met her tragic end: during the afternoon of May 5, 1917 she was torpedoed and sunk in the Atlantic on passage from Belfast to New York. Fortunately, her crew was picked up and landed safely at Balderic in northwest Ireland.

Europa

Type:	three-masted clipper
Tonnage:	1,911 tons
Dimensions:	length overall 258 ft 9 in (78.9 m); beam 42 ft 0 in (12.8 m); draught 23 ft 7 in (7.2 m)
Speed:	not available
Armament:	none
Complement:	unknown number of passengers and about 35 men

Yorkshire Lugger 1900

Otherwise known as the Yorkshire farm, or as the five-man boat because it was generally owned and sailed by five men, the Yorkshire lugger was a notably sturdy three-masted lugsail vessel designed for the herring drifter and line fishing roles. The Yorkshire lugger was used most importantly by Yorkshire fishermen during the years before and after 1800, and is generally regarded as the successor to the square-rigged buss, a two- or three-masted type of between 50 and 70 tons.

Now best known from an excellent model of about 1800, held in the collection of the Science Museum in London and exemplifying what is believed to be a larger example of the breed, the Yorkshire lugger was a clinker-built and fully decked vessel. Key features of the design were a bluff bow with a curved stem, a straight keel and

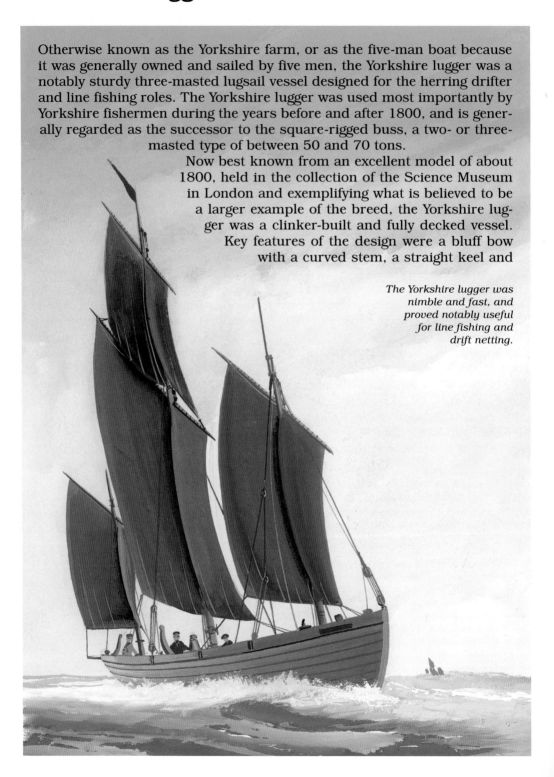

The Yorkshire lugger was nimble and fast, and proved notably useful for line fishing and drift netting.

a fine run to the underside of the hull, round bilges and slightly hollow floors, short bilge keels, and a lute stern. On the assumption that the model is an accurate representation, the Yorkshire lugger carried large but comparatively low-peaked dipping lugsails on the fore and mainmasts, a smaller topsail on the mainmast, and a small but more sharply peaked standing lugsail on the mizzen mast. The mizzen lugsail's sheet was rove through a sheave at the outboard end of an outrigger extending over the stern. There was no bowsprit, but a topmast was a prominent feature on each of the three masts. Intended for the hauling of drift nets rather than the working of the boat, a capstan was fitted on the deck abaft the main mast.

Drawings of Yorkshire luggers in the 19th century indicate a number of variations from this "standard," most notably a fuller head to provide volume for the carriage of the catch, and in some cases a bowsprit. The Yorkshire lugger was built in fairly large numbers. A late example, with lines that were probably finer than those of earlier craft, was the *York* built by Robert Skelton at Scarborough in 1848. This vessel was 63 ft 6 in (19.35 m) long and 17 ft 3 in (5.25 m) in beam.

In the period between March and September, the Yorkshire luggers were generally used for the line-fishing of cod and other larger fish on the edge of the Dogger Bank or even further afield. During the autumn the luggers switched to the herring drift netting role off the coast of Norfolk, and at the end of this season were laid up for the winter. Though they were generally owned by a consortium of five men, the luggers often carried seven men when line fishing and eight or more when drift netting. Fishing was undertaken with the aid of two square-stern cobles (carvel-built and flat-bottomed boats) carried out to the fishery on deck. The seaworthiness of the Yorkshire lugger was attested by the fact that in heavy weather the craft could often lie to rather than run for shelter, and a lucrative hidden occupation was smuggling, for the luggers were fast as well as handy, and therefore able to outrun revenue cutters.

In 1825 there were some 45 Yorkshire luggers working out of ports such as Filey, Flamborough, Robin Hood's Bay, Runswick Bay, Scarborough and Staithes, this last having the largest fleet, namely 17 vessels. This highpoint in the career of the Yorkshire lugger reflected the fact that fish prices were high in the aftermath of the Napoleonic Wars, which ended in 1815, and between this date and 1820 some 25 examples of the Yorkshire lugger were built.

Yorkshire lugger (typical larger type)

Type:	three-masted fishing lugger
Tonnage:	not available
Dimensions:	length 61 ft 0 in (18.6 m) between perpendiculars; beam 19 ft 6 in (5.9 m); draught 7 ft 6 in (2.3 m)
Speed:	not available
Armament:	none
Complement:	7-10 men

Preussen 1905

Built in 1902 by J. C. Tecklenborg of Geestemünde in Germany as the second ship of this name for the Reederei F. Laeisz, the *Preussen* (Prussia) was one of only four five-masted square-rigged vessels, the only five-masted ship square-rigged on all her masts, and the largest ship without an auxiliary powerplant. Built for the nitrate trade, in which large quantities of guano (bird dropping) fertilizer were shipped from Chile to Europe, the steel-hulled *Preussen* was at her birth a major source of pride to the German merchant marine. The ship had five masts each carrying six yards, and could set 43 sails with an overall area of 59,848 sq ft (5560 m²), and with a favorable wind the *Preussen* was capable of exceeding 17 kt: in one 24-hour period during 1903, the ship covered 424 miles (682 km) for an average speed of 15.3 kt. Although with their longer and therefore more capacious hulls five-masted ships were able to carry a greater weight (almost 8,000 tons) of freight than four-masted vessels, the square-rigged ship offered little increase in speed over the mixed square and fore-and-aft rig of the barque, and had the economical disadvantage of needing larger crews, which made such ships more costly to man.

Whatever the economic pros and cons of the ship versus the barque rig, the *Preussen* was certainly a fast ship, especially under the impetus of a driving skipper such as Captain Boye R. Petersen, who was the *Preussen's* master between her completion in 1902 and 1909. The *Preussen* sailed from Europe to Chile on 12 occasions, with an average passage time of 65 days (on one occasion in 1903 setting a record of only 55 days from the English Channel to Iquique), and her 13 return passage times averaged 73 days. In 1908 the ship was chartered by the Standard Oil Company, and sailed from New York on the northeastern coast of the USA to Yokohama in Japan via the Cape of Good Hope, and in the course of this passenger

Square-rigged on five masts, the Preussen was a hugely impressive ship.

achieved 3,476 miles (5595 km) in one 11-day period at an average of slightly more than 11.4 kt.

On November 7, 1910, outward bound to Chile under command of Captain J. Heinrich H. Nissen, the *Preussen* rammed the SS *Brighton*, a British cross-Channel steamer which was making 17 kt in foggy conditions as the *Preussen* was making 4 kt. The ship's bowsprit ripped away one of the steamer's two funnels and tore a hole in her hull. With her bows stove in by the collision, the *Preussen* was taken in tow by the steam tug *Alert*. Some 21 miles (33 km) from Dover, Nissen tried to anchor his ship in the lee of Dungeness, but the ship's anchor chains parted in a squall and Nissen was forced to run for Dover. Attempting to enter Dover harbor with the aid of three tugs, the *Preussen* was so unwieldy as a result of the windage of her top hamper that the towing lines snapped. Setting sail in an effort to back out of the shallows around Dover harbor, the *Preussen* lodged her bow on rocks in Crab Bay. All attempts to free the ship proved fruitless, and the *Preussen* was battered to pieces.

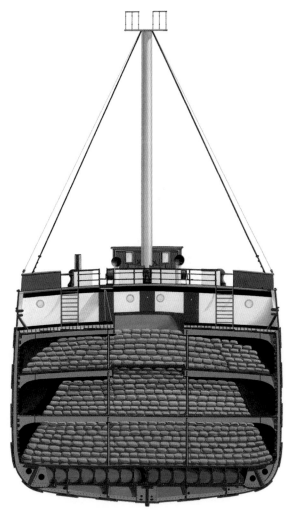

A section of the Preussen's hull in line with the mizzen mast reveals, from top to bottom, the chart room, crew's and officers' quarters flanking the galley, cargo of the lower and orlop decks and in the hold, and the water ballast above the cellular bottom.

Preussen

Type:	five-masted ship
Tonnage:	5,081 gross registered tons
Dimensions:	length 407 ft 11 in (124.3 m); beam 53 ft 6 in (16.3 m); draught 27 ft 3 in (8.3)
Speed:	17 kt
Armament:	none
Complement:	48 men

Gjøa 1905

Roald Amundsen, who was born in 1872 at Borgo in southern Norway and died in 1928, was one of the greatest of all polar explorers. As a boy he had been inspired by accounts of the efforts of Sir John Franklin, and as a young man abandoned a career in medicine to serve as seaman in Arctic waters and so gain his mate's certificate. He was trapped in the Antarctic ice during the winter of 1897-98 with the rest of the crew of de Gerlache's *Belgica* expedition, and on his return in 1899 secured his master's certificate. Amundsen felt he was now ready to lead his own expedition, and decided that his first goals would be the first passage through the Northwest Passage, and the reaching of the northern magnetic pole.

With the encouragement of Fridtjof Nansen, a slightly older Norwegian Arctic explorer, Amundsen bought the *Gjøa*, an old fishing smack, and in this became the leader of the first expedition to transit the Northwest Passage. Named for a Valkyrie, and built by Kurt Johannesson Skaale of Rosendal in the Hardanger region of Norway in 1872, the *Gjøa* had worked for 28 years under Asbjørn Sexe of Hangesund and, from the mid-1880s, H. C. Johanneson of Tromsø. Amundsen bought this shallow-draft smack in 1900 and spent the following year on trials between Norway and Greenland, after which he gave the vessel a sheathing of oak some 3 in (7.5 cm) thick, added an iron strapping on the bow, and installed a 13-hp (9.7-kW) kerosene-fuelled internal combustion engine driving a single propeller.

Evading his ever more pressing creditors, Amundsen sailed from Christiania (now Oslo) on June 16, 1903 with a six-man crew. At Godhavn on the western side of Greenland the *Gjøa's* crew loaded sleds, dogs and kayaks. The little

The Gjøa was a small but sturdy (and reinforced) sloop-rigged fishing smack which made the first passage from the Atlantic to the Pacific Ocean's round the north of Canada and Alaska.

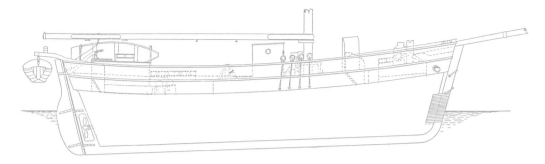

Amundsen's revisions of the Gjøa were designed to provide the capability to move through pack ice and to survive the pressures of being trapped in the ice.

vessel then crossed Melville Bay, passed through Lancaster Sound, and moved south into Peel Sound between Somerset and Prince William Islands before reaching King William Island on September 12, 1903. The expedition remained two years at this Gjøa Haven to take observations which, it hoped, would allow the expedition to establish both the current location and the steady movement of the magnetic north pole. On August 13, 1905 the *Gjøa* headed west between continental Canada and the south shore of Victoria Island, and on August 26, off Banks Island met an American whaler, the *Charles Hanson*, which had sailed from the Pacific, and knew that the expedition had passed through the Northwest Passage. The *Gjøa's* crew wintered again off King Point, and from her Amundsen trekked up the Porcupine and Yukon rivers to Eagle, Alaska, where he telegraphed the news of his success to the world. The *Gjøa* reached Nome in Alaska on August 31, 1906, and then as a short pause sailed to San Francisco, where the expedition was given a hero's welcome by the city even though it was recovering from a devastating earthquake.

Despite an invitation to become the first vessel to pass through the newly completed Panama Canal, Amundsen agreed to the idea of the Norwegian community in San Francisco and handed the *Gjøa* over to the city for display in Golden Gate Park. The vessel remained there for 30 years in slowly deteriorating condition, and a reconstruction was delayed by other imperatives in World War II (1939-45) and completed only in 1949. The *Gjøa* remained in San Francisco until 1974, when she was returned to Norway for permanent display at the Norsk Sjøfartsmuseum in Oslo.

Gjøa

Type:	single-masted fishing sloop revised for Arctic exploration with an auxiliary engine
Tonnage:	67 gross registered tons
Dimensions:	length 70 ft 0 in (21.3 m); beam 20 ft 7 in (6.3 m); draught 7 ft 9 in (2.3 m)
Speed:	not available
Armament:	none
Complement:	7 men

Reliance 1909

The largest single-masted vessel ever built, a tour de force of imaginative design and phenomenal engineering, but also a racing yacht so extreme as to approach the downright dangerous, the *Reliance* was the fourth America's Cup defender designed by Nathanael (sometimes rendered Nathaniel) Herreshoff, and was one of the earliest examples of the yacht as an outright racing machine.

Nathanael Greene Herreshoff was born in 1848 near Bristol, Rhode Island, on the edge of Narragansett Bay, as one of the six sons and three daughters of Charles and Sarah Herreshoff. John Brown Herreshoff, Nathanael's elder brother by seven years, had from a very early age revealed a distinct flair for boatbuilding and marine

engineering, and was primarily responsible for encouraging Nathanael along the course. Before Nathanael was 12 years old, the brothers had designed and built a 22-ft (6.7-m) sailing boat, the *Sprite*, which proved herself a steady winner for a number of years in local regattas.

Following a course in mechanical engineering, as the subject nearest to naval architecture available at this time at the Massachusetts Institute of Technology, Nathanael was employed for the years between 1866 and 1875 by the Corliss Steam Engine Company at Providence, Rhode Island, largely on the design team. His own genius for boat design resulted in 1876 in his 30-ft (9.1-m) racing catamaran, the *Amaryllis*. This type of craft was new to the waters of Narragansett Bay, and proved herself wholly superior to all the

The hull of the Reliance was totally dwarfed by the yacht's truly enormous sail plan.

local sandbagger yachts (shallow, wide-beam boats with movable ballast in the form of bagged sand) until a change in the racing rules prohibited the catamaran.

With the formation of the Herreshoff Manufacturing Company, Nathanael turned to the design of steam yachts and launches together with their machinery, while continuing to design a succession of beautiful racing yachts. Although by this time he had become blind as a result of a Herreshoff family genetic weakness, his brother John was an equally active partner and was the inventor of a new type of coil boiler used for high-speed yachts and naval torpedo boats. After 1891 the Herreshoff company, unwilling to become involved with the gasoline-fuelled internal combustion engine that was beginning to supplant steam machinery in pleasure craft, came to concentrate its efforts on the design and construction of sailing yachts with Nathanael drawing the lines of the yachts and John checking the hulls with unerring accuracy using only his hands. Nathanael's talent for innovation found expression in both design and light-construction techniques, and the switch to high-performance racing yachts was reflected, during 1891, in Nathanael's design for the 70-ft (21.3-m) yacht *Gloriana*, which had a waterline of only 45 ft (13.7 m) and revolutionized the design of racing yachts with a profile that swept easily from the stem head to the bottom of the keel.

It was with this stage in its life that the company found its true metier, and from the Herreshoff yard there came a series of yachts characterized by outstanding performance, among them the 30-, 40-, 50-, 65- and 70-ft one-design classes for the New York Yacht Club. The construction of several yachts to exactly the same stan-

With the victory of the Reliance over the Shamrock III in 1909, the America's Cup remained safely in the hands of the New York Yacht Club.

dard was facilitated by the brothers' introduction of the novel and labor-saving practice of building the yachts with their keels uppermost before turning them over to have the deck and interior arrangements installed, thereby introducing what was to become the standard quantity production method in yacht building. Among the more celebrated sailing yachts designed and built by the firm were the successful America's Cup defenders *Vigilant* (1893), *Defender* (1895), *Columbia* (1899 and 1901), *Reliance* (1903) and *Resolute* (1920). Afflicted in his latter years with inherited blindness, Nathanael died at Newport, Rhode Island, in 1938.

Designed and built for a syndicate headed by C. Oliver Iselin, the commodore of the New York Yacht Club, the *Reliance* was an open, unfinished hull with exposed frames and no trick spared in the creation of a radical hull shape in which waterline length and underwater size were reduced to the minimum to cut wetted area and drag. But the *Reliance's* speed was not the result of drag-reduction alone, for underneath her highly polished skin of 3/16-in (4.7-mm) bronze plates, the *Reliance* was a magician's tour of structural and mechanical ingenuity.

To lessen his yacht's displacement, Herreshoff saved on weight

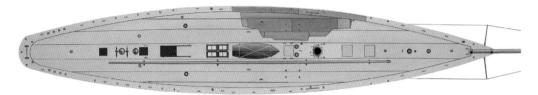

With the yacht worked largely from the below-decks area, the Reliance's deck plan was notably clean. The area to port of the mast is shown with the cork linoleum removed to reveal the aluminium plates.

until the yacht's framework looked more like that of a modern aeroplane than a yacht of the first decade of the 20th century, when wood still predominated over metal as the primary structural medium. The hull's key structural members were T-shaped web frames 8 in (203 mm) wide, made of 0.125-in (3.2-mm) nickel steel spaced 80 in (2.03 m) apart with lighter L-shaped frames of 2-in (51-mm) steel located at 20-in (51-cm) intervals between them. To support the tremendous weight of the mast and carry the huge loads transmitted down it to the hull by the massive area of canvas which the mast carried, Herreshoff designed an enormous steel keelson to carry its foot, and added extra web frames on each side. The yacht's fragile framework was then stiffened and strengthened by a lattice of steel reinforcement members including transverse steel-tube braces within the web frames. The deck was made of 0.25-in (6.4-mm) aluminium plates laid over a network of 0.3125-in (7.9-mm) steel straps and itself covered with a 0.125-in (3.2-mm) layer of cork linoleum to provide a good foothold.

In his determination to create a yacht strong enough for its task yet light enough to possess phenomenal performance, Herreshoff carefully considered every aspect of the *Relian-ce* and all her equipment. Rather than use stock fittings, therefore, Herreshoff designed every cleat, hook, shackle and turnbuckle for adequate strength yet minimum weight, and to ensure that the spars and fittings did actually possess the required strength, prototypes were tested to destruction on three machines in Herreshoff's home and yard. Herreshoff was also very far-sighted in the aids he created to ease the task of the crew. Thus a foot-operated brake on the steering gear was introduced to lighten the helmsman's task in a race that would certainly last for hours, and an indicator was provided to show the helmsman the rudder's exact angle. The rudder itself was hollow, which was not uncommon for the time, but contained a rubber bladder which could be filled with air by a foot pump when the *Reliance* was carrying a lee helm, the theory being that the added buoyancy would reduce the forces to be overcome by the helmsman; with a weather helm, the air in the bladder was allowed to escape so that the rudder filled with sea water. The standard practice of the day was to entrust all sail-trimming to the brawn of the on-deck members of the crew, but Herreshoff had other ideas and led the halyards and sheets belowdecks through fair-leads to nine two-speed winches, which were of the self-releasing type and each designed for a specific task. This marked a major step forward in the technology associated with yacht racing, and the winches were so admirably designed that identical winches were used by the America's Cup defenders for the next 34 years.

The *Reliance* was the first America's Cup yacht with belowdecks winches, and this gave her a major advantage over the British challenger, Sir Thomas Lipton's *Shamrock III*, which relied on abovedecks brawn in the traditional manner. Whatever the ingenuity of the hull and its structure, the feature which dominated the *Reliance's* appearance was her huge sail plan. The yacht had a sparred length of 201 ft 6 in (61.4 m) from the tip of the bowsprit to the after end of the boom, her topmast towered 199 ft 6 in (60.8 m) above the waterline, and her spinnaker pole was 83 ft 9 in (25.5 m) long. The total area of the canvas that could be spread was 17,730 sq ft (1647.1 m²), and this gave the *Reliance* a speed of 17.5 kt or more.

Skippered by Captain Charles Barr, the *Reliance* easily bettered the *Columbia*, which had defended the America's Cup against Lipton's *Shamrock* in 1899 and Shamrock II in 1901, during the defender's trials. In the first race against Lipton's third challenger, the William Fife-designed *Shamrock III*, in August 1903, the *Reliance* won by 7 minutes and 3 seconds. Lipton closed the gap in the second race, losing by only 1 minute and 18 seconds. The third race was sailed in light breezes and neither yacht finished within the allotted time. The *Reliance* finished her only racing season undefeated, and in the following year she was broken up. By this point, the "90-footer" America's Cup yachts, so-called for their waterline length, were deemed to have become so costly and even dangerous, that Herreshoff was asked to devise a new rating rule, and his Universal Rule was first employed in the next America's Cup challenge, held between *Resolute* and *Shamrock IV* in 1920.

The design of the Reliance was optimized for the lightest possible weight and the combination of a short waterline length and a long overall length.

Reliance

Type:	single-masted racing cutter
Tonnage:	189 tons displacement
Length	144 ft 0 in (43.9 m); beam 25 ft 9 in (7.9 m); draught 19 ft 7 in (6.0 m)
Speed:	more than 17.5 kt
Armament:	none
Complement:	66 men

Morecambe Bay Prawner 1910

So known even though its primary catch was shrimp, the Morecambe Bay prawner was an extremely elegant variant of the cutter-rigged fishing smack used round much of Great Britain's coast. The Morecambe Bay prawners were based mainly at Morecombe, Fleetwood, Southport and in the Mersey estuary, and trawled for shrimps between the Solway Firth and north Wales. The first such vessels were clinker- or carvel-built with a vertical stem and a transom stern as well as a centerboard in many of the boats, but from the late 19th century the type became more standardised, at lengths between 23 ft 0 in (7.0 m) and 40 ft 0 in (12.2 m), with a rounded stem, cutaway after hull, rockered keel, wide beam with sharp bilges and a coaster (or tug) stern.

The Morecambe Bay prawner was stable yet handy and fast, and could point well up into the wind. This combination made the prawner admirably well suited to the task of negotiating the twisty channels

The Morecambe Bay prawner was well suited to the conditions in which it operated, but could be very wet in any sort of sea.

between coastal sand banks, yet its seaworthiness meant that it was also capable of coping well with the short and quickly whipped-up seas typical of the shallow waters of regions such as Morecambe Bay. Another feature of the design, as reflected in the wide beam and basically flat bottom, was its ability to settle safely on the bottom as the tide dropped in anchorages such as Southport, and then lifting safely as the flood tide arrived.

The prawners were only partially decked, most particularly in the bows, and carried a coal-fired boiler to process the catch as the boat returned to harbor. The boats were rigged as pole-masted cutters carrying a gaff main sail of about 500 sq ft (46.5 m²) and two headsails (including a jib on a sliding bowsprit) totalling some 400 sq ft (37.2 m²); there was also a jackyard staysail above the gaff main sail.

The Morecambe Bay prawners were built in several yards right into the 1930s, primarily with a keel and frames of oak or elm and planking of larch. Later boats were completed

Among the working boats of the world, the Morecambe Bay prawner stands out as being considerably more pleasing in aesthetic terms than many other boats.

with an auxiliary engine of the type that was also retrofitted in such of the older boats as had survived.

Morecambe Bay prawner (typical)

Type:	single-masted shrimp-trawling cutter
Tonnage:	not available
Dimensions:	length 32 ft 0 in (9.75 m); waterline length 28 ft 0 in (8.5 m); beam 9 ft 0 in (2.75 m); draught 3 ft 0 in (0.9 m)
Speed:	not available
Armament:	none
Complement:	1 man and 1 boy

Wavertree 1910

Laid down in 1885 by Oswald Mordaunt & Co. of Southampton on the south coast of England as the *Toxteth* to the order of R. W. Leyland and Company of Liverpool, the ship eventually known as *Wavertree* was one of the last and largest iron-hulled ships of the full-rigged types ever to be completed. Her builders sold her to Chadwick and Pritchard shortly after her launch, and the ship spent the first three years of her commercial existence in the jute trade between India and Great Britain as the *Southgate*. Although she had already changed hands, in 1888 Leyland and Company bought back the ship and renamed her as the *Wavertree* for a suburb of the port city of Liverpool. The *Wavertree* was sailed in the general cargo role, sailing the world's

oceans to delivery contracted cargoes and in search of the same or alternatively for cargoes of opportunity. The ship was therefore used for the carriage of all sorts of cargo. On her first voyage for Leyland and Company, for example, she sailed from Port Pirie in Australia with 122,900 bushels of wheat which, it is believed, was the greatest load ever carried by a sailing ship to that time. On other voyages, the *Wavertree* carried a cargo of salt from Hamburg to Calcutta, of guano (nitrate fertilizer) from Chile to England, of coal from Calcutta to Mauritius, and of case oil from New York to a destination in the Far East.

In 1908 the ship sailed from Portland, Oregon, for Liverpool with provisions for $3\frac{1}{2}$ months despite the fact that her owners knew the passage

The Wavertree is depicted in storm conditions with only the minimum of canvas aloft to steady the ship and provide steerage way.

The Wavertree is caught by the camera in Stanley in 1910 after a Cape Horn storm had removed her mainmast, part of her fore mast and all but the lower part of the mizzenmast.

would take at least six months. The crew was reduced to eating biscuits and then wheat taken from the cargo and boiled using cut-up spars and the like after the coal had been exhausted. Much of the crew was in the early stages of scurvy, but some three days out from Liverpool a fishing boat was sighted and the ship's master was able to buy fish. The *Wavertree* was sold on two occasions during 1910, and on May 26 of that year sailed from Cardiff for Valparaiso with a cargo of coal. Severely damaged while trying to round Cape Horn, the ship put back to Montevideo for repairs. with the repairs completed, the ship headed south once more toward Cape Horn, and was again driven back by fearsome weather conditions including boarding seas. With five of her crew badly injured and her masts, spars and rigging in total disarray, the

Wavertree managed to make Stanley in the Falkland Islands. Here the ship was condemned, but in the following year the ship was sold to Chilean interests and towed to Punta Arenas for use as a wool storage hulk. In 1948, her hull still sound, she was towed to Buenos Aires, and here the old ship was used for something approaching 20 years as a sand barge.

In 1966, returning from a survey of *Great Britain* at Stanley, Karl Kortum found the *Wavertree* in a backwater of the Riachuelo. Negotiations to buy the ship were begun by the newly established South Street Seaport Museum in New York City, and in August 1970 the *Wavertree* was towed to New York, where she was steadily restored toward a near-pristine beauty.

Wavertree (formerly *Don Ariano N*, *Wavertree* and *Southgate*)

Type:	three-masted ship
Tonnage:	2,170 gross registered tons
Dimensions:	length 268 ft 6 in (81.8 m); beam 40 ft 3 in (12.3 m); depth in hold 24 ft 6 in (7.5 m)
Speed:	not available
Armament:	none
Complement:	28 men

Mediterranean Bateau-Boeuf 1911

The *bateau-boeuf* (ox-cart boat) was the type of lateen-rigged boat used in along the French part of the Mediterranean Sea, between the ports of Agde and Marseilles, to fish in the Golfe du Lion right into the 20th century. The *bateaux-boeuf* were created as trawlers, and always operated in pairs towing the net between them (hence the cart horse analogy) and the large capstan on the clear deck area abaft the single pole mast located about 22 ft 4 in (6.8 m) abaft of the stem head. The "standard" *bateau-boeuf* had a length of some 51 ft 8 in (15.75 m) on deck, but there was also a slightly smaller model with a length of 42 ft 8 in (13.0 m). The boat itself

was comparatively broad-beamed and flat-bottomed, and the capability to set a large area of canvas was provided to ensure that there was adequate "power" for trawling operations. The boat was controlled with the aid of a tiller-operated rudder.

Each *bateau-boeuf* was crewed by between 16 and 18 men as this type of fishing was always labor-intensive, and the net had two sides 27.5 yards (25 m) in length with, at the end, a pocket 6.5 to 9.5 yards (6 to 8 m) long with a semi-circular iron collar opening whose flat edge was dragged over the sea bed.

With a standard rig of two triangular sails (in the form of one large

A bateau-boeuf scuds before a quartering breeze with all sail set.

lateen sail and a large jib extending between the top of the bowsprit and the mast head), the *bateau-boeuf* had no provision for reefing. In the event of a wind too strong for continued safety under normal sail, the jib was set on the smaller of the two lengths of yard normally lashed together to create the lateen sail's yard: this was some 41 ft 0 in (12.5 m) long by comparison with the other section's length of about 40 ft 0 in (15.25 m). With this amount of sail set, the *bateau-boeuf* can run before the wind in a controllable manner. It is worth noting that lashed together to create the single spar for the lateen sail, the two sections of spar had an overall length of 70 ft 6 in (21.50 m). There was also provision for a number of other sails to improve sailing performance in light airs.

Gravel was used for ballast, and the boats never carried an

anchor as they always returned to port rather than tried to anchor at sea. Other features of the *bateau-boeuf* were a small dinghy lashed upside-down on the foredeck, and four large sweeps, each with a length of 32 ft 10 in (10 m), for continued mobility when otherwise becalmed. The ribs were 4 in (10 cm) square, spaced at 12-in (0.3-m) intervals, while the deck beams, curved downward from the centerline to ensure that any water drained outward and over the sides of the boat, were spaced at twice the timbers' width.

As well as its lateen main sail and large jib, the bateau-boeuf had provision for a number of additional sails to exploit lighter winds.

Bateau-boeuf (larger size)

Type:	single-masted lateen-rigged fishing boat
Displacement:	not available
Dimensions:	length 51 ft 8 in (15.75 m) on deck; beam 16 ft 1 in (4.9 m); draught 5 ft 3 in (1.6 m)
Speed:	not available
Armament:	none
Complement:	16-18 men

Leigh Bawley 1912

Operating from harbors in the southern part of the North Sea and on both sides of the Thames estuary, most typically Gravesend, Harwich, Leigh, the Medway and Southend, the bawley was decked smack designed for shrimping during the summer months. The bawleys were therefore equipped from the 1850s with a coal-fired copper boiler in which the catch could be processed before the bawley returned to port in time for its catch to be put onto the late train service to London. In the winter, when there was no shrimping, the bawley was used for stow-boating (fishing for sprats).

Certainly in existence by 1760, the bawley was straight-stemmed boat with a transom stern, considerable beam and a tall-masted cutter rig based on a loose-footed gaff main sail which was stowed or reduced in area with brails, with a topsail above it, and in the fore triangle a staysail and jib. The bawleys initially worked comparatively close to London and were comparatively small, clinker-built boats. But as these waters were fished out and pollution from London reduced their fecundity, the boats had to operate farther out into the estuary. This placed a greater emphasis on speed, and as a result the boats became larger (and, in the case of boats operating from Southend and Leigh but often built in Brightlingsea and Harwich, carvel- rather than clinker-built) with comparatively greater sail area. The bawley's bow had a somewhat

The broad-beamed bawley had a tall mast and could carry a large area of canvas for its size.

260

The bawley was an economic artery for coastal communities such as those at Leigh on the northern side of the Thames estuary from about 1750.

were very delicate, and were worked with the aid of a large deck-mounted capstan (initially man-powered but later fitted with small engines) and carefully control of the boat's speed through use of the brails.

Although the last of the bawleys were not retired from shrimping until the 1950s, the heyday of the fleets was in the 1890s, when there were 86 such craft based at Leigh and another 20 at Southend. The economic importance of the bawley fleets to the communities which operated them was great, and therefore the rivalry between them was intense. This rivalry was further increased as the advent of the train allowed Londoners to make day and holiday visits to the port towns on the Thames estuary, and on these trips shrimps were considered a delicacy not to be missed.

hollow entrance rapidly opening into a broad beam, and it was the combination of this beam and up to 15,680 lb (7110 kg) of ballast which allowed the bawley to carry up to 875 sq ft (81.3 m²) of sail on its tall mast without excessive heel. The nets

Leigh bawley (typical)

Type:	gaff-rigged shrimping and stowboating cutter
Tonnage:	not available
Dimensions:	length 36 ft 0 in (11.0 m); beam 13 ft 0 in (34.0 m); draught 4 ft 4 in (1.3 m)
Speed:	not available
Armament:	none
Complement:	not available

Dutch Botter 1912

The *botter* was a traditional type of Dutch fishing boat normally based between Volendam and Harderwijk in the southwestern part of the Zuider Zee. The *botter* was normally something in the order of 45 ft 3 in (13.80 m) long, wide in the beam and characterized by a flat bottom. The boat had a high, curved stem, a low, narrow stern, a tiller-operated rudder, and two leeboards which were long and narrow, and designed to provide the *botter* with the capability to fish effectively and safely in offshore waters, which can often kick up very rough. A notable feature of the design was the incorporation of a free-flooding well (or trog) amidships so that the catch could be kept alive and therefore in prime condition during extended fishing forays and long runs back to port. The *botter* was designed for extended periods away from home, so the area forward of the mast was fully decked to create a substantial forecastle volume providing modestly comfortable accommodation (with a coal-burning stove and sleeping benches)

and also a separate compartment for storing the nets. The decking was extended abaft the mast to create a shelter, and ended just forward of the stern well from which the boat was worked.

Supported by just two shrouds and single fore and back stays, the single pole mast carried a basic plan of one gaff main sail and one stay sail, these two sails possessing a combined area of some 430.5 sq ft (40.0 m²). There was also provision for a jib set on the forward tip of the long bowsprit. This jib could be a small unit with an area of 161.5 sq ft (15.0 m²) or a large unit with an area of 269.1 sq ft (25.0 m²), the decision about which of these jibs to set being dictated by the weather conditions. The gaff main sail was loose footed, but its clew at attached to the after end of a boom carrying the block for the sheet. At the stern of the boat a triangular stay sail could be hanked to the

With its high stem and effective leeboards, the botter was also capable of fishing in the coastal area of the open sea as well as in the Zuider Zee.

The botter generally fished with a dragnet. This could be worked by two boats in co-operation, or by a single boat towing the net from the end of a spar.

mast's back stay with the clew of its loose foot sheeted to the after end of an outrigger pole.

Although the *botters* were traditionally of wooden construction, later in their lives many of the boats were sheathed with iron to prolong their lives, and some of the boats were also fitted with an auxiliary engine. As the type ceased to be economically viable as a fishing boat, many *botter* craft were sold for use as yachts, a role made feasible by their possession of adequate internal volume for conversion into comfortable accommodation. The process of conversion from fishing boat to pleasure yacht not infrequently saw the removal of iron sheathing and in virtually every case a loving external restoration.

MK 63 (Zuider Zee botter)

Type:	single-masted fishing boat
Tonnage:	not available
Dimensions:	length overall 44 ft 3 in (13.5 m); beam 13 ft 9 in (4.2 m); draught 3 ft 3 in (1.0 m)
Speed:	not available
Armament:	none
Complement:	2 or 3 men

"Q" Trawler WW1

At the beginning of World War I in August 1914, a large part of the fishing fleet supplying Britain with much of her fresh food were sailing vessels of many types, including ketches which operated from ports such as Brixham in Devon, Ramsgate in Kent and Lowestoft in Suffolk. The Lowestoft vessels habitually trawled in a North Sea area between 20 and 60 miles (32 and 97 km) to the southeast of their home port, a fact that caught the attention of the German navy in the summer of 1915. The fishing fleet was a worthwhile target, and in the summer of 1915 there appeared in this fishing area the first of the "UB"

class of coastal submarines, which carried an armament of two torpedoes and, sometimes, a small deck gun. The "UC" types that followed were equipped for minelaying with six tubes for 12 or 18 mines and, while having no torpedo tubes in the first two classes, did have a deck gun. It was this last which was the threat to the British trawlers, for the U-boats could use their greater speed and the threat of the gun to force the trawlers to heave to, and then put aboard them an explosive charge.

The first victims of this tactic were the *E. & C.*, *Boy Horace* and *Economy* on June 3-4 1915, and sinking con-

In its "Q-ship" form, the Lowestoft trawler had to entice a target to short range before having any real chance of success with its light gun.

tinued until September 1915 before an autumn pause but a renewal of the German offensive in January 1916. In an effort to counter the German offensive, in August 1915 four Lowestoft trawlers had been taken in hand for adaptation into "Q-ship" armed decoys with a concealed 3-pdr gun worked by some five naval ratings. Within a few days the new "warships" were in action: the G. & E. tackled a "UB" class U-boat, the Inverlyon sank the UB-4, the Pet fought off another U-boat, and the Inverlyon was again in action on September 7.

In the first week of March 1916, six Lowestoft trawlers had been boarded and sunk by U-boat crews, and on March 23 the men of the armed trawler Telesia were spoiling for a fight. The skipper, W. S. Wharton, spotted a U-boat on the surface at a distance of some 3 miles (4.8 km). The U-boat then closed to within 50 yards (45 m) of the Telesia before submerging and keeping watch through her periscope. Then, quite extraordinarily, the U-boat pulled back and fired a torpedo, which was an extremely expensive way in which to seek the destruction of a low-value target which could have been cheaply despatched by an explosive charge or a few rounds from the deck gun. The torpedo just missed, and Wharton ordered the 3-pdr gun into action, 15 rounds being fired at the periscope of the U-boat, which pulled back but then returned 30 minutes later to fire a second torpedo. This too missed, but Wharton's gunners now managed to score two hits on the partially surfaced German boat, which crash-dived and made off. By April 23, when she made her next foray, the Telesia had become the Hobbyhawk and was under naval command, as was the similar Cheero. Working together like a pair of trawlers, the two smacks were to trial a new weapon, namely a 600-yard (550-m) wire that appeared to be a trawl wire but was fitted with impact-fused explosive charges. An immediate success was achieved by the Cheero as the minelaying UC-3 became tangled in the wire, triggered one of the charges and was then destroyed by the explosion of her own mines. On May 13 the Hobbyhawk and another conversion, the Revenge, had a similar encounter, but the U-boat escaped.

The idea of the armed fishing smack spread and was further developed in larger fishing vessels, but its utility was short lived after the Germans appreciated what the British were doing. All the U-boat had to do was stand off beyond the range of the "pop gun" carried by the sailing vessel and destroy her with its own larger-caliber weapon.

"Q" Lowestoft trawler

Type:	disguised anti-submarine vessel
Tonnage:	46 tons
Dimensions:	length 72 ft 0 in (21.95 m); beam 20 ft 0 in (6.1 m); depth in hold 9 ft 6 in (2.9 m)
Speed:	not available
Armament:	one 3-pdr gun, one 0.303-in (7.7-mm) machine gun and, on some vessels, mines attached to the trawls
Complement:	8 men for fishing supplemented by 5 men for 'Q' ship service

Thames Barge 1920

The Thames barge was the classic bulk transport of the river, estuarine and coastal waters of southeast England between the Yare river in Norfolk and the Stour river in Kent. Although the barge was a square-rigged vessel in its original incarnation, this was soon developed into the "classic" barge, as typified by the two-masted, flat-bottomed Thames or spritsail barge. Of the masts, one was large and rigged with a spritsail and a jib-headed or occasionally a jackyard staysail, and the other very small, ketch-set forward of the rudder head and rigged with a spritsail. The rest of the sail plan comprised a fore staysail and generally a jib. Other features of the barge were leeboards rather than a keel, and the stepping of the mast on deck in a lutchet, which was a type of tabernacle. The flat bottom and leeboards allowed the barge to negotiate very shallow waters and to settle on the bottom without any heel, yet still possess adequate windward per-

formance, while the arrangement of the mast allowed this to be lowered on deck for the barge to proceed under bridges.

This Thames barge layout had been introduced in its basic form by 1800 with a rig based on a single head sail and two spritsails, and at about decade intervals between 1810 and 1900 the hull was decked with a single large covered hatch over the cavernous hold, the original swim bow was replaced by a rounded bow, the overhanging stern gave way to a square-cut transom stern, the tiller was superseded by a wheel, a main topsail was added, and the addition of a bowsprit opened the way to the setting of additional headsails. The spritsails were easy to handle with a crew of just two persons, and the additional advantage of having no boom on the mainmast meant that access to the hold was unhindered once the sail had been brailed up.

Thames barges were built up to 1931, initially with wooden but latterly steel hulls, but by that time the end was in sight as a result of the development of motor and rail transport as well as

With its two-man crew, the Thames barge for many years provided the cheapest means of delivering bulk cargoes to and from the ports of southeastern England and the towns on the major rivers debouching into the southern end of the North Sea.

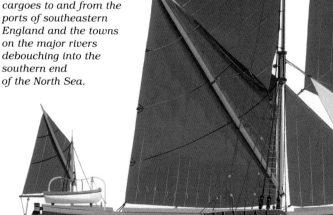

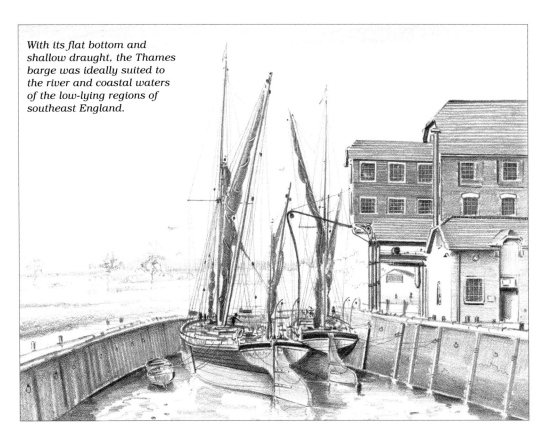

With its flat bottom and shallow draught, the Thames barge was ideally suited to the river and coastal waters of the low-lying regions of southeast England.

more economical shipping, and in an effort to maintain the viability of the barge many were fitted with an auxiliary powerplant. The importance of the Thames barge peaked just before World War I (1914-18), when there were considerably more than 2,000 such vessels, many of them being able to ply across the English Channel to enter the rivers and canals of northern France. By the outbreak of World War II (1939-45), the number of Thames barges had dropped to about 600, and by the early 1980s there survived only some 50 Thames barges converted as museums, yachts and the like. By 2005 only 31 were still able to sail. Possessing a sort of stately elegance, the Thames barge nonetheless retains a strong hold on the emotions of persons who retain a feeling for the slower-paced life typical of the late 19th and early 20th centuries.

Thames barge (typical)

Type:	two-masted spritsail cargo barge
Tonnage:	49 gross registered tons
Dimensions:	length 77 ft 0 in (23.5 m); 19 ft 0 in (5.8 m); draught 3 ft 3 in (1.0 m)
Speed:	not available
Armament:	none
Complement:	2 men

Brixham Trawler 1922

The term Brixham trawler covers several type of sailing vessel which operated from this Devon port in the southwest of England. The basic design was that of a cutter-rigged fully decked vessel of 30 to 40 tons, with a full bow, broad beam and long straight keel, and characterized by a fine run to a flared transom. The trawlers were notably sturdy in their construction and had a good record of longevity, and seem to have appeared before the middle of the 18th century as sloop-rigged vessels. Operating at first in waters close by Brixham and Torbay, the fleet grew so much that soon some of the vessels were fishing off the south coast of Wales and along to the eastern end of the English Channel. When the laws designed to curtail smuggling were relaxed to allow cutter-rigged vessels, many of the Brixham trawlers were revised to this standard but always known as sloops.

The vessels fishing off south Wales worked mainly out of Tenby, and were known as Mumble-bees for their numbers and their adoption of a number of features of Mumbles boats. The vessels which worked the eastern end of the Channel were based at Rye, Dover and Ramsgate, and by 1850 were also to be found in the southern part of the North Sea. All of these vessels were worked by a crew of three men and an apprentice or later by four men, and had notably heavy beam trawls whose warp was hauled by deck-mounted capstan or a hand-spike windlass.

By the 1890s the Brixham trawler had been overtaken in importance by the mule, which was a faster type designed to delivery its catch in time to catch the train services that would make deliveries to more distant markets feasible. The introduction of a larger sail plan was the obvious solution, but was danger-

The "big sloop" type of Brixham trawler was notable for its combination of a deep hull and a sail plan designed to yield a speed of about 4 kt with the beam trawl deployed.

The "big sloop" was the ultimate expression of the fishing vessel concept that had first seen the light of day as the Brixham trawler, and was immensely successful.

ous for the Brixham trawler, so the mule introduced a ketch rig. Relaxation of the regulations governing the size of the trawl beam in the years leading to the end of the 19th century paved the way for another change, this time to the "big sloop," which was a smack of greater size so that it could work effectively in more distant waters and also carry the steam capstan that made it possible to use larger and heavier trawls. These could be hauled in a mere 15 minutes by comparison with the time of two hours or more required by the Brixham trawler's smaller trawl. The "big sloop" was ketch-rigged and had a registered tonnage of between 40 and 70 tons. The type proved very successful, and was widely copied in fishing ports right round the coast of Great Britain, generally as the dandy, as well as in Belgium and northern France, where it was known as the "dundee." The type survived into the 1930s as the fishermen of the English southwest lacked the financial resources to buy steam machinery and the internal combustion engine was not yet sufficiently developed. In 1913 there were more than 200 dandies, 20 to 25 mules, and 78 mumble-bees, but the number had fallen to 25 by the middle of the 1930s and effectively died in World War II (1939-45).

"Big sloop" (typical)

Type:	two-masted ketch-rugged fishing trawler
Tonnage:	70 gross registered tons
Dimensions:	length overall 78 ft 0 in (23.8 m); length 69 ft 0 in (21.0 m) between perpendiculars; beam 18 ft 3 in (5.6 m); draught 11 ft 0 in (3.35 m)
Speed:	not available
Armament:	none
Complement:	4 men

Colchester Oyster Smack 1923

Given its size and nature as the approach to London from the sea, the tidal estuary of the River Thames and the southern part of the North Sea along the coast of Essex have been of vital importance to the English and British capital over a period of many centuries. Given this importance, the nature of the estuary with its tributaries, creeks, mud flats and sand banks, and the fish and shellfish which can be caught and gathered along its northern and southern shores, it is inevitable that the Thames estuary and Essex coast have seen the development of large numbers of sailing vessels.

Typical of this tendency, which saw the creation of a multitude of types of specialized vessel in a large assortment of sizes, was the Colchester oyster smack intended for the lucrative oyster dredging trade. A classic example of this type is the *Secret*, which was built at Wivenhoe on the Essex coast during 1856 for work over the oyster beds of the Thames estuary. In common with the other Colchester oyster smacks, the *Secret* was cutter-rigged and, as a comparatively early example of the breed, had a greater draught than later smacks: the draught forward was 3 ft 6 in (1.1 m) increasing to 5 ft 9 in (1.75 m) aft. Another difference from the standard of later smacks was a comparatively short mast carrying a topmast rather than a taller mast without a topmast. The primary characteristics of the Colchester oyster smack were a notably low freeboard aft to facilitate the lifting of the oyster dredges aboard; the flush deck

A Colchester oyster smack heads for the mouth of the River Crouch in Essex with its main sail slightly shortened in a brisk south-easterly wind.

without any cockpit, providing ample space on deck for the handling of the dredges, and an arched tiller of distinctive shape.

These smacks form were among the small number of types of fishing vessel with the cutter rig. This was unsuitable for the general fishing role because of the weight of the spars and the gear aloft, the intricacy of the rigging, the impossibility of lowering the mast

The sail plan of the Colchester oyster smack included a loose-footed gaff main sail, a fore staysail and a jib.

on deck, and the lack of any separate riding sail aft. What the cutter rig did provide, however, was speed and handiness under sail, and the ability to come up into the wind in a narrow channel with greater ease than any other rig. It was as a result of these qualities that the cutter was favored by the men of Essex, who worked in waters which were shallow and typified by strong tides, and were based in harbors often located toward the head of creeks that were both winding and tidal.

Secret

Type:	cutter-rigged oyster-dredging smack
Tonnage:	11 tons
Dimensions:	length overall 33 ft 0 in (10.1 m); beam 10 ft 0 in (3.05 m); draught 5 ft 9 in (1.75 m)
Speed:	not available
Armament:	none
Complement:	3 men

Bluenose 1925

Designed by William J. Roue and built in 1921 by Smith & Rhuland of Lunenburg, Nova Scotia, the wooden schooner *Bluenose* was created specifically for the International Trophy, a prize offered by W. H. Dennis, a local newspaper publisher, in response to criticism that the America's Cup was for yachts rather than working vessels. The *Bluenose's* first skipper was Angus Walters, a very successful Grand Banks fisherman who had made a name for himself in the trials for the first International Fishermen's Trophy race of October 1920. The *Bluenose* beat all comers with ease, and was selected as Canada's entrant in the race against the US defender, the *Elsie*. In the October 1921 contest the *Bluenose* soundly beat the *Elsie*. In the following year, the *Bluenose* defeated the *Henry Ford,* and the 1923 series

Fast and handy, the Bluenose was a schooner whose elegance did not disguise that fact that she had been designed and built as a working vessel.

against the *Columbia* was drawn. The *Columbia* won the first race. In the second the schooners fouled each other and the *Bluenose* won by 90 seconds. The *Bluenose* was first over the line in the third race, but because Walters had not rounded one of the marks, as the committee had ordered following the earlier collision, he was said to have forfeited the race. Walters refused to race again.

In 1930 the *Bluenose* was beaten by the *Gertrude L. Thebaud* for the Sir Thomas Lipton Cup. During the following year the *Thebaud* challenged the *Bluenose* for the International Trophy, held off Halifax, and was beaten easily. Two years later, the *Bluenose* sailed up the St. Lawrence River and through the Great Lakes to represent Canada at the Chicago Exposition. In 1935 the schooner was again on show, this time in England where she was placed third in a race around the Isle of Wight. In

The Bluenose was a topsail schooner of the classic Grand Banks cod-fishing type with gaff sails on two masts.

1936 the schooner was fitted with auxiliary diesel machinery and, two years later, in the International Trophy race off Massachusetts, the *Bluenose* took the trophy outright by winning three of the scheduled five races against the Thebaud.

With the outbreak of World War II (1939-45), the German U-boat force was deemed a significant threat even to the Grand Banks schooners, so the *Bluenose* was taken out of commission and in 1942 sold to the West Indies Trading Company. Skippered by Captain Wilson Berringer, the schooner operated in the warmer water of the Caribbean Sea as a trading vessel between the islands until 1946, when she went aground off Haiti, broke her back and sank. Although built to race, the *Bluenose* had been conceived as a working vessel, and the greater part of her life was spent in the long-line cod fisheries over the Grand Banks off Newfoundland. She raced only after the fishing season had ended. Even before World War II, images of the this extremely beautiful schooner had graced Canadian stamps and coins, and her loss did not erase the fond memories of the Canadian people. Thus in 1963 the government of Nova Scotia built the *Bluenose II*, a careful replica to serve as the province's goodwill ambassador.

Bluenose

Type:	two-masted schooner
Tonnage:	285 tons displacement
Dimensions:	length 143 ft 0 in (43.6 m); beam 27 ft 0 in (8.2 m); draught 15 ft 9 in (4.8 m)
Speed:	not available
Armament:	none
Complement:	22-28 men

Padua and Kruzenshtern 1926

Built in 1926 by J. C. Tecklenborg of Geestemünde for the Reederei F. Laeisz, the *Padua* was one of the last large square-rigged vessels built specifically to trade under sail. Captained by J. Hermann Piening, the steel-hulled *Padua* recorded some of the fastest passages of the period after World War I (1914-18) with cargoes of nitrates and grain. In 1933, for instance, the *Padua* sailed from Hamburg for the Spencer Gulf of Australia in a mere 63 days. The *Padua's* last deep-water voyage for the Laeisz line was from Bremen to Glasgow via Valparaiso in Chile and Port Lincoln in South Australia. After her grain cargo had been unloaded, the *Padua* sailed to Hamburg in ballast and arrived there on August 8, just before the start of World War II (1939-45). In 1946 the *Padua* was seized by the USSR and renamed *Kruzenshtern* for the Russian admiral who had led the expedition of the Neva and Nadezhda, which sailed for the Pacific via Cape Horn in 1803, explored the northern Pacific and returned to Kronshtadt via the Cape of Good Hope. The barque was operated by the ministry of fisheries for sail training with 230 cadets and crew. Active primarily in European waters, the barque also visited New York for the USA's bicentennial celebrations in 1976 and the Statue of Liberty Centennial in 1986. With the dissolution of the USSR in the early 1990s, the *Kruzenshtern* passed to the Estonian ministry of fisheries.

Padua (later *Kruzenshtern*)

Type:	four-masted trading and sail training barque
Tonnage:	3,064 gross registered tons
Dimensions:	length 320 ft 6 in (97.7 m); beam 46 ft 1 in (14.1 m); draught 25 ft 5 in (7.7 m)
Speed:	not available
Armament:	none
Complement:	crew of unknown size and 40 cadets

Passat 1926

of Germany's war reparations to that country, but was then sold back to the Laeisz line at the end of the same year. In the 1920s she was involved in two serious accidents in the English Channel: during 1928 she rammed and sank the French steamer *Daphne*, and in 1929 collided with another steamer, in both instances being repaired at Rotterdam. With synthetic fertilizers replacing natural products in the 1920s, in 1931 Laeisz sold the *Passat* to one of the last great operators of sailing ships, Gustaf Erikson, and it was therefore under the Finnish flag that the steel-hulled barque took part in the last stages of the grain races between Australia and Europe up to the start of World War II (1939-45). In 1949 she sailed with the *Pamir* from Australia to Europe for the last time, and was then sold as a training vessel which also sailed between Argentina and Europe with grain. Retired in 1957, she has been a floating camp at Lübeck since the spring of 1966.

Built by Blohm & Voss of Hamburg in 1911 as a sister of the *Peking*, the *Passat* (trade wind) was created for use in the nitrate trade between Chile and Europe, and in her four voyages before World War I (1914-18) achieved the extremely creditable averages of 79 and 90 days for her outbound and homebound passages respectively. Held by the Chilean authorities at Iquique during World War I, she was surrendered to France in 1921 as part

Passat

Type:	four-masted trading and sail training barque
Tonnage:	3,091 gross registered tons
Dimensions:	length 322 ft 0 in (98.1 m); beam 47 ft 3 in (14.4 m); draught 22 ft 0 in (6.7 m)
Speed:	not available
Armament:	none
Complement:	not available

English Sailing Pilot Boat 1930

Although now much reduced in importance by the availability of accurate charts and effective navigation aids such as the Global Positioning System, pilotage (derived from the Dutch word for a sounding lead) was vital until recent times as the means of ensuring that ships passed safely through shallow coastal waters to reach their destination ports. Posses-sing excellent local knowledge of the channels and shoals (together with land and sea marks) and also of the tides and currents and other factors which could affect safe navigation, the pilot was put aboard an incoming or outgoing vessel to navigate it into or out of harbor. Licensed pilots were available at most ports, and were put on board a ship at a specified location.

Typical of the type of sailing pilot cutter that operated in the waters round England and Wales right up to the period of World War II (1939-45) was the Isle of Wight Pilot Cutter No. 1.

In all maritime nations the control of pilotage was allocated to a national authority which specified the conditions under which a pilot had to be taken on board and the fee to be levied, and in many navigable waters and harbors it was compulsory for ships over a certain size to embark a pilot. Before radio equipment became standard, pilots waited near specified major points of entry pilot cutters, from which they could go on board an incoming vessel or onto which they could be disembarked by an outboard vessel. At smaller ports, an inboard ship anchored off the entrance, hoisted the flag signal requesting a pilot, who arrived in a launch that was then towed by the ship. The masters of ferries and other similar vessels which invariably sailed in pilotage waters were generally qualified pilots, and thus needed no further assistance. The master retained responsibility for his vessel's safety, but had to follow the pilot's instructions.

The authority for all aspects of pilotage in English waters was entrusted to Trinity House, which was initially a guild of established in 1517 by King Henry VIII (1509-47) with responsibility for the "relief, increase and augmentation of the shipping of this our realm of England." Queen Elizabeth I (1558-1603) extended Trinity House's responsibilities to the institution of sea marks, and since that time the Corporation of Trinity House has been responsible for lighthouses, lightships, buoys and other aids to navigation within the waters surrounding the coast of England and Wales, the Channel Islands and Gibraltar, and also licenses pilots. In 1604 the membership of Trinity House was divided into Elder Brethren and Younger Brethren. The former were responsible for the corporation's practical duties and also acted as nautical assessors in the Admiralty Division of the High Court. They numbered 13 men in the form of 11 elected from the merchant service and two appointed from the Royal Navy, and persons of distinction were admitted from time to time as honorary Elder Brethren. The Younger Brethren had no responsibility in Trinity House's practical duties, but had a vote in the election of the master and wardens.

The traditional method for getting a pilot onto or off a vessel was by pilot cutter, which had to be notably seaworthy as pilots were required under any and all sea and weather conditions with the single notable exception of fog. These cutters were crewed by extremely capable skippers and men who built up an enviable reputation for sailing their craft effectively under the worst of conditions.

English sailing pilot cutter

Type:	two-masted pilot cutter
Tonnage:	not available
Dimensions:	length overall 69 ft 10 in (21.29 m); length on the waterline 62 ft 6 in (19.1 m); beam 14 ft 0 in (4.3 m); draught 7 ft 0 in (2.1 m)
Speed:	not available
Armament:	none
Complement:	3 men plus 1 or more pilots

Swedish Galleas 1930

The *galleas* was the typical small trading vessel of the Baltic Sea, and was certainly in existence in its definitive form by the middle of the 18th century as a fully decked ketch-rigged vessel characterized by boomed gaff sails on her main and mizzen masts, a square top sail on her mainmast, and a long pole bowsprit braced by martingales or a bobstay and a dolphin striker. Later changes were the replacement of the square top sail by a top sail above the gaff, and the replacement of the pole bowsprit by a

The galleas was evolved as a trading vessel but lately has acquired another existence as a pleasure yacht.

short bowsprit often extended by a jib-boom, a combination which allowed the setting in the fore triangle of a stay-sail (often boomed) and one or two jibs. Trading vessels of the *galleas* type were built in substantial numbers throughout the countries edging the Baltic Sea at least into the 1920s, and remained in profitable use until the interruption of World War II (1939-45). Many of the vessels survived the war, however, and from 1945 were still used to a limited extent as trading vessels between remoter coastal communities ill-served by any other form of transportation, but gradually to the related but somewhat different task of providing sail experience of the type which was often demanded by the mercantile marines of some Baltic states. As the *galleas* vessels gradually faded from such service in reflection of the reduced regard paid to sail training experience, the surviving *galleas* vessels were frequently bought for conversion into pleasure yachts.

The traditional construction of the *galleas* was based on pine planking over frames of sawn oak, beams of oak or pine, and a backbone of beech and oak with iron fastenings. This created a structure which was relatively straightforward to build, and which provided considerable strength. This latter was of great importance in a vessel designed for the workaday trading role, which was facilitated by the vessel's low length to beam ratio. This latter made for a capacious hold, which was accessed by means of a large hatch in the deck between the main and mizzen masts. The ballast was carried internally, and generally comprised pigs of cast iron stowed in the bilges above the basically flat bottom. The stern was of the flat transom type, and steering was the task of a wheel-operated rudder. The later *galleas* vessels often incorporated an auxiliary engine, in some cases a donkey engine winch in place of the original windlass for the handling of cargo, and metal rather than the original wood for the spars and sometimes the masts.

There was nothing remarkable about the *galleas* in terms of its design, construction and materials, but its longevity as a trading vessel is attributable to the fact that it was exactly suited to the requirements of Baltic trading folk and the nature of the Baltic Sea itself, whose coastline also provided all the materials that were needed to built and maintain these vessels. The *galleas* could be handled effectively and economically by a small crew, and it is this last factor that combined with the capacious hull to make the galleas suitable for conversion as a comfortable cruising yacht with the erstwhile hold added to the existing accommodation.

Galleas (typical)

Type:	two-masted ketch-rigged trading vessel
Tonnage:	100 tons Thames Measurement
Dimensions:	length overall 67 ft 8 in (20.6 m); beam 20 ft 4 in (6.2 m); draught 6 ft 6 in (2.0 m)
Speed:	not available
Armament:	none
Complement:	3 or 4 men

Mercator 1931

Designed by G. L. Watson Ltd., the *Mercator* (named for the great Flemish geographer of the 16th century) was built by Ramage & Ferguson Ltd. of Leith in Scotland during 1932 to a contract placed by the government of Belgium for a sail training vessel. At the same time the Belgian government terminated its subsidies, which were now considered too great to represent a useful return on the investment, for the altogether larger *L'Avenir*, the 2,754-ton four-masted and steel-hulled barque which had been built in Germany during 1908 as the third ship owned by ASMAR (Association Maritime Belge) of Antwerp as a cargo-carrying vessel which also undertook the sail-training role. This cessation of subsidy forced the sale of the barque to the Hamburg-America Linie as the *Admiral Karpfanger*.

The *Mercator* was completed with a steel hull and an auxiliary diesel engine driving a single propeller. At the end of her four-day maiden voyage, on delivery from Leith to Ostend, the *Mercator* limped into port with her rigging all slack and decidedly down by the head as a result of the flooding of a forward compartment. In this initial and not very successful form, the vessel was rigged as a topsail schooner, carrying on her foremast a course, single topsail and single topgallant as well as a fore-and-aft foresail, but was then extensively revised before re-emerging from repairs at a French yard as a barquentine with her foremast now carrying a course, lower and upper topsails and a topgallant.

The Mercator was of typical barquentine rig, and therefore had square sails only on her foremast.

This transformed the vessel's capabilities, and during the 1930s she made no fewer than 22 sail-training voyages, including several return passages across the Atlantic. During February 1940 the barquentine called in the Belgian Congo on the west coast of Africa while returning from South America. Germany invaded and conquered Belgium, as well as the Netherlands and France, from May 10 of the same year, so the *Mercator* was kept in West Africa and placed in service for hydrographic rather than training work along the somewhat poorly charted coast of West Africa. The *Mercator* was transferred to the Royal Navy in 1943 for continued service, in this instance as a submarine depot ship in Sierra Leone, and finally returned to Belgian control only in 1948, three years after the end of World War II. The *Mercator* required considerable refurbishment, and therefore resumed her sail training role only in 1951. The *Mercator* retained her training role for some 10 more years before entering on a different but related final career on 1961 as a floating but still "sailable" museum ship administered by the Belgian transport ministry, first at Antwerp and later at Ostend, and also at Rotterdam in the neighboring Netherlands.

A photograph of the Mercator's foremast reveals the overlap of the mast and top mast as well as the mechanical link between the masts and the yards in place of the rope-and-truck parrel previously used for the same task.

Photo: John Batchelor.

Mercator

Type:	three-masted barquentine
Tonnage:	770 gross registered tons
Dimensions:	length 209 ft 9 in (63.9 m); beam 35 ft 0 in (10.7 m); depth in hold 16 ft 9 in (5.1 m)
Speed:	not available
Armament:	none
Complement:	100 men

Gorch Fock 1933

To replace its sail training vessel *Niobe*, a jackass-barque which sank in July 1932, the German navy was able to order a replacement partially funded by a public subscription. The result was the three-masted barque named *Gorch Fock*, which was the nom-de-plume of the poet Johann W. Kienau, born in Hamburg-Finkenwerder in 1880 and killed on the cruiser *Wiesbaden* at the Battle of Jutland in May 1916. The new vessel was laid down in January 1933 by the great Blohm und Voss shipbuilding company of Hamburg in north Germany, launched in May of the same year and commissioned a little less than eight weeks later on June 27. The vessel had a 360-hp (268-kW) or later 550-hp (410-kW) auxiliary engine driving a single propeller, the latter providing a speed of 7 kt, but her primary propulsion was provided by a sail plan totalling 19,989 sq ft (1857 m²) and comprising 23 sails including 10 square sails

for the fore and main masts. From 1936 there followed five near-sister ships, namely the *Horst Wessel*, *Albert Leo Shchlageter* and uncompleted *Herbert Norkus* for the German navy and the *Mircea* for the Romanian navy before World War II (1939-45), and the *Gorch Fock II* for the German navy in 1958. All but the Mircea were some 25 ft (7.6 m) longer than the *Gorch Fock*.

The vessels were built to the highest possible steel-hulled standard and with very fine lines, and particular emphasis was placed on their stability to avoid the type of capsizing that had caused the *Niobe's* loss. A number of innovatory features were incorporated, these including the use of many welded rather than riveted elements in the structure, and the use of prefabricated sections. The *Gorch Fock* was therefore built very rapidly and launched with her lower masts stepped, her topmasts in place and the standing rigging already set up. The sail plan was nicely conceived but

The original sail plan of the Gorch Fock included a single-gaff spanker and provision for six staysails between the fore and main masts, and the main and mizzen masts.

was not notably tall as the barque was designed to pass under the bridges over the Kiel Canal without striking her topmasts and upper yards. On the fore and main masts all of the vessels set a course, lower and upper topsails, a topgallant and a royal, but only the *Gorch Fock* had a single- rather than double-gaff spanker on the mizzenmast. Before the war the *Gorch Fock* sailed regularly on training cruises, mainly in the Baltic and North Seas together with once transatlantic voyage each year, with 66 permanent crew and 180 cadets, and remained in commission through most of the war before being scuttled off Stralsund by German army engineers, using demolition charges, on May 1, 1945. As part of the Allied division of German spoils, the USSR was allocated three German sail training vessels including the *Gorch Fock*. After two failed attempts, the vessel was raised in June 1947, repaired at Rostock in what was now East Germany, and then rebuilt at Wismar before entering Soviet service as the

Tovarich with a double-gaff spanker. This operated in the Black Sea with the *Mircea*, which the Soviets had captured from the Romanians in August 1944, and on the dissolution of the USSR in the early 1990s passed into the hands of the Ukrainians. In the early part of the 21st century Ukraine decided that the continued upkeep of the barque was too expensive for its economy, and in August 2003 passed the *Gorch Fock* back to German ownership in the form of the Tall-Ship Friends e.V.

Gorch Fock

Type:	three-masted sail training barque
Tonnage:	1,760 tons displacement
Dimensions:	length overall 269 ft 4 in (82.1 m); beam 39 ft 5 in (12.0 m); draught 17 ft 2 in (5.2 m)
Speed:	not available
Armament:	none
Complement:	66 men plus 180 cadets

St. Malo Fishing Boat 1935

Given the nature of the northwestern coast of France with waters that shoal rapidly and are both rocky and littered with offshore reefs, it was always very important for the fishing boats of the area to by notably sturdy and possess good sailing performance, especially in terms of windward performance so that they could claw their way off a lee shore. This was especially true of the traditional fishing boats of St. Malo, which were capable sailing craft that survived into the 1930s.

The key features of the design were its rig and also its robust and fully decked hull with ver-

tical stem, comparatively flat bottom over the forward part of the hull and a deep run ending in a cut-off transom stern occupied by the helmsman at the tiller of the powerful rudder. The sailing rig was based on a notably tall and slightly forward-raked mast, the latter comprising a lower mast supported on each side by a pair of shrouds and a topmast without any support. This carried a gaff main sail, which was of the boomed type with an area of 484.4 sq ft (45.0 m²), a battened lower leech and four sets of reef points. Above this was a jib-seated staysail with an area of 158.2 sq ft (14.7 m²). The fore triangle was filled by a staysail with an area of 87.7 sq ft (8.15 m²), and above the very long bowsprit could be set any of three jibs with an area thereby variable between 52.75 and 247.6 sq ft (4.9 and 23.0 m²) to suit the conditions.

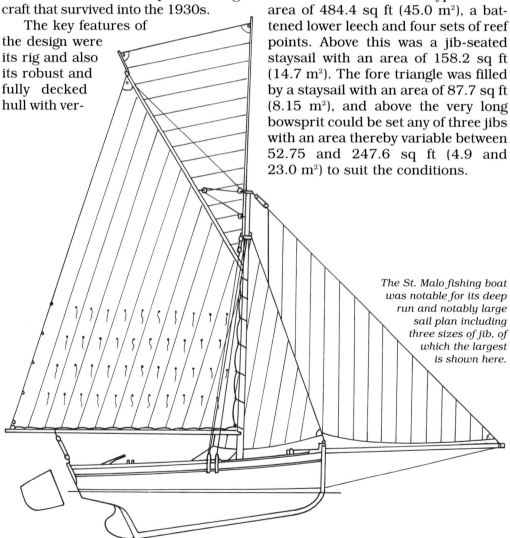

The St. Malo fishing boat was notable for its deep run and notably large sail plan including three sizes of jib, of which the largest is shown here.

Included in the equipment carried by each boat was a wooden dinghy. This was generally some 9 ft 10 in (3.0 m) long and quite wide in the beam, and had three thwarts. The St. Malo fishing boat was built completely of wood other than metal fastening and fixtures, and the precise nature of the structure and even the details of their vessels were jealously guarded secrets of the families which built them. Only in this way, they believed, could they maintain exclusivity in the features which gave their particular vessels a perceived advantage over other vessels and therefore, it was felt, a useful commercial edge.

The St. Malo fishing boat was well ballasted, and therefore did not heel strongly even in a stiff breeze.

St. Malo fishing boat

Type:	single-masted fishing boat
Tonnage:	7 tons displacement
Dimensions:	length overall 26 ft 1 in (7.95 m); waterline length 24 ft 5 in (7.45 m); beam 9 ft 8 in (2.95 m); draught 4 ft 9 in (1.45 m)
Speed:	not available
Armament:	none
Complement:	3 or 4 men

Cap Pilar 1937

A wooden-hulled barquentine built in St. Malo, northwestern France, by G. Gauthier during the course of 1911, the *Cap Pilar* was designed as a vessel to become part of the French cod-fishing fleet over the Grand Banks off Newfoundland. Named after an inhospitable spur of land jutting out into the Pacific Ocean at the western end of the Strait of Magellan, not far from Cape Horn at the southern end of Chile's long coast, the *Cap Pilar* was bought in 1936 from Louis Laisney by Adrian Seligman, a well experienced British sailing man who had served for three years in Gustaf Erikson's fleet of Finnish-flagged sailing vessels, including the *Olivebank*, a steel-hulled four-masted barque of 2,824 gross registered tons built by Mackie & Thompson of Glasgow in 1892 as the sister of the *Cedarbank* for Andrew Weir and Company, which later became the Bank Line.

The *Olivebank* sailed in the general trade role over a period of 21 years, carrying cargoes (including coal, nitrate and wheat) to Europe and the Pacific ports of South America. In 1913 the vessel passed into the ownership of Akties Olivebank of Norway, which retained the vessel in general trade for three years, but in 1916-22 the vessel was sold another three times, the last to a Norwegian owner who renamed her as the *Caledonia*, laid up at Sandefjord in Norway for 18 months before she found a new owner, the Finnish Gustav Erikson who operated the last significant fleet of square-rigged ships. Erikson resumed the name *Olivebank*, and used the vessel in the Australian grain trade. The vessel was a poor sailer but much liked, and during the late 1920s carried cadets for the Lithuanian merchant marine. Inward bound off Jutland, on September 8, 1939, just a week after the start of World War II (1939-45), the *Olivebank* struck a mine and went down with 14 of her crew.

Even before he had the *Cap Pilar*, Seligman advertised for six crew to join him and his fiancée on a voyage

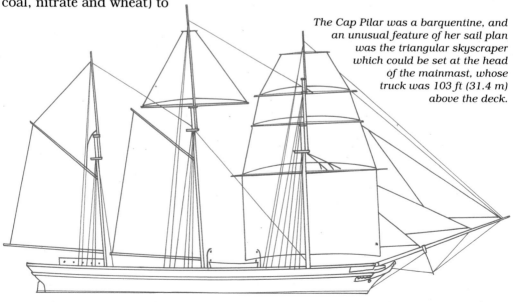

The Cap Pilar was a barquentine, and an unusual feature of her sail plan was the triangular skyscraper which could be set at the head of the mainmast, whose truck was 103 ft (31.4 m) above the deck.

*In 1937-38, after a career in the cod fishing and general trading roles,
the Cap Pilar was used as a "yacht" for a round-the-world honeymoon voyage.*

round the world. On September 29, 1937, the *Cap Pilar* sailed from London with a crew of 19 whose experienced hands included Seligman himself and an Erikson shipmate, Lars Paersch. The *Cap Pilar* sailed south through the Atlantic Ocean with halts at Madeira, Tenerife, Cape Verde, Rio de Janeiro, Tristan da Cunha, Cape Town, and Simons Town, the crew changing periodically. After an eastward passage to Sydney in Australia, the vessel sailed in short stages across the South Pacific Ocean via Auckland, where Mrs. Seligman gave birth to a daughter, the Gambier and Marquesas Islands, Peru, and the Galápagos Islands, before passing through the Panama Canal and thence to Jamaica, the Cayman Islands, New York and Halifax. The *Cap Pilar* reached England once more on September 12, 1938 at Falmouth.

The vessel was to be sold to the Nautical College of Haifa in Palestine during 1939, but this plan was terminated on the outbreak of World War II and the *Cap Pilar* was sadly left to rot at Wyvenhoe.

Cap Pilar

Type:	three-masted fishing and trading barquentine
Tonnage:	295 gross registered tons
Dimensions:	length 117 ft 10 in (35.9 m); beam 27 ft 6 in (8.4 m); depth in hold 12 ft 9 in (3.9 m)
Speed:	not available
Armament:	none
Complement:	19 or 20 men

Amerigo Vespucci 1931

In the late 1920s the Italian navy decided to order a pair of identical sail training ships to give officer cadets a thorough experience of working a ship at sea under all weather conditions. These two sister ships were the *Cristoforo Colombo* and *Amerigo Vespucci* to a design based on a 74-gun third-rate line-of-battle ship and ordered from the Royal Shipyard at Castellamare di Stabia near Naples. The *Amerigo Vespucci* was launched on March 22, 1930 and commissioned on May 15, 1931.

Though based on a three-masted ship design from the days of sailing navies, the two new vessels had a number of more modern features including a steel hull, steel masts and yards, lower and upper topgallants in place of a single topgallant, auxiliary power in the form of a 1,900-hp (1417-kW) Fiat/Marelli diesel-electric arrangement powering a single shaft for a speed of 10.5 kt, and a number of other more modern devices including, in recent years, two navigation and surface-search radars. The *Cristoforo Colombo* was named after the Genoese explorer who, in Spanish service, became the first European since the time of the Vikings to reach the Americas, while the *Amerigo Vespucci* was named after the Florentine explorer for whom the 16th century German cartographer Martin Waldseemüller named the newly discovered transatlantic lands to the west of Europe.

Derived from those of a warship, the full lines which characterized the *Cristoforo Colombo* and *Amerigo Vespucci* were singularly different from those of most sail-training vessels of the time, which were based on more recent experience and therefore

The only truly discordant feature of the Amerigo Vespucci is the tall funnel beneath the main staysails.

possessed the finer lines typical of 19th century trading ships. The two ships were completed with hulls of black broken by two broad longitudinal bands of white along the positions where the two gun decks would have been, and dotted with ports purposefully designed to give the impression of gun ports. The ships' bows and sterns were elaborately decorated with a mass of gingerbread gilt work and large figureheads, and included in each ship's complement were no fewer than 40 servants to cater to the comfort of 150 cadets. The ships were each square rigged on three masts, and the total plain sail area (26 square and fore-and-aft sails) was some 30,400 sq ft (2824 m²), and the height of the mainmast truck above deck level was 151 ft (46.0 m). All of the sails were of traditional heavy and closely woven canvas, and the standing and running rigging, extending to an overall length of some 18.6 miles (30 km), was of vegetable (hemp) cordage. Only in comparatively recent times was a measure of synthetic material introduced for the mooring lines to comply with modern port regulations.

After the end of World War II (1939-45), the *Cristoforo Colombo* was allocated to the USSR as part of Italy's war reparations and renamed as the *Dunai*, but soon discarded, whereas the *Amerigo Vespucci* was retained by the Italian navy and has continued in sail-training service with voyages to many parts of the world. The *Amerigo Vespucci* is currently the only three-decked square-rigged ship in existence.

Amerigo Vespucci

Type:	three-masted sail-training ship
Tonnage:	4,146 tons full load
Dimensions:	length overall 270 ft 0 in (82.4 m); beam 51 ft 0 in (15.5 m); draught 22 ft 0 in (7.0 m)
Speed:	not available
Armament:	none
Complement:	285 men plus 165 cadets

Gratitude 1957

The Swedish Cruising Club Sail Training Foundation was created at Göteborg in 1957 to teach young people the arts of sailing and navigation. The foundation owns three gaff ketches in the form of the *Gratitude*, 97 ft 3 in (29.6 m) *Gratia* and 86 ft 0 in (26.2 m) Atlantica. The oldest of these is the *Gratitude*, which was conceived as a sailing trawler and built of oak at Porthleven in Cornwall, southwest England, during 1903. In 1932 she was sold, still for fishing, to a Swedish owner who renamed her as the *Ostanvag*. Four years later she received her first engine, and in 1945 she was subjected to a major refit before re-emerging as a cargo vessel for continued commercial service in Swedish coastal waters up to 1952 or thereabouts. The *Ostanvag* was then laid up, sold several times, and during this time steadily deteriorated until, in 1956, she was lying at Hono, to the west of Göteborg, before being broken up. This ketch-rigged vessel was saved at the last moment, in 1958, by the newly formed foundation, which arranged for the vessel to be towed to the shipyard at Nordviksstrand, and here the hull and deck were completely restored, the interior was converted into accommodation, a new diesel engine was installed, and the original gaff-ketch rig was restored. In this form the *Ostanvag* now became the *Gratitude* once more.

The Gratitude is one of three ketches operated by the Swedish Cruising Club Sail Training Foundation to provide young people, especially teenagers, with experience of sailing and navigating.

The *Gratitude* started work as a sail-training vessel in 1959, and is still in service as one of the oldest and longest-serving traditional vessels involved with the youth sail training concept.

The *Gratia* was the foundation's second vessel, and is the oldest of the three as she was designed by A. E. Payne and built by H. S. Hansen & Co. of Cowes in 1900 as a classic Victorian gaff yawl yacht with the name *Bertha*. She was later renamed *Aziade* and then *Blue Shadow* before being laid up at Svendborg in Denmark during the early 1930s. In 1936 she was bought by the Swedish ship-owner Einar Hansen, who renamed her *Cinderella*. The yacht was refitted at Svendborg in 1936-38 with a new teak deck, refurbished accommodation and two-masted schooner rig. Hansen owned the *Cinderella* for 26 years before giving her to the foundation in 1964. Revised for a crew of seven and 18 trainees, the vessel was renamed *Gratia* and in 1974 revised as a gaff ketch.

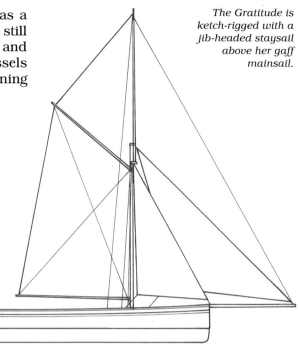

The *Gratitude* is ketch-rigged with a jib-headed staysail above her gaff mainsail.

In 1979 the foundation decided to build a new vessel and, because of its success with the sailing trawler concept, opted for a similar design for the *Atlantica*, which is in essence a scaled-up *Gratitude*. The foundation placed its 1980 order with the Karstensens yard in Denmark, and the *Atlantica* (so named for the insurance company which made the single largest contribution to her building cost) was completed in October 1981 with accommodation for a crew of seven and up to 24 trainees.

Gratitude

Type:	two-masted sail training ketch
Tonnage:	100 tons displacement
Dimensions:	length overall 77 ft 9 in (23.7 m); waterline length 68 ft 7 in (20.9 m); beam 19 ft 8 in (6.0 m); draught 9 ft 6 in (2.9 m)
Speed:	not available
Armament:	none
Complement:	7 persons plus 20 trainees

Chesapeake Bay Skipjack 1960

In the middle of the 19th century, the standard workboat of the great Chesapeake Bay on the eastern seaboard of the USA was the sharpie. This had originated in about 1830 as an oyster dredger in the area around New Haven in Connecticut. The sharpie was a flat-bottomed type with single chines and a large retractable centerboard of wooden construction, and was a versatile design that was built in hull lengths between 30 and 60 ft (9.1 and 18.3 m) according to the specific requirement, and with a ketch rig with jib-headed sail but no headsails. The type's concept soon moved south along the coast to Chesapeake Bay, where it gained great popularity.

From about 1860 the sharpie was comparatively swiftly replaced by the skipjack as the standard workboat of Chesapeake Bay and other parts of the USA's eastern coast. The original name was *bateau* (the French word for boat), and the adoption of the name skipjack seems to have come soon after 1900, for no discernible reason. The skipjack was again a utilitarian design with a hard-chine hull and of basically wooden construction with a large wooden centerboard, but was sloop-rigged on a single mast with a jib-headed mainsail of notably low aspect ratio (short luff and long foot) running up and down the mast on hoops so that it could be dropped quickly in the event of a squall's

Skipjacks in the shallow waters of Chesapeake Bay in light airs.

A skipjack converted as a comfortable cruising yacht.

approach, and a self-tending foresail set on a long bowsprit: the result was very easy manning requirements and therefore economy of operation. In its classic form as a workboat, the skipjack had it mast raked well back, by as much as 25°, so that the main halyard could be used to hoist cargo on board. With a wide, shallow-draught hull and a comparatively generous sail area, the skipjack could sail in air light that other types could make no headway, and therefore gained a great popularity that was enhanced by its ability to turn almost on a sixpence.

The skipjack reached the peak of its popularity in 1901, when there were perhaps 2,000 such craft on Chesapeake Bay, but thereafter declined in importance, many of the craft being snapped up for conversion as very comfortable yachts as their commercial owners disposed of them. The main change in this process was a significant reduction in the mast's rearward rake. In 2002 only some dozen or so skipjacks were still working as oyster dredgers.

Skipjack (typical)	
Type:	single-masted oyster-dredging and general-purpose sloop
Displacement:	not available
Dimensions:	length overall 38 to 45 ft (11.6 to 13.7 m); beam not available; draught not available
Speed:	not available
Armament:	none
Complement:	2 or 3 men

Sir Winston Churchill and Malcolm Miller 1967

Virtually identical schooners owned and operated by the Sail Training Association up to 2000 for the sail training of young Britons, the *Sir Winston Churchill* and *Malcolm Miller* are three-masted topsail schooners designed by Camper & Nicholson and built on the basis of a steel hull and three single-piece aluminium alloy masts of identical height with their heads 97 ft 9 in (29.8 m) above the deck. The vessels each carry 7,104 sq ft (660 m²) of working canvas in the form of 14 sails. The vessels typically carry a gaff mainsail and jib-headed topsail on the fore mast and main mast, a Bermuda mainsail on the mizzenmast, and up to four fore sails in the form of a boomed staysail and one, two or three jibs set on the bowsprit. An option is up to two square sails, in the form of a course and a topsail, on the fore mast. Forsafety reasons and the requirements of maneuvring in the confined waters of ports, the design incorporated an auxiliary powerplant driving two propellers. The ships

were designed to be sailed easily and safely by a reduced crew in the event of heavy weather, which would probably incapacitate the trainees, but also to have a good turn of speed.

The slightly older of the two vessels is the *Sir Winston Churchill*, which was laid down on November 21, 1966 Dunstons Scarr Shipyard at Hessle-on-the-Humber, close to Kingston-upon-Hull. Just before the vessel was launched, late in 1954, she was toppled on the ways and had all three of her masts broken, but this did not impose a major delay in the programme and the schooner entered service early in 1965, as originally planned. The second vessel is the *Malcolm Miller*, so named in honor of the son of Sir James Miller, a former Lord Mayor of London and the current Mayor of Edinburgh, whose financial donation allowed the start of work on the new schooner at the Aberdeen yard of

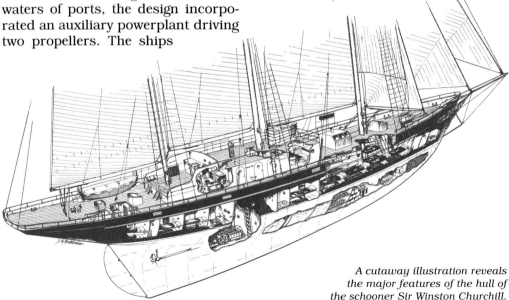

A cutaway illustration reveals the major features of the hull of the schooner Sir Winston Churchill.

John Lewis & Sons, Ltd. in 1967, with the new schooner completed in the following year. The two schooners were homeported at Portsmouth, and though they sometimes sailed together, main in tall ships races, they generally cruised separately in British and European waters, between them completing some 30 cruises each year and carrying about 1,260 young people.

The success of the *Sir Winston Churchill* and *Malcolm Miller* in catching the attention of an ever-increasing number of young persons was reflected in the decision late in the 20th century to replace them on the strength of the Sail Training Association, now incorporated within the Tall Ships Youth Trust, by a pair of larger brig-rigged vessels. Thus the two vessels were sold in 2001 and 2000 respectively as they were replaced by the newly built *Prince William* and *Stavros S. Niarchos*.

Built at the Appledore Shipyard in 2000-01, these are the largest sailing vessels built in the United Kingdom for more than 100 years, and each have a crew comprising a six salaried and 13 volunteer personnel as well as up to 48 trainees. The vessels are brig-rigged with 18 sails available for 10 yards on two masts to a maximum area of 12,508 sq ft (1162 m²), and there are more than 9 miles (14.5 km) of wire and rope in the standing and

The schooner Sir Winston Churchill under easy sail as she sails to windward.

running rigging. Each of the brigs has an overall length of 195 ft 0 in (59.4 m), waterline length of 133 ft 3 in (40.6 m), beam of 32 ft 6 in (9.9 m), draught of 14 ft 9 in (4.5 m) and mast head height of 147 ft 8 in (45.0 m). The tonnages are 493 gross registered tons and 635 tons displacement, and the brig had made more than 13 kt under sail, with 10 kt available from the two 445-hp (330-kW) MTU auxiliary diesel engines.

Winston Churchill

Type:	three-masted sail training topsail schooner
Tonnage:	328 tons displacement
Dimensions:	length overall 134 ft 9 in (41.1 m); waterline length 103 ft 1 in (31.4 m); beam 24 ft 9 in (7.5 m); draught 16 ft 1 in (4.9 m)
Speed:	not available
Armament:	none
Complement:	7 persons plus 40 trainees

HMS Rose 1970

Bearing one of the names used most frequently in British naval service, the first such vessel dating back to 1322, HMS *Rose* was a 24-gun frigate built by Hugh Blades of Hull in South Yorkshire from 1756 and commissioned in the following year as one of the "Seaford" class of the Royal Navy's smallest rated fighting ships. Completed at the outset of the Seven Years' War (1756-63), the *Rose* was employed primarily for patrolling the coast of France, in the course of which she made several attacks on French harbors, and in Caribbean operations, in which she was involved in the capture of Havana from the Spanish and Martinique from the French. In 1768, the ship was considered for possible service in Captain James Cook's first South Seas expedition, but could not be made ready in time and therefore replaced by HMS *Endeavour*. Later in

the same year, the *Rose* was dispatched to the coast of North America under the command of Captain Sir Benjamin Caldwell, and was notably active in the impressments of seamen from merchant ships.

In 1774 the *Rose* was dispatched to Narragansett Bay under Captain James Wallace to suppress the smuggling trade which had been largely instrumental in elevating Newport, Rhode Island, to the position of fourth richest city in the American colonies. She was so successful that the merchants of Newport were forced to appeal to Rhode Island's colonial legislature for the formation of a navy to combat the frigate, while they themselves fitted out the merchant sloop *Katy*, which they renamed as the *Providence*, to patrol their waters while Rhode Island, in its own turn, requested the Continental Congress of

The Rose is a near replica of the smallest type of British frigate of the middle of the 17th century.

With her high bowsprit and comparatively simple sail plan, the Rose exemplifies the smaller type of warship in the definitive period of sail.

the rebellious colonies to establish a Continental Navy. In July 1776 the *Rose* was involved in the British campaign to expel General George Washington's Continental Army from New York, and also saw action against shore batteries along the Hudson river.

In 1779 the *Rose* aided the defence of Savannah, Georgia, which the British had just captured but was now threatened with attack by a French fleet. On September 9, 1779 the *Rose* was scuttled to block the river and so prevent a French naval advance. The city remained in British hands until the end of the American Revolution in 1782, when the hulk of the *Rose* was broken up so that regular mercantile commerce could start once more.

In 1970 John Fitzhugh Millar ordered a replica of the ship, for the US bicentennial of 1976, from a Canadian builder, the Smith and Ruland Shipyard of Lunenburg, Nova Scotia. The ship had fallen into a state of considerable disrepair by the late 1970s, but the new *Rose* was then bought by Kaye Williams and towed to Captain's cove Seaport in Black Rock Harbor, Connecticut. The ship was then restored by the HMS Rose Foundation from 1985, and took part in the centennial celebrations for the Statue of Liberty. Further work completed the repair of the hull and the addition of two new auxiliary diesel engines. The ship was then placed in service as a sail training vessel and dockside attraction, voyaging from her base at Bridgeport, Connecticut, to ports from the Great Lakes to Europe as the USA's largest sailing school vessel.

HMS *Rose*

Type:	three-masted frigate
Displacement:	430 tons
Dimensions:	length 108 ft 0 in (32.9 m); beam 30 ft 1 in (9.2 m); draught 9 ft 6 in (2.9 m)
Speed:	not available
Armament:	20 9-pdr guns
Complement:	160 men

Eagle 1980

Built by Blohm und Voss of Hamburg in 1936, the *Horst Wessel* was launched on June 30, 1936 and later commissioned as a German sail training vessel. Among her features were a sail area of 21,345 sq ft (1985 m²) with 22 sails, and the fore and main mast trucks were each 150 ft 0 in (45.7 m) above sea level, and the yards for the fore and main courses were each 78 ft 9 in (24.0 m) long. The vessel had some than 20 miles (32 km) of standing and running rigging, and also an auxiliary diesel engine providing a speed of 10 kt. The hull was fabricated of steel plates 0.4 in (10 mm) thick, and included two full-length steel decks, with a platform deck below and a raised forecastle and quarterdeck above. The weather decks were also of steel under an upper layer of teak 3 in (75 mm) thick.

This *Horst Wessel* was the second of four near-sister barques, whose other units were the *Gorch Fock* (later the Soviet *Tovarich*), *Albert Leo Schlageter* (later the Portuguese *Sagres*) and Romanian *Mircea*. The *Horst Wessel* made only a few training voyages up to 1939, and during World War II (1939-45) saw useful service as a transport and training vessel in the Baltic. After the end of World War II, the USA acquired the vessel as part of Germany's war reparations. The barque was allocated to the US Coast Guard, which had made considerable and notably successful use of the Danish training ship *Danmark*, built for the training of mercantile marine officers, in the course of World War II

The elegant barque Eagle of the US Coast Guard is here depicted under slightly shortened sail.

Dressed for the occasion, this is the Eagle on a visit to Weymouth on the south coast of England.

Quite fittingly, the figurehead of the Eagle is a gilt eagle also emblematic of the USA.

and thus welcomed the advent of its own vessel. Renamed as the USCGB *Eagle*, the vessel was homeported at the US Coast Guard Academy in New London, Connecticut, and became the seventh vessel of the name to serve the USA, the first having been a vessel commissioned in 1792, a mere two years after the establishment of the Revenue Marine, which was the forerunner of the US Coast Guard.

Commissioned into US service on May 15, 1946 and homeported on the Thames River in New London, the *Eagle* was for many years one of a very limited number of sail training vessels of any size in the USA. Right from the beginning she proved herself invaluable in the all-important task of inculcating in young men and, later, young women, an elemental understanding of the sea and the wind, and also the vital importance of team

efforts as any major maneuve requires the co-ordinated movement of more than 200 lines. For more than 50 years, now, the *Eagle* has shown the "Stars and Stripes" of the USA in ports throughout the Americas and also in Europe and other parts of the world. It was on the express instruction of President John F. Kennedy that the *Eagle* have her hull painted in a color scheme (orange chevron and blue shield) over the white hull of smaller US Coast Guard cutters, and this is now a characteristic of all US Coast Guard vessels. The vessel usually makes two cruises each summer, the academy's first and third classes having a long voyage to somewhere in South America or Europe, and the second and fourth classes having a shorter cruise. All the trainees sleep in hammocks.

USCGB *Eagle*

Type:	three-masted sail training barque
Tonnage:	1,816 tons full load
Dimensions:	length overall 295 ft 0 in (89.9 m); waterline length 231 ft 0 in (70.4 m); beam 39 ft 1 in (11.0 m); draught 17 ft 0 in (5.2 m)
Speed:	17 kt
Armament:	none
Complement:	65 persons plus 180 trainees

Bali Jukung 2000

In its sense as a fairly substantial piece of wood held out from one or other side, or indeed each side, of a canoe-like hull of great length to beam ratio to provide a considerable degree of additional stability when under sail in stiff breeze, the outrigger has a venerable and important history. It is believed that the origins of the outrigger lie in Southeast Asia, and thence extended through the local archipelagos to reach the Indian and Pacific Oceans, allowing the spread of the local cultures into deep-water and even transoceanic voyages. Yet the outrigger is marvellously simple and economical in concept and execution, for outrigger canoes effectively combine the attributes of the compartmented bamboo pole to float, the stability of the multi-hull notion of hull layout, and the simplicity and straightforward manufacture of the dug-out log canoe, the whole very considerably exceeding the sums of the individual components.

From this it might be imagined that the outrigger canoe would almost inevitably have followed a simple evolutionary process that would have reduced variations to an absolute minimum. Yet this was and indeed is still not the case, and the variations on the theme of the outrigger canoe are enormous not just in detail but in a number of fundamental and also geographical ways.

One of the most elegant and also efficient variations of the basic concept

The jukung is light, handy and fast, but has poor windward performance,
the Balinese always gybing rather than tacking and using currents
and other expedients to move their craft up to windward.

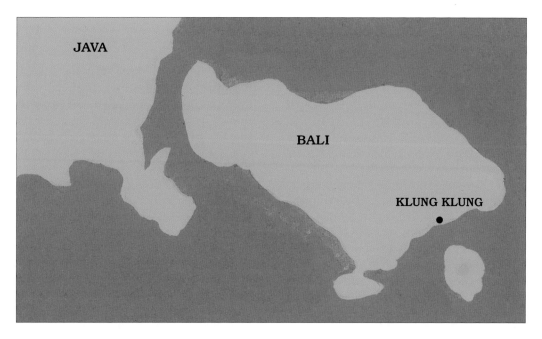

Bali lies to the east of Java, and one of the jukung havens is Klung Klung.

is to be found in the *jukung* used by the islanders of Bali in the Indonesian archipelago. In keeping with virtually every aspect of Balinese culture, the *jukung* is characterized by the bringing of a high degree of elegance to what is in effect a completely utilitarian type of coastal craft. Classic examples of this type of craft about in the small community of Klung Klung. Here the *jukung* is based on a central canoe crafted out of a log of belalu wood. This is a light softwood which can be worked easily, with obvious advantages in the fabrication of this core unit, but requires that the *jukung* must be allowed to dry thoroughly between voyages. The central canoe can have its sides raised by single strakes on each side, and is completed in structural terms by V-shaped pieces at the stem and stern, all adzed from solid wood and joined, where necessary, by treenails. The hull is always beautifully painted, the bow normally depicting an open-mouthed predatory fish.

The *jukung* is know as a five-part canoe, and the other four parts are the two outriggers and the two cross beams. The outriggers are selected from bamboo poles with a diameter of some 6 in (15 cm), with the right curvature to lift their fronts and backs out of the water by an identical distance in each float, and are painted to prevent them from absorbing water. The outriggers are connected to the central hull by a pair of cross-armed adzed from sturdy waru wood, with grown shapes selected to provide the right gull-wing curve out and up from the hull before curving down to the outriggers. Again symmetry, this time lateral rather than longitudinal, is all-important. The *jukung* is completed by its triangular sail now made from strips of cheap woven plastic material, its luff and foot supported by light and flexible bamboo spars, and the whole assembly is balanced on a short mast set well forward. Steering is effected with a steering oar.

301

Wilhelm Pieck and Greif 1975

Built in 1951 on the basis of a steel hull, the *Greif* was the first sail training ship built in Germany after World War II (1939-45), and was also the first new-build training brigantine to enter service anywhere in the word during the period after World War II's conclusion. The brigantine was designed by Wilhelm Schröder as a two-masted topsail schooner. Intended as the East German state yacht, the vessel was to have been built as a gift from the population of Mecklenburg to Wilhelm Pieck, the first president of the German Democratic Republic (East Germany) on the occasion of his 75th birthday. The bitter irony of the whole notion was that Pieck, as young social democratic leader of the 20th century's earlier stages, had been among those who spoke out most harshly and bitterly against the expenditure of last sums of public money on yachts for Kaiser Wilhelm II while the German empire still existed. In this circumstance, therefore, it was hardly surprising that Pieck said that the new vessel should instead be completed for the young people of East Germany

for sail training service. The vessel was therefore considerably adapted internally to provide the required accommodation and equipment, and the rig was changed to that of a brigantine with 6,135 sq ft (570 m²) of canvas carried by a mainmast (four square sails with provision at the very top for a triangular skyscraper) and a mizzenmast (gaff mainsail and jib-headed topsail) as well as fore sails.

The *Wilhelm Pieck* was the first vessel of steel construction to be built in East Germany after World War II. The vessel was laid down at the Warnow Shipyard at Warnemünde on February 27, 1951, launched on May 26, of the same year, and completed on August 2, still in the same year. Given the number of German ships which had been sunk in World War II or seized by the victorious Allied powers, and the parlous state of the East German economy as this communist state was rebuilt from the ravages of the war, the *Wilhelm Pieck* was one of only three sea-going vessels then wearing the East German flag. The brigantine's primary task was the training of young seamen for the service in the new East German navy and merchant marine, and generally she undertook short training voyages within the confines of the Baltic Sea, although later, in 1957, she sailed some 9,2000 miles (14805 km) from East Germany round western Europe to pass through the Dardanelles and Bosporus to enter the Black Sea. With East Germany's steadily growing

The Greif is of the classic brigantine rig, square rigged on the mainmast and fore-and-aft rigged on the mizzenmast, and with a long bowsprit setting a number of jib sails.

determination to be seen as a member of the community of nations in her own right, the *Wilhelm Pieck* took part for the first (and in fact only) time in a Sail Training Association "Tall Ships Race" during 1974. During her service under the East German flag, the *Wilhelm Pieck* GDR flag she sailed about 129,000 miles (207600 km), and was instrumental on the training of some 6,000 young people for a life at sea.

When the East and West parts of Germany were reunified in October 1990, the brigantine's continued existence seemed problematical give the fact that West Germany was contributing a greater number of larger ships to the combined training effort. However, a campaign to save the brigantine was launched in her home port of Greifswald with the active support of local political figures and the Pamir-Passat Foundation of Lübeck. This effort was successful, and in February 1991 the *Wilhelm Pieck* was given to Greifswald and renamed as the *Greif* (griffin), a fact signalled by the depiction of a griffin on her fore topgallant.

In 1991 the *Greif* underwent a major refit in Rostock. Her hull and rig remained unaltered, but internally she was completely refurbished and new auxiliary machinery was installed. In this improved form the *Greif* returned to trailing service as a sail training vessel for young people of both sexes up to the age of 16. After a period of more than 50 years in continuous training service under sail, she is still in superb condition and a magnificent example of the brigantine.

The Greif is seen here in her original form as the East German Wilhelm Pieck, running easily before a quartering breeze.

Greif

Type:	two-masted sail training brigantine
Tonnage:	not available
Dimensions:	length: 134 ft 6 in (41.0 m); beam 25 ft 0 in (7.6 m); draught 11 ft 10 in (3.60 m)
Speed:	not available
Armament:	none
Complement:	14 persons plus 30 trainees

Sagres

The barque *Sagres II* is the naval sail training replacement of the original Sagres, which had been built in 1860 at Bremerhaven in Germany as the *Rickmer Rickmers*, and underwent several changes of name before being bought by the Portuguese navy as the *Sagres*, so named for the town near Cape St. Vincent in which Prince Henry "the Navigator" established the first European school of navigation in the 15th century. The *Sagres* served until 1962, and is now a museum vessel in Hamburg under her original name. For some time, the *Sagres II* has been easily the most readily identifiable of the world's surviving "tall ships" as a result of the distinctive red crosses on her square sails.

The origins of the vessel are not Portuguese, however, for the barque was launched on October 30, 1937, at the Blohm und Voss shipyard in Hamburg, as the German navy's sail training vessel *Albert Leo Schlageter*, a barque with 20,410 sq ft (1896 m²) of canvas. Damaged by mines during World War II (1939-45), the vessel was laid up and seized at Bremerhaven by US forces as World War II ended. Since the USA had her undamaged sister ship, which became the US Coast Guard service's *Eagle*, in 1948 the *Albert Leo Schlageter* was sold to Brazil to become that nation's sail training vessel *Guanabara*, which remained in service up to 1961. In that year the vessel was sold to

The Sagres II is readily identifiable from her sister ships by the red crosses on her square sails.

the Portuguese navy, which renamed her as the *Sagres II* and homeported her at Alfeite, near Lisbon.

The steel-hulled ship undertakes two training cruises each year in a form that now includes 23 sails carried on three masts, of which the main mast rises to 146 ft (44.5 m) above the waterline. The vessel also has a 50-hp (559-kW) auxiliary diesel powerplant, which provides a speed of 10.5 kt. The hull is painted white with a blue stripe, and her mizzenmast carries three fore-and-aft sails. Another distinctive feature is the small exhaust pipe for spent gases from the diesel engine: this is located at the forward end of the long poop, which extends almost to the main mast. Four large lifeboats, two to a side, hang from davits or rest atop a small deckhouse at the after end of the forecastle.

Sagres II	
Type:	three-masted sail training barque
Tonnage:	1,784 gross registered tons
Dimensions:	length overall 295 ft 3 in (90.0 m); waterline length 231 ft 0 in (70.4 m); beam 39 ft 5 in (12.0 m); draught: 17 ft 0 in (5.2 m)
Speed:	not available
Armament:	none
Complement:	162 persons plus 90 cadets

Star Flyer and Star Clipper

Partnering the Star Clippers company's five-masted ship *Royal Clipper* in today's sail cruising role, which is becoming an aspect of increasing commercial importance as people seek to rediscover the adventure of sail without any sacrifice of creature comforts, are two slightly smaller barquentines. These are the sister vessels *Star Clipper* and the *Star Flyer*, which were built in a Dutch shipyard and launched in the early 1990s. These were created specifically for cruising under sail in the more benign, and therefore sunnier and warmer, waters of areas such as the Caribbean Sea and Indian Ocean. Like their larger compatriot, the vessels are Swedish-owned by the Fred. Olsen Travel Ltd. company and registered in Luxembourg after completion to the highest technical standard as certified by Lloyds. The vessels are based on a steel hull of notably fine lines, and

have an auxiliary powerplant based on one Caterpillar 12-cylinder diesel engine driving a single propeller. This ensures that in the event of unsatisfactory conditions the vessels can proceed under motor power to make the voyage as comfortable as possible for the passengers, and also to guarantee that timetables can be met.

As noted above, the vessels are barquentine-rigged on four masts, the mainmast rising to a height of 226 ft (68.9 m) and making these the tallest sailing ships currently in service anywhere in the world. As comfort rather than speed is the watchword of the vessels' operation, there is only a modest sail area. Thus these masts carry some 36,000 sq ft (3344 m²) of Dacron embodied in 16 sails including five square sails (course, lower and upper topsails, topgallant and royal) set on the fore mast, and there is also provision for four headsails as

A scene typical of the image projected by a cruising holiday on one of the "Star" class barquentines: sun, calm blue water, and the romance of the Far East.

well as seven fore-and-aft sails set on or between the four masts. This wardrobe of sails was specially designed for ease of handling, with the aid of several mechanical systems, by an operating crew of the smallest possible size.

The barquentines as based on a substantial hull designed for maximum volume and thus large public areas as well as comfortable staterooms and cabins. The hull has four decks, the uppermost being the Sun Deck divided between three blocks, of which the midships and after sections each incorporate a swimming pool and also a pair of large lifeboats in davits. The accommodation is organized with its most luxurious element (eight staterooms) on the Sun Deck and the Main Deck immediately below it, where there is also a piano bar, tropical bar and library. One level lower, on the Clipper Deck, is somewhat less costly accommodation of three standards as well as the dining and conference room, right aft, and the owner's suite. Finally, on the Commodore Deck, just above the waterline, are further passenger cabins in four classes.

The two "Star" class barquentines are seen in company under all plain sail.

The vessels were completed to the highest standards of comfort and facilities for both the passengers and crew, and all the latest mechanical and electronic equipment was incorporated to ensure safety and the smoothest possible sailing.

"Star" class barquentine

Type:	four-masted sail cruising barquentine
Tonnage:	3,025 gross registered tons
Dimensions:	length 360 ft 0 in (109.7 m); beam 50 ft 0 in (15.2 m); draught 18 ft 6 in (5.6 m)
Speed:	not available
Armament:	none
Complement:	70 persons plus 170 passengers

Mirabella V

Listed in 2005 in the *Guinness World Records* as the yacht, or perhaps "super yacht," holding three world records, the *Mirabella V* was designed in Ireland by Ron Holland Design and built in the United Kingdom by VT Halmatic at Southampton for the American Joe Vittoria, previously head of the Avis vehicle rental company, and charter-operated by Jacqui Beadon Yachts of France at a rate, at the beginning of 2005, of $250,000 per week excluding food, drink and a crew gratuity. Intended to provide both good performance, including a speed of 20 kt or more and a good windward capability under sail, the *Mirabella V* was designed from the outset in terms of superlatives. No expense was spared in the completion of this, the world's largest single-masted yacht, with the utmost of comforts and appointments for up to 12 very discerning and demanding charter customers, whose luxurious accommodation is entirely separate from the very comfortable and well appointed quarters for the 12 members of the crew. The crew have their own boats, and when these have been hoisted outboard, their under-deck wells can be filled to create a 20-person Jacuzzi and a 21-ft (6.4-m) swimming pool with a pump-created current to increase the apparent length of the pool.

Among the passenger facilities are extremely comfortable staterooms with full bathing facilities rather than showers, a saloon and other facilities including a 600-bottle wine cellar, an indoor/outdoor cinema, a gym, the Jacuzzi and dip pool mentioned above, as well as powered boats, jet-skis, sailing dinghies and diving gear. Passenger access to the yacht is provided

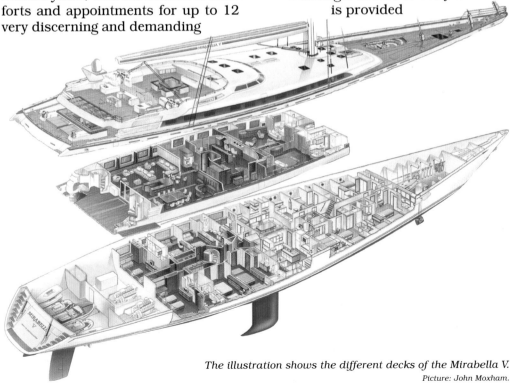

The illustration shows the different decks of the Mirabella V.
Picture: John Moxham.

by a launch with waterjet propulsion, and this uses a well accessed by a hatch in the transom.

The *Mirabella V* is a sloop of composite carbon and glass fiber construction including a carbon fiber mast, and among her many features are a keel which can be retracted to reduce the draught from 33 ft (10.0 m) to 13 ft (4.0 m). The *Mirabella V* is sloop-rigged with three forestays, and her sails were made by Doyle Sailmakers of the USA. Among these is the world's largest single sail, a genoa with an area of 19,730 sq ft (1833 m²). The other world-record figure for the *Mirabella V* is the height of her mast, which is 290 ft (88.5 m) supported by shrouds and four sets of jumper struts.

The operation of so large a craft by a small crew is facilitated by the careful design with three identical control positions in strategic locations, considerable use of TV cameras and both electric and hydraulic power, and a hydraulically powered platform able to lift three persons to a point near the masthead. All of the ropework and winches are located below deck, leaving the maximum possible area of clear deck for the passengers, and the yacht has no less than 54 miles (70 km) of electrical wiring as well as a desalinization plant capable of producing 30 tons of

Pictures show the difference in height between the Mirabella V and Nelson's Column. Picture of Mirabella V: Nevil Swinchatt.

fresh water per day. Naturally enough the yacht also has auxiliary diesel propulsion and electricity generating capability.

The *Mirabella V* was launched on November 26, 2003, and early assessment revealed that the yacht was within 1% of her weight estimate. The immense mast, somewhat taller than Nelson's Column in Trafalgar Square, was stepped in December of the same year with the sails first bent on during February 2004, and the yacht first set sail on April 15, 2004.

Mirabella V

Type:	super yacht
Displacement:	753 tons half load
Dimensions:	length 247 ft 0 in (75.2 m); beam 48 ft 6 in (14.8 m); draught 33 ft 0 in (10.0 m) with the keel lowered
Speed:	more than 20 kt
Complement:	12 plus provision for 12 passengers

Royal Clipper

In 1902 the largest and fastest sailing ship the world had ever seen was launched at the yard of J. C. Tecklenborg at Geestemünde in Germany. This vessel was the five-masted ship *Preussen* (Prussia), the second ship of this name built for one of the last and greatest of operators of sailing vessels, the Reederei F. Laeisz. The *Preussen* was one of only four five-masted square-rigged vessel, the only five-masted ship, and the largest ship without auxiliary engines ever to sail. The primary data for the *Preussen* included a tonnage of 5,081 gross registered tons, length of 407 ft 9 in (124.3 m), and complement of only 48 men.

A legend almost as soon as she took to the water, the *Preussen* dominated the final days of sail as an economic force to be reckoned with, but was lost after only a few years when she went aground on the southern coast of the England in 1910. It is arguable that neither before nor since has there been so magnificent a sailing ship. The only contenders of recent years are the three vessels of the Royal Clipper line. The first of these were the sisters *Star Clipper* and *Star Flyer*, four-masted barquentines of 2,298 tons, dimensions including a length of 360 ft 0 in (109.7 m), and 26,000 sq ft (3344 m²) of Dacron in 16 sails set on four masts reaching a maximum height of 226 ft 0 in (68.9 m). The ships each carry 170 passengers and a crew of 72.

These two vessels were later joined by an even more impressive third ship, the *Royal Clipper* which is the largest and only five-masted sailing ship built since the *Preussen*. Setting 42 Dacron sails with an area of 54,360 sq ft (5050 m²), the *Royal Clipper* is certainly an impressive

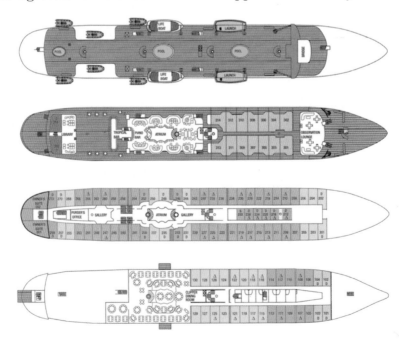

The four decks of the Royal Clipper used by passengers are, from top to bottom, the Sun Deck, Main Deck, Clipper Deck and Commodore Deck.

There is no doubt that the Royal Clipper is thoroughly modern in her construction, systems and appointments, but combined with a hull shape and a rig redolent of more leisurely times.

sight, but she is also a vessel very carefully conceived in terms of factors such as her state-of-the-art systems (including navigation and anti-roll tanks) and modern levels of accommodation and comfort.

For the devotees of cruising under sail, the *Royal Clipper* offers perhaps the final word by today's standards in sea-going experience and luxury, with an expression of sailing tradition served up with magnificent service, amenities and accommodations of the finest modern yachts. The *Royal Clipper* carries just 227 passengers. The deck area of 18,940 sq ft (1760 m²), studded with three swimming pools, provides a spacious open-air environment, and passengers can climb the masts to one of the comfortably appointed "crows-nests." Internally, the *Royal Clipper* is stunning, with a three-deck atrium that pours the light of the sun into smartly appointed dining room. Another feature is the marina platform which descends from the stern for water sports and diving. There is also the so-called Captain Nemo Lounge, which is laid out as a spa and health club, and features underwater glass portholes.

Royal Clipper

Type:	five-masted cruising holiday ship
Tonnage:	5,000 gross registered tons
Dimensions:	length 439 ft 0 in (133.8 m); beam 54 ft 0 in (16.5 m); draught 18 ft 6 in (5.6 m)
Speed:	not available
Armament:	none
Complement:	106 persons plus 227 passengers

Orcelle 2010

Given the likelihood of a decrease in the availability of fossil fuels and their rapid rise in cost, it is only sensible to consider the ways in which renewable energy can be exploited. So far as maritime transport is concerned, such energy sources are waves, wind and sun light, any or all of which are be considered for use in advanced-technology ships that could be used for the delivery of bulk cargoes which are not radically time-critical. Such a vessel would lack any conventional engines, and would therefore require no fossil fuel and release no noxious emissions into the air or sea. One of the first such vessels could well be a cargo ship to transport loads such as some 10,000 motor vehicles over distances such as that between the Far East and Europe and, if successful in operational and commercial terms, this technology could be adapted for other vessels such as ferries and cruise ships.

In this proposed first vessel, wave energy would be harnessed by 12 fins on the vessel's hull, wind energy by three large, swept fin-like sails, and light energy by solar panels on the sails. The power generated from the energy so garnered would provide a cruising speed in the order of 15 kt, and stability would be entrusted to the so-called "pentamaran" layout with a slim cargo-carrying central monohull balanced by an in-line arrangement of two smaller stabilizing sponsons on each side. The harnessed wave, wind and solar energy would be combined with hydrogen and stored in fuel cells to power the vessel's engines.

Conceived by a Scandinavian bulk cargo company, Wallenius Wilhelmsen, which specializes in the delivery every year of 160,000 cars, from Southampton in southern England to destinations such as Australia, New Zealand and Far Eastern countries. As currently conceived, the new-technology vessel would have a cargo deck equivalent in area to 14 football pitches to embark up to 10,000 cars.

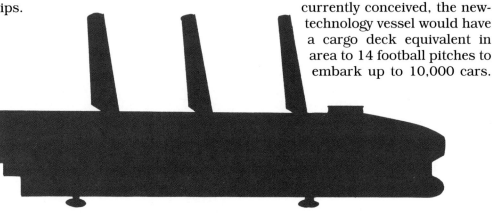

Illustration comparing the size of the Orcelle and the Queen Elizabeth 2.

312

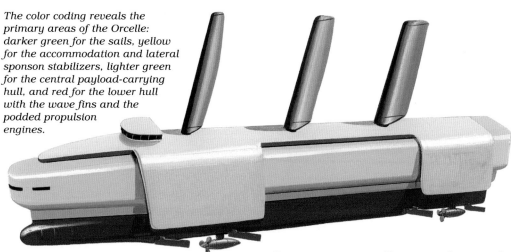

The new vessel would be the ES *Orcelle*, the prefix standing for Environmentally Sound Ship, and the orcelle being the French name for one of the world's most notably endangered aquatic mammal, the Irrawaddy dolphin.

The design means that the vessel, built of aluminium alloys and thermoplastic composites with eight cargo decks including some adjustable in height, would not need to take on ballast water for the stability needed in conventional monohull vessels, and this would be another "plus," as the intake and discharge of ballast water has been a maritime practice which has worried marine conservationists for many years. Many fragile species can be drawn inadvertently into the hull ballast tanks as a vessel takes thousands of tons of water from the sea, and when discharged back into the ocean, generally many thousands of miles away, many species are dumped in alien environments that threaten their survival. The discharged water has also been contaminated in many cases.

Wallenius Wilhelmsen has a fleet of some 60 modern vessels delivering about 17 million vehicles per year, and revealed a model of the *Orcelle* at a world trade fair in Japan during April 2005. The company's chief executive revealed that a vessel with some of the *Orcelle's* best qualities could be launched within five years, but that a vessel incorporating all of the features would be unlikely before 2025. And while such a vessel would be more expensive to build that the current diesel-powered equivalent, the cost would drop as the technology matured, and the "fuel" would be entirely free.

Orcelle (provisional)

Type:	renewable-energy bulk car carrier
Tonnage:	34,000 tons full load
Dimensions:	length 820 ft 3 in (250.0 m); beam 164 ft 0 in (50.0 m); draught 29 ft 6 in (9.0 m)
Speed:	20 kt
Armament:	none
Complement:	not available

John Batchelor

Index

A

Amundsen, Roald 248-249
Arnold, General Benedict 134-135

B

Bainbridge, Captain William 178
Barbary corsair 124-125
Barron, Captain James 178
Beaglehole, Captain 209
Bell, James 234
Bellamy, Samuel "Black Sam" 110-113
Blackwood, Captain Henry 174
Bligh, Captain William 133
Broke, Captain Philip 187
Brown, William H. 214
building a wooden ship 156-157

C

Christian, Fletcher 142-143
Clerke, Captain Charles 133
Collingwood, Admiral Sir Cuthbert 175
Cook, Captain James
120-123, 132-133, 142-143
Crozier, Francis 204-205

D

Darwin, Charles 196-197

F

FitzRoy, Lieutenant Robert 196-197
Franklin, Sir John 205, 248
Furneaux, Commander Tobias 132-133

G

Gore, Lieutenant John 133
Gower, Captain R. H. 158-159
Groselliers, Médard, 98-99

H

Herreshoff, Nathanael 250-253
Heyerdahl, Thor 26-27
Hybertson, Henrik 94

I

Iselin, C. Oliver 151

J

Jacobson, Henrik 94
Jones, Captain John Paul 136-139

L

Lambert, Captain Henry 182
Lapenotiere, Commander John 174-175
Lawrence, Captain James 187
le Maire, Isaac 90-91
le Maire, Jakob 90-91

M

Morris, Commodore Richard 187

N

named vessels
Adventure 132, 196
Aeolus 181
Africa 181
Alert 178
Alliance 139
Amaryllis 250
Amerigo Vespucci 288-289
Atlantic 244-245
America 214-217
Amsterdam 91, 102
Anne 110-113
Asra 241
Aurora 215
Avondster 103
Beagle 196-197
Belvedira 181
Bethia 142
Blessing 103
Blossom 143
Bluenose 272-273
Bonhomme Richard 139
Boston 138
Bounty 142-143
Bucentaure 168
Camilla 216
Cap Pilar 286-287
Captain 167
Carolina 114-115
Challenge 212-213
Chatham 152-153
Cherub 179

Index

Chesapeake	180, 186-187		L'Etoile	121
Christopher	78		La Boudeuse	121
Columbia Rediviva	152		Levant	183
Congress	135, 180		Lotos	241
Constellation	180		Macassar	153
Constitution	179, 180-183		Malcolm Miller	294-295
Cutty Sark	224-227		Marigold	78
Cyane	183		Mary Anne	111-113
Discovery	133, 150-153		Mary Rose	70-71
Dolphin	121		Mauritius	102
Drake	138		Mayflower	92-93
Dunbrody	206-207		Memphis	216
Duyfken	102-103		Mercator	280-281
Eagle	298-299		Mexicana	152
Eaglet	99		Mirabella V	308-309
Earl of Pembroke	120		Nautilus	175, 181
Eendracht	90-91		Neptune	169
Elizabeth	78		Niña	52-55
Endeavour	120-123, 132		Nonsuch	98-99
Erebus	204-205		Orcelle	312-313
Essex	178-179		Padua	274
Essex Junior	179		Passat	275
Europa	240-241		Peacock	186
Ferreira	226		Pelican	78
Fisher	111-113		Peregrine Galley	114-115
Gjøa	248-249		Philadelphia	134-135
Gloriana	251		Phoebe	179
Golden City	213		Pickle	174-175
Golden Hinde	76-79		Pinta	52-55
Golden Swan	78		President	180
Gorch Fock	282-283		Preussen	246-247
Gratitude	290-291		Principe de Asturias	167
Great Britain	17		Providence	138-139
Great Harry	68-69		Punjaub	224
Greif	302-303		Queen of France	138-139
Guerrière	181		Ra	27
Hector	126-129		Ra II	27
Heemskerck	96-97		Ranger	136-139
Henry Grâce à Dieu	68-69		Redoutable	168
Hollandia	102		Reliance	250-253
Hoorn	90-91		Resolution	123, 132-133
Hornet	179, 187		Rose	120, 296-297
Java	182		Royal Caroline	114-115
Jullanar	234		Royal Charlotte	115
Jhelum	208-209		Royal Clipper	310-311
Kon-Tiki	26		Royal Savage	135
Kruzenshtern	274		Royal Sovereign	168

Index

Sagres	304-305
Salvador del Mundo	167
San Josef	167
San Nicolas	167
San Ysidro	167
Santa María	56-59
Serapis	139
Shamrock III	253
Shannon	181, 186-187
Sir Winston Churchill	294-295
Snow Squall	218-219
Sobraon	222-223
Speedwell	93
Star Clipper & Star Flyer	306-307
Sussex	104-107
Sutil	152
Téméraire	168
Terror	204-205
The Tweed	224
Thermopylae	224
Thistle	234-235
Tingira	223
Transit	158-159
Tryal	120
Tuscaloosa	218
United States	180
Vasa (Wasa)	94-95
Vicar of Bray	210-211
Victoria and Albert	215
Victory	166-169, 183
Volunteer	235
Washington	135
Wavertree	256-257
Whydah	110-113
Wilhelm Pieck	302-303
Zeehaen	96-97
Nelson, Admiral lord	166-169, 174-175

P
pirate ships	144-145
Porter, Captain David	178-179
Preble, Commodore Edward	178, 180
Puget, Lieutenant Peter	152-153

R
Radisson, Pierre	98-99
Rodgers, Commodore John	181

Ross, James	204-205
rated warships	11

S
sailing vessels	
barque	19, 20
barquentine	13, 19, 20
bateau-boeuf	258-259
bergantin	67
bireme	8, 32
boeier (boier)	100-101
bomb ketch	148-149
boomie ketch	236-237
botter	262-263
brig	19, 190-191
brigantine	13, 19, 20
Brixham trawler	268-269
caravel	9, 64-67
caravela da annada	65
caravela de armada	67
caravela latina	52-53
caravela rotunda (redonda)	
	52-53, 65, 67-68
carrack	9, 11
chasse-marée	170-171
Chesapeake Bay skipjack	292-293
Cinque Port ship	44-45
clipper	13, 19
Colchester oyster smack	270-271
corbita	15
crab claw boat	188-189
crompster	88-89
Crusader ship	48-49
dhow	232-233
East Indiaman	12
Egyptian	28
English pilot boat	276-277
færing	238-239
felucca	130-131
fluyt (flute)	108-109
frigate	162-165
galleas	278-279
galleass	82-83
galleon	9, 82-83, 84-87
galley	82-83
gaulus	9
Greek merchant ship	30-31

Index

Hansa cog	50-51	Venetian galley	72-75	
high-charged vessel	18	Viking longship	8, 40-43	
hoy	202-203	wall-sided ship	9	
jacht	96, 102-103	whaling vessel	198-201	
jekta	184-185	Yorkshire lugger	242-243	
jukung	300-301	*zomp*	228-229	
junk	62-63	sailing vessel features		
Khufu vessel	7, 28	after castle (poop)	9, 18	
koff	230-231	bowsprit	18	
Kvalsund	28-39	fore-and-aft rig	18 f	
lateen-rigged	60-61	forecastle	9, 18	
Leigh bawley	260-261	lateen rig	60-61	
lugger	170-171	mast	18, 25 f	
mediaeval	9	rigging	21 f	
monoreme	32	running rigging	23 f	
Morecambe Bay prawner	254-255	standing rigging	22 f	
muletta (muleta)	116-117	rudder	9	
Mumbles oyster boat	220-221	sails	18 f, 24 f	
ndrua	172-173	square rig	17 f	
Nile boat	130-131	Schouten, Willem	90-91	
origins	7	shipbuilding		
papyrus/reed boat	26	carvel	15	
patache	67, 83	clinker	15	
periague gunboat	176-177	iron construction	17	
periauger (petiauger)	140-141	Egyptian	14	
Phoenician war galley	8	Phoenician	14	
Poole Seal ship	46-47	Roman	15	
Q trawler	264-265	Slade, Sir Thomas	166	
revenue cutter	154-155	Spanish Armada	80-81	
Roman	36-37	Stevens, John C.	214	
round ship	15	Stewart, Captain Charles	182	
saetta	67			
sailing packet	194-195	**T**		
schooner	17, 21, 158-159	Tasman, Abel	96-97	
skaerbaat	118-119			
skerry boat	118-119	**V**		
sloop	146-147	Visscher, Franchoys	96-97	
snow	192-193			
Spanish armada vessels	82-83	**W**		
Spanish treasure galleon	84-87	Warren, Sir William	98	
St. Malo fishing boat	284-285	Waterman, Captain Robert	212	
staten jacht	103	Watson, George	234	
Tarshish ship	9	whaling vessels	198-201	
Thames barge	266-267	wooden ship, building of	156-157	
tjalk	100-101			
trireme	8, 32-35			
urca	83			